The Race to Commercialize Biotechnology

In the early 1970s the demonstration of recombinant DNA offered new possibilities for making drugs and other products. Entrepreneurs in the US responded almost immediately, forming dedicated companies to commercialize the new technology. Prospective Japanese entrepreneurs, however, faced imposing regulatory hurdles and a drug pricing system that deterred entry into pharmaceutical applications. Consequently, US entrepreneurs raced ahead, establishing a lead that Japan has never been able to fully close.

This comparative study looks at the early development of biotechnology in the US and Japan. Drawing on primary and secondary sources it traces the historical roots of recombinant DNA technology, discusses the tensions between regulation and promotional policies and identifies the major actors and strategies that launched biotechnology in both countries. Developing several strands of theory in economic history, science and technology policy, the book proposes a simple model that relates the differences in the two countries' response to variations in the availability of institutional, financial, and organizational resources needed to commercialize the new technology.

Written in an accessible style, *The Race to Commercialize Biotechnology* is designed for those with research interests in Asian Studies, Public Policy and Comparative Politics as well as Science and Technology.

Steven W. Collins is Associate Professor in the Interdisciplinary Arts and Sciences Program at the University of Washington.

The Nissan Institute/RoutledgeCurzon Japanese Studies Series

Other titles in the series:

The Myth of Japanese Uniqueness
Peter Dale

The Emperor's Adviser
Saionji Kinmochi and pre-war Japanese politics
Lesley Connors

A History of Japanese Economic Thought
Tessa Morris-Suzuki

The Establishment of the Japanese Constitutional System
Junji Banno, translated by J.A.A. Stockwin

Industrial Relations in Japan
The peripheral workforce
Norma Chalmers

Banking Policy in Japan
American efforts at reform during the occupation
William M. Tsutsui

Educational Reform in Japan
Leonard Schoppa

How the Japanese Learn to Work
(Second edition)
Ronald P. Dore and Mari Sako

Japanese Economic Development
Theory and practice: second edition
Penelope Francks

Japan and Protection
The growth of protectionist sentiment and the Japanese response
Syed Javed Maswood

The Soil, by Nagatsuka Takashi
A portrait of rural life in Meiji Japan
Translated and with an introduction by Ann Waswo

Biotechnology in Japan
Malcolm Brock

Britain's Educational Reform
A comparison with Japan
Michael Howarth

Language and the Modern State
The reform of written Japanese
Nanette Twine

Industrial Harmony in Modern Japan
The intervention of a tradition
W. Dean Kinzley

Japanese Science Fiction
A view of a changing society
Robert Matthew

The Japanese Numbers Game
The use and understanding of numbers in modern Japan
Thomas Crump

Ideology and Practice in Modern Japan
Edited by Roger Goodman and Kirsten Refsing

Technology and Industrial Development in Pre-war Japan
Mitsubishi Nagasaki shipyard, 1884–1934
Yukiko Fukasaku

Japan's Early Parliaments, 1890–1905
Structure, issues and trends
Andrew Fraser, R.H.P. Mason and Philip Mitchell

Japan's Foreign Aid Challenge
Policy reform and aid leadership
Alan Rix

Emperor Hirohito and Shôwa Japan
A political biography
Stephen S. Large

Japan
Beyond the end of history
David Williams

Ceremony and Ritual in Japan
Religious practices in an industrialized society
Edited by Jan van Bremen and D.P. Martinez

Understanding Japanese Society
(Second edition)
Joy Hendry

The Fantastic in Modern Japanese Literature
The subversion of modernity
Susan J. Napier

Militarization and Demilitarization in Contemporary Japan
Glenn D. Hook

Growing a Japanese Science City
Communication in scientific research
James W. Dearing

Architecture and Authority in Japan
William H. Coaldrake

Women's *Gidayû* and the Japanese Theatre Tradition
A. Kimi Coaldrake

Democracy in Post-war Japan
Maruyama Masao and the search for autonomy
Rikki Kersten

Treacherous Women of Imperial Japan
Patriarchal fictions, patricidal fantasies
Hélène Bowen Raddeker

Japanese–German Business Relations
Competition and rivalry in the inter-war period
Akira Kudô

Japan, Race and Equality
The racial equality proposal of 1919
Naoko Shimazu

Japan, Internationalism and the UN
Ronald Dore

Life in a Japanese Women's College
Learning to be ladylike
Brian J. McVeigh

On the Margins of Japanese Society
Volunteers and the welfare of the urban underclass
Carolyn S. Stevens

The Dynamics of Japan's Relations with Africa
South Africa, Tanzania and Nigeria
Kweku Ampiah

The Right to Life in Japan
Noel Williams

The Nature of the Japanese State
Rationality and rituality
Brian J. McVeigh

Society and the State in Inter-war Japan
Edited by Elise K. Tipton

Japanese–Soviet/Russian Relations since 1945
A difficult peace
Kimie Hara

Interpreting History in Sino-Japanese Relations
A case study in political decision making
Caroline Rose

Endô Shûsaku
A literature of reconciliation
Mark B. Williams

Green Politics in Japan
Lam Peng-Er

The Japanese High School
Silence and resistance
Shoko Yoneyama

Engineers in Japan and Britain
Education, training and employment
Kevin McCormick

The Politics of Agriculture in Japan
Aurelia George Mulgan

Opposition Politics in Japan
Strategies under a one-party dominant regime
Stephen Johnson

The Changing Face of Japanese Retail
Working in a chain store
Louella Matsunaga

Japan and East Asian Regionalism
Edited by Syed Javed Maswood

Globalizing Japan
Ethnography of the Japanese presence in America, Asia and Europe
Edited by Harumi Befu and Sylvie Guichard-Anguis

Japan at Play
The ludic and logic of power
Edited by Joy Hendry and Massimo Raveri

The Making of Urban Japan
Cities and planning from Edo to the twenty-first century
André Sorensen

Public Policy and Economic Competition in Japan
Change and continuity in antimonopoly policy, 1973–1995
Michael L. Beeman

Modern Japan
A social and political history
Elise K. Tipton

Men and Masculinities in Contemporary Japan
Dislocating the Salaryman Doxa
Edited by James E. Roberson and Nobue Suzuki

The Voluntary and Non-Profit Sector in Japan
The challenge of change
Edited by Stephen P. Osborne

Japan's Security Relations with China
From balancing to bandwagoning
Reinhard Drifte

Understanding Japanese Society
(Third edition)
Joy Hendry

Japanese Electoral Politics
Creating a new party system
Edited by Steven R. Reed

The Japanese–Soviet Neutrality Pact
A diplomatic history, 1941–1945
Boris Slavinsky translated by Geoffrey Jukes

Academic Nationalism in China and Japan
Framed by concepts of nature, culture and the universal
Margaret Sleeboom

The Race to Commercialize Biotechnology
Molecules, markets and the state in the United States and Japan
Steven W. Collins

The Race to Commercialize Biotechnology

Molecules, markets and the state in the United States and Japan

Steven W. Collins

LONDON AND NEW YORK

First published 2004
by RoutledgeCurzon
11 New Fetter Lane, London EC4P 4EE

Simultaneously published in the USA and Canada
by RoutledgeCurzon
29 West 35th Street, New York, NY 10001

RoutledgeCurzon is an imprint of the Taylor & Francis Group

Typeset in Sabon by LaserScript Ltd, Mitcham, Surrey
Printed and bound in Great Britain by
Antony Rowe Ltd, Chippenham, Wiltshire

British Library Cataloguing in Publication Data
A catalogue record for this book is available from the British Library

Library of Congress Cataloging in Publication Data
Collins, Steven W. (Steven Wayne), 1960–
The race to commercialize biotechnology : molecules, markets and the state in the United States and Japan / by Steven W. Collins
p. cm. – (The Nissan Institute/RoutledgeCurzon Japanese studies series)
Includes bibliographical references.
1. Biotechnology industries–Japan. 2. Biotechnology industries–United States. 3. Pharmaceutical industry–Japan. 4. Pharmaceutical industry–United States. 5. Pharmaceutical biotechnology industry–Japan. 6. Pharmaceutical biotechnology industry–United States.
[DNLM: 1. Biotechnology–economics–Japan. 2. Biotechnology–economics–United States. 3. Genetic Techniques–history–Japan. 4. Genetic Techniques–history–United States. 5. Biotechnology–history–Japan. 6. Biotechnology–history–United States. 7. Biotechnology–legislation & jurisprudence–Japan. 8. Biotechnology–legislation & jurisprudence–United States. 9. Public Policy–Japan. 10. Public Policy–United States. 11. Technology Transfer–Japan. 12. Technology Transfer–United States. QZ 52 C699r 2004] I. Title. II. Series: Nissan Institute/RoutledgeCurzon Japanese studies series.
HD9999.B443J33 2004
338.4′76606′0952–dc22

2003015381

ISBN 0–415–28339–6

Contents

Illustrations

Figures

Tables

Series editor's preface

The Nissan/RoutledgeCurzon Japanese Studies Series was launched in 1986 and has now passed its sixtieth volume. It seeks to foster an informed and balanced, but not uncritical, understanding of Japan. One aim of the series is to show the depth and variety of Japanese institutions, practices and ideas. Another is, by using comparisons, to see what lessons, positive or negative, can be drawn for other countries. The tendency in commentary on Japan to resort to out-dated, ill-informed or sensational stereotypes still remains, and needs to be combated.

Since the ending of the Cold War international relations in the Asia Pacific have been slowly evolving to conform to new global realities. No doubt the most important adjustment has been towards a world dominated by the United States as the sole "hyperpower." But in what takes on the appearance of a unipolar world the United States shows some surprising vulnerabilities. This is most obvious in respect of international terrorism, and also in the acute difficulties it is facing in its efforts to rebuild Iraq.

By comparison with the Middle East, the Asia Pacific generally receives less media attention (with the current exception of North Korea). The Asian economic crisis of the late 1990s, and the Middle Eastern crises of the early 2000s (so sharply involving the United States), tended to reduce coverage of the region for a prolonged period. Meanwhile, however, the Asia Pacific was regaining much of its economic dynamism, manifested especially in the spectacular development of the Chinese economy. Japan, after a decade of relative economic stagnation, was gradually resuming its economic growth and showing some signs of greater political activism in relation to external threats. The crisis over North Korean nuclear weapons (real or imagined, but probably real), that emerged in the later months of 2002, gave a sense of urgency to the task of rethinking the international politics of the Asia Pacific region. Despite the extreme reticence of its foreign policy since the 1950s, Japan, as the second largest economy in the world, seemed destined to play a pivotal role in such a reassessment.

The Japanese, being a proud people and heirs to an ancient civilization, have long been concerned to map out their own path in the world. It is too simple to assume that they will simply follow a road designed for them by

Washington, even though current Government policy is broadly pro-American. There is a pattern in Japanese history whereby adaptation to external norms of behaviour is tempered by the maintenance of structures and practices based on indigenous cultural experience. Little in the currently fashionable debate about globalization would appear likely to negate this approach.

This is the second book in the present series to discuss biotechnology in Japan. The first was by Malcolm Brock, entitled *Biotechnology in Japan*, and was published in 1989. Brock wrote his book at a time when the Japanese economy appeared to be forging ahead in an unstoppable fashion, and biotechnology was one area of scientific and commercial development where Japan was expected to achieve spectacular developments. He showed the extent and character of Government involvement in the promotion of progress in this field.

Since the late 1980s the Japanese economy has in general performed at less than its potential level. In the present volume Steven Collins takes biotechnology as an example of how Japan has fallen behind, particularly by comparison with the United States. He analyses the effects of path dependency on the development of biotechnology in Japan, and shows how the wrong sort of government involvement seriously inhibited the progress of the industry. Nevertheless, he concludes that by complex processes of adaptation the biotechnology industry has made significant achievements in certain areas.

J.A.A. Stockwin

Preface and acknowledgements

Seventeen years ago, as a young chemical engineer fresh out of engineering school, I had my first serious encounter with Japanese technology. I was in the employ of a large multinational corporation that, like many others in the US at that time, had slowly awakened to the fact that American manufacturers had much to learn from their Japanese counterparts in such fields as production and quality management. Being one of the few engineers in my division to have some expertise in applied statistics, I was given the opportunity to participate in a series of seminars on something called "statistical process control," a subject that sounded for all the world like an engineering student's worst nightmare. Although the course packet explained that the concepts we were about to learn were among the main contributors to Japan's stunning economic and technological achievements, I had little appreciation of what that meant. To be sure, I was well aware that Japanese companies made nifty cars, motorcycles – oh how I loved my Honda 650 with the water-cooled engine – and stereo components, not to mention the instrumentation and control systems my employer was using in increasing quantity in its factories. But a seminar on Japanese methods of quality control? Taught by a consulting firm dedicated to spreading the ideas of W. Edwards Deming, the American management expert who had evangelized Japan in the technique of statistical process control in the early postwar period? Steeped in the ethos that the US had little to learn from other countries in science, technology, or management, I had a hard time keeping a straight face. Then the instructor passed out our "textbook": David Halberstam's *The Reckoning*, a riveting account of the rise of the Japanese automobile industry. Though asked to read only a few sections, I could not put the book down but read it through to the end. It would change forever the way I thought about Japan. Indeed, it changed my life, for it inspired me eventually to take up the study of Japan and East Asia, first as a graduate student, now as a college professor.

Despite Japan's compelling technological and managerial achievements, several political economists had by the late 1980s begun drawing attention to another side of the economy: the industries in which Japanese firms had little or no global presence. They included industries protected from competition through cartels or trade barriers, dependent on costly factor inputs, regulated by the government, or dependent on scientific knowledge not easily generated or readily obtainable. Consider the chemical industry. As a chemical engineer, I was acutely aware that Japan's chemical industry had nothing like the global presence of its automobile and machinery sectors. Why not? Why had the technological and managerial prowess that had enabled Japan's automobile industry to challenge the leadership of America's Big Three not worked the same magic in the chemical and pharmaceutical industries? If lean production, quality circles, cross-functional teams, close contractor–subcontractor relations, just-in-time production scheduling, and market-conforming industrial policies were responsible for the success of the automotive, shipbuilding, machinery, and electrical equipment sectors, why would these same institutions, or variants thereof, not also have conferred competitive advantage on the chemical sector, or, for that matter, the food processing, telecommunications, computer software, and biotechnology sectors? Such noted scholars as Richard Samuels, Kent Calder, and Frances Rosenbluth had by the late 1980s already revealed the sources of Japan's competitive disadvantages in declining industries, petrochemicals, agriculture, finance, and other sectors whose governance was captive to the political process. But what accounts for the difficulty Japan has experienced in fielding globally competitive firms in biotechnology, pharmaceuticals, and other science-intensive industries? Conversely, why was the US political economy able to give rise to and sustain a world-leading biotechnology sector, even while its manufacturing base was crumbling in the face of growing international competition in the 1970s and 1980s?

When *The Reckoning* was published in the mid 1980s, the competitive position of many of America's core manufacturing industries had fallen to a point where reasonable people could countenance the possibility of the US and Japan trading positions in the world economy. Yet even as arrogance and rigidity were stifling America's mainline manufacturing firms, a quiet revolution in biology was unfolding in the research laboratories of American universities. This book tells the story of that revolution, and it seeks to explain both why it happened first in the US and why it had happened differently in Japan.

In the course of writing this book, I have accrued many debts. I first developed the core ideas in graduate seminars led by my mentors, Professors Leonard Schoppa and Herman Schwartz in the Department of Politics at the University of Virginia; I have continued to benefit greatly from their mentorship over the past decade. Professors John Echeverri-Gent and Gary Allinson provided additional valuable support as I developed the theoretical framework into a doctoral dissertation. Field research commenced in fall 1991, when I was guest researcher at Japan's National Institute for Science and Technology Policy (NISTEP), now a part of Japan's Ministry of Education, Science, and Culture. A second period in residence at NISTEP in fall 1998, followed by regular visits ever since, has afforded the privilege of maintaining fruitful contact with this eminent body of Japanese researchers on science and technology policy. I am grateful for the assistance the staff at NISTEP has rendered over the years. In particular, the late Dr. Kinji Gonda, a research director at NISTEP and professor at Tokai University, provided valuable direction during the early and middle stages of the project. Yoshiki Shigihara, formerly with the Science and Technology Agency and now professor at Tokyo University of Agriculture, introduced me to the science and technology policy community in Japan when I was a graduate student, and he has remained a generous mentor. Professor W.D. Kay has been a continual source of inspiration since I was a graduate student and a model of mentorship. Professor Richard Samuels afforded me the first opportunity to present a part of this work to a broader audience through the MIT Japan Program Working Paper Series and provided much helpful feedback in the process. Professors Vicki Golich and Leonard Lynn have also provided valuable advice and support. No less valuable has been the support from the editorial staff at RoutledgeCurzon, whose enthusiasm and patience in seeing me through this project have never wavered.

This book would never have seen the light of day had it not been for the continual encouragement of Professors Jane Decker and JoLynn Edwards of the University of Washington, Bothell. Their bold vision and energy have been instrumental in leading a newly established campus successfully through its first decade, and they have worked tirelessly to create opportunities for a young faculty in a teaching-intensive program to advance their scholarship.

Finally, no words can fully convey the appreciation and love I feel for Ali, Stephanie, Heidi, and Sophia. Their unconditional love and support over the years have made it possible for me to persevere with this project, even at the cost of missed family meals, bedtimes, and countless special events. It is to them, my wife and daughters, that I dedicate this book.

Steven W. Collins
Ishikawa Prefecture, Japan
August 2003

Abbreviations

ARS	Agricultural Research Service
BERI	Biomolecular Engineering Research Institute
BIO	Biotechnology Industry Organization
BMS	Bristol-Myers Squibb
BRAIN	Bio-oriented Technology Research Advancement Institution
BSCC	Biotechnology Science Coordinating Committee
CDC	Center for Disease Control
CRADA	Cooperative Research and Development Agreement
CST	Council for Science and Technology
CSTP	Council for Science and Technology Policy
DBCs	Dedicated Biotechnology Companies
DNA	Deoxyribonucleic Acid
DOD	Department of Defense
DOE	Department of Energy
EPA	Environmental Protection Agency
EPO	Erythropoietin
FCCSET	Fenderal Coordinating Council for Science, Engineering, and Technology
FDA	Food and Drug Administration
GSF	Granulocyte Colony Stimulating Factor
HGF	Hepatic Growth Factor
HGH	Human Growth Hormone
HHS	Department of Health and Human Services
IBCs	Institutional Biosafety Committees
IPO	Initial Public Offering
JETRO	Japan External Trade Organization
JKTC	Japan Key Technology Center
JTEC	Japanese Technology Evaluation Center
MAFF	Ministry of Agriculture, Forestry, and Fisheries
METI	Ministry of Economy, Trade, and Industry
MEXT	Ministry of Education, Culture, Sports Science, and Technology
MHW	Ministry of Health and Welfare
MHLW	Ministry of Health, Labour, and Welfare

MITI	Ministry of International Trade and Industry
MSG	Monosodium Glutamate
NAS	National Academy of Sciences
NASA	National Aeronautics and Space Administration
NBFs	New Biotechnology Firms
NCE	New Chemical Entity
NCI	National Cancer Institute
NIH	National Institutes of Health
NIS	National Innovation System
NISTEP	National Institute for Science and Technology Policy
NMR	Nuclear Magnetic Resonance
NSF	National Science Foundation
OECD	Organization for Economic Cooperation and Development
ORTA	Office of Research and Technology Application
OSHA	Occupational Safety and Health Administration
OSRD	Office of Scientific Research and Development
OSTP	Office of Science and Technology Policy
OTA	Office of Technology Assessment
PARC	Policy Affairs Research Council
PCR	Polymerase Chain Reaction
PERI	Protein Engineering Research Institute
PhRMA	Pharmaceutical Research and Manufacturers Association
PLA	Product License Application
PTO	Patent and Trademark Office
R&D	Research and Development
RAs	Research Associations
RAB	Research Association in Biotechnology
RAC	Recombinant DNA Advisory Committee
RDLP	Research and Development Limited Partnership
SNPs	Single-Nucleotide Polymorphisms
SSC	Superconducting Supercollider
STA	Science and Technology Agency
STTR	Small Business Technology Transfer
TLOs	Technology Licensing Organizations
TNF	Tumor Necrosis Factor
TPA	Tisse Plasminogen Activator
USDA	(United States) Department of Agriculture

1 Introduction

In the middle 1980s, the United States Office of Technology Assessment released an alarming report on the competitive status of the newly formed biotechnology industry.[1] Its conclusions had a familiar ring at a time of great anxiety over the health of the US economy: American firms, which had only a decade earlier kicked off the revolution in commercial biotechnology, were at serious risk of being overtaken by new competitors in Japan. Why? Because the Japanese government was targeting biotechnology, as it had steel, machine tools, semiconductors, and computers in preceding years, vowing to make the life sciences a centerpiece of Japan's industrial and technology policies over the coming decade. The fledgling American industry, by contrast, faced serious regulatory and scientific hurdles, along with capricious investors uncertain about the potential of this new technology. A few years later came the first reports of Japanese firms taking equity stakes in, or even acquiring, biotechnology firms in the US; many more were projected to follow. The fear was that technology transfer would be one-sided: from the US to Japan. Concern reached a peak when the National Research Council warned that the biotechnology industry in the US would "lose its strong leadership position in several industry segments at the end of the decade unless concrete steps are taken by government, industry, and universities."[2]

American firms did not yield their early technological leadership in biotechnology. On the contrary, they continue to set the pace of research and commercialization in most segments of the industry, especially pharmaceuticals and agricultural products made using recombinant DNA techniques. Propelled by the advances in molecular biology and genetics that had accumulated since the 1950s, US firms acquired an early head start when the technology first began to be commercialized by Genentech and other small start-ups in the second half of the 1970s. Japanese industry, caught off guard by the speed with which recombinant DNA technology had leapt from lab bench to product development, and hobbled by a dense thicket of regulations that banned or severely limited research using genetically modified organisms, spent the next decade struggling to catch up. It is still doing so more than two decades later.

Today, the image of powerful Japanese firms storming into the American market, swallowing up tiny, cash-starved biotechnology start-ups and acquiring control over a large swath of the underpinning science base, seems absurd, a relic of a bygone era. Instead, quite the opposite scenario has played out: foreign firms have gained not only increasing shares of Japan's domestic product markets in biotechnology, they own or control a commanding share of the underlying intellectual property. Indeed, rare in Japan is an industry survey or policy analysis that fails to point out the extent to which Japan continues to lag the US in the development and commercialization of biotechnology. Among the facts cited to support a dismal assessment is the country's relatively minor contribution to the international project that by the end of 2000 had produced a draft sequence of the human genome: Japanese researchers provided only 7 percent of the sequence data, compared to the US's 67 percent and UK's 22 percent.[3] Nor has Japan kept pace with other countries in building a portfolio of patents, ownership of which has proved a more important source of competitive advantage in biotechnology than in other sectors. Between 1990 and 1998, Japan's patent office processed only 20 percent of all patent applications related to biotechnology filed worldwide, well behind America's 52 percent;[4] in the newer subfields of bioinformatics and protein analysis, Japan's share of patents filed worldwide in 1999 was a mere 12 percent, a percentage point above China's.[5] In pharmaceuticals, the industry most impacted by biotechnology, foreign companies developed or licensed 69 percent of new drugs introduced into Japan between 1996 and 2001, enabling foreign drug companies to establish a growing presence in Japan's domestic market.[6] Finally, although Japanese universities have recently begun spinning out biotechnology start-up companies at a growing rate, the number of venture-financed biotechnology firms in Japan remains comparatively low: 334 in spring 2003, or about a quarter the number of comparable firms in the US, and less than one-fifth the number in the European Union.[7]

On the other hand, that Japan's firms failed to conquer world markets and set industry standards in biotechnology as they had earlier done in automobiles does not mean that their investments have been fruitless. Japan's achievements in biotechnology on many measures pale only in comparison with the US, which is not surprising considering that US government spending on research in the life sciences exceeds that of Japan by a factor of seven, while American universities churn out six times the number of graduates with degrees in the life sciences.[8] Indeed, one could plausibly argue that, given the enormity of America's cumulative investments, Japanese institutions have made more productive use of the far smaller investments they have made to date. If anything, Americans run the risk of underestimating Japan's research achievements in the life sciences and the determination among scientists, industry, and policy makers to close the gap. The scientific and policy-making communities in Japan experienced embarrassment and frustration over the country's comparatively small and belated contribution to the Human Genome Project;[9] they are determined not to fall behind again in the post-genomics era dawning at the beginning of the twenty-first century. That determination extends to the government, which in early 2003 was proposing to boost spending on the life sciences by 5 percent, despite the otherwise severe budgetary climate.[10]

The stakes are high. Two recent incidences of alleged theft of intellectual property by Japanese researchers in the US serve as stark reminders of the intensity of the competition to harness the economic potential of biotechnology. The first surfaced in spring 2001 when two Japanese molecular biologists were charged under the 1996 Economic Espionage Act with the theft of trade secrets from an American laboratory for the purpose of benefiting a foreign government, in this case the government of Japan. According to the indictment, the scientists conspired to steal samples of DNA and cell-line reagents from the Cleveland Clinic, where one of them had been researching Alzheimer's disease, and ship them to the Institute of Physical and Chemical Research (Riken), one of Japan's premier research institutes. The Federal Bureau of Investigation determined that the Cleveland Clinic suffered $2 million worth of damage through the loss of trade secrets.[11] Although the former Cleveland Clinic researcher returned to Japan before he could be apprehended, his accomplice remained in the US, agreeing in May 2002 to cooperate with prosecutors in investigating his former partner in return for pleading guilty to a lesser charge of giving false statements to investigators. The incident has received considerable media attention in both countries; it threatens to undermine trust between Japanese and American researchers and deter Japanese scientists pursuing research projects in the US.[12]

In a second case that came to light in June 2002, a Japanese researcher and her Chinese husband were arrested for allegedly stealing genetic material related to their work on the control of the immune system from a laboratory at Harvard University and shipping it to a pharmaceutical company in Japan.[13] Although details of the couple's relationship with the drug firm remain unclear, it seems certain that they failed to follow proper procedure in disclosing to their supervisor several important discoveries of genes that control immune system function. Media accounts in Japan have seized on this incident to draw attention to the heated competition in the US to secure ownership of genes and other biological materials,[14] the considerable differences between Japanese and American academic laboratories in the management of intellectual property and attitudes toward the intellectual property implications of scientific research, and the degree to which Japan lags the US in building a legal framework to protect intellectual property and prosecute intellectual property theft.[15]

These differences have only grown more pronounced: Japanese researchers complain that patents held by Americans in such key technologies as the polymerase chain reaction (PCR) and the DNA chip have effectively walled off large sectors of biomedical research from other scientists whose added contributions would advance the technology.[16] The recent spying cases thus underscore both the centrality of intellectual property in biotechnology innovation and the cut-throat nature of the competition over it.

In short, the commercialization of biotechnology has no less the character of a global race today than it had in the 1980s. Although Japanese policy makers may no longer be targeting American industry with the same approaches and policy instruments they deployed in the 1960s and 1970s, there is no reason to believe that the "technonationalism" Richard Samuels finds at the core of Japan's technology policies from the Meiji Era through the 1980s is any less evident today than it was two or three decades ago.[17] Indeed, the stakes are even higher today: Japan's rapidly aging population portends a lucrative market for new drugs and therapies for diseases associated with aging; serving that market, however, threatens to sink the country's national health insurance system, which is one rationale driving government support of biotechnology. If the market for new therapies based on biotechnology develops in accordance with the government's forecast, by 2010 health expenditures will be 10 percent less than what they would be in the absence of biotechnology.[18] Moreover, structural changes taking place in the economy make the maintenance of the country's high living standards contingent upon shifting resources into new technologies, among which biotechnology is expected to play a leading role. More than ever before, Japan's economy needs the shot in the arm that a dynamic, innovative biotechnology sector could provide.

Nor is the pressure to succeed any less in the US. There, investors and managers fret over the length of time required to move new drugs through the process of clinical development, the recent slowdown in new product approvals by the Food and Drug Administration (FDA), and the sluggish pace with which knowledge of the human genome is being translated into corporate profits. In 2002 the FDA, for example, approved only seventeen "new molecular entities," or drugs made from novel chemical compounds, the fewest since 1983.[19] Nine of every ten drugs that enter clinical trials fail to reach the market. Since the typical biotechnology firm is developing only one or two products, the odds of succeeding are small indeed.[20] Moreover, to date biotechnology has produced few "blockbuster" drugs – drugs that attain annual sales of $1 billion or more: only three of the fifty blockbusters on the market today are made using recombinant DNA, the oldest and most commonly used technique in modern biotechnology.[21] Consumers and insurers, meanwhile, agonize over soaring health care costs. Spending on prescription drugs has been growing at an exponential rate since 1994, topping US$ 149 billion in the year to February 2003, a 17 percent jump over the figure for the previous year; that is more than the total spent in Britain, Germany, France, Canada, Italy, Spain, and Japan combined.[22] It is by no means clear that the nation's prodigious investment in biomedical research will ever deliver the goods at costs the system can bear.

Despite the enormous risks, the market for biotechnology products is growing rapidly. Global revenues are approaching US$ 35 billion. A commanding 91 percent of those revenues flow to firms headquartered in the US or Europe (70 percent to the US alone); a tiny 3 percent is shared among firms in Asia, including Japan.[23] The overall pie, however, is still strikingly small, especially in light of the hundreds of billions of dollars spent on research and development in the life sciences over the past three decades; American pharmaceutical giant Merck earns almost as much in global sales as the entire biotechnology industry. Yet the well has hardly begun to be tapped: hundreds of drug candidates and genetically modified crops are working their way through clinical trials and regulatory review. Determined to tap it further, policy makers in Japan, the US, and Europe alike have made scientific leadership and commercial success in biotechnology a national imperative.

A race it has been, and a race it will likely continue to be.

This book is about the beginning stages of that race. It is the story of the emergence and take-off of commercial biotechnology in the US, and the belated but determined efforts in Japan to catch up. In particular, it aims to explain why Japan's attempts to exploit new techniques in recombinant DNA and other new innovations in the life sciences from the 1970s through the 1990s fell short of the goal of catching up with the US, and why the early pessimism over American prospects proved over the long run to be unwarranted. In outline, the argument is simple: a highly developed infrastructure supporting biomedical research and the transfer of the fruits of that research to industry, coupled with a fluid industry structure and flexible regulatory environment, primed American industry for rapid take-off in commercial biotechnology and ultimately to global dominance. Japan, in contrast, possessed few of the institutional and organizational prerequisites for quick exploitation of the economic opportunities the new technology provided. Although it benefited from a long history of successful process innovation in fermentation technology, Japan's innovation system was weak in many of the core elements the US experience had shown were essential to successful commercialization in the fields most likely to earn the highest returns to investment. These elements included competitive, well-funded academic research in molecular biology; a technology transfer system linking academic research to entrepreneurial agents capable of commercializing it; and factors of production – capital, knowledge, and researchers – mobile enough to find the point in the chain of value creation where they could most productively be used. Nor did public policy respond with the speed and flexibility needed to ensure smooth and rapid catch-up with the US once the industry there had begun to develop. To be sure, Japanese researchers have made important contributions, especially in fermentation and bioreactor technologies, but also in the newer fields of regenerative medicine, livestock cloning, and plant genomics; they are well poised to play a leadership role in green biotechnology, proteomics, and in applications that bring together nanotechnology and biotechnology. Nonetheless, the center of gravity of innovation in biotechnology is not likely to shift away from the US, at least in the near future.

The approach

This book is not merely a descriptive account of biotechnology's beginnings in two countries. It aims rather to situate the stories of biotechnology in the US and Japan within an analytical context that facilitates cross-national comparison of technological change and provides insight into differences in outcomes. To understand the diverging paths of biotechnology innovation in the US and Japan requires asking broader questions about how countries generate, absorb, and diffuse new technologies; it demands that we theorize about the relationships among knowledge, institutions, and geography. Technological innovation is a major source of productivity growth in most industries. Yet national economies differ markedly in their capacity to generate and absorb new technologies. What accounts for differences in technological development and performance across countries? What kinds of organizations influence innovation? How do these organizations interact and change over time? With these questions as a guide, this book seeks to compare biotechnology's beginnings in the two countries in the context of a general theory of how new technology emerges and is shaped by the social, political, and economic forces within the broader society.

Attempts to model the relationship between technology and society have given rise to a varied literature spanning several disciplines. Political economists tend to stress the role of governing structures and institutions that support research and development (R&D), coordinate industry governance, control allocation of finance, and promote international competitiveness of industry.[24] Market structure, regimes of intellectual property protection, institutional linkages across interacting members of an innovation community, the evolutionary and path-dependent nature of technological change, and means of coordinating and organizing market transactions are among the factors stressed by economists and business historians.[25] A few theorists have focused on politics and the discourse of science and technology, explaining policy outcomes in biotechnology in terms of discursive practices that privilege certain meanings and interpretations of how a technology should be developed and applied.[26] Others have adopted an ethnographic approach, drawing insights about the social processes underpinning scientific research in corporate, government, and academic laboratories based on direct observation of everyday life in the laboratory.[27] Finally, some scholars point to an eclectic mix of characteristics that determine national competitiveness and shape technological change to meet national objectives; these range from management strategy and inter-firm rivalry to the quality of university R&D, national technology policies, and national ideology.[28]

Each of these approaches illuminates a part of the complex set of relationships linking science and technology to the social, political, and economic milieu that shapes and is shaped by them. Missing in the literature, however, is a satisfactory explanation of why countries whose innovation systems elevate firms to technological leadership in some industries fail utterly to do so in others. This book aims to fill this gap. In doing so, it leans toward the eclectic approach noted above, though drawing freely from the other perspectives. Using biotechnology in the US and Japan as cases, I seek to relate differences in national patterns of innovative performance to the characteristics of institutions and organizations involved in scientific research and technological innovation.

Stated in general terms, my argument runs as follows: nations prosper when the human, material, and knowledge resources within their borders continually give rise to new industries and reinvigorate old ones. New industries emerge and prosper when entrepreneurial agents, be they new or existing firms, respond successfully to new technological opportunities. Those opportunities may spring from an individual act of invention or insight, tinkering with an existing technology in the workshop or on the factory floor, or formal scientific research performed in academic, government, and corporate laboratories. Regardless of the opportunity's origin, entrepreneurial agents are apt to respond to it successfully when they possess appropriate organizational, managerial, and knowledge resources, or have ready access to those they are lacking. Because technological change is difficult to predict and internal resources costly to develop, these agents need help: they look to the resources available to them in the "national innovation system" (or NIS) of which they are part. National innovation systems, however, contain a limited range of resources; no country's NIS is likely to propel its firms to global dominance in every technology. Rather the forces of history, public policy, demographics, stage of development, politics, ideology, natural resource endowment, and many other factors conspire to compel the NIS to become specialized in structure and orientation. Depending on the nature of the technology, the resources available within the NIS may not be sufficient to guarantee success; some opportunities will by necessity have to be foregone. Faced with a new technological opportunity, entrepreneurs thus have the greatest probability of success when the innovation system in which they are embedded provides the institutional, organizational, and knowledge resources needed to solve the problems posed by that particular technology.

Applying this model to the particular cases of biotechnology in the US and Japan leads to the following argument. As a technological opportunity, biotechnology sprang from decades of scientific research in molecular biology and genetics, the culmination of which was the demonstration in the early 1970s of the successful transfer of genes from one organism into the genome of another organism of a different species. Most of this research had been carried out in the US under the sponsorship of the National

Institutes of Health (NIH) and in the UK with the support of the Medical Research Council; the US-based Rockefeller Foundation also played an important role in the creation of the new field of molecular biology. It quickly dawned on the scientists involved in this research, as well as a few perceptive venture capitalists, that the recombinant DNA technique could be used to induce simple cells such as bacteria and yeast to produce therapeutically valuable proteins that had hitherto been too costly or impossible to produce. They started companies; investors flocked to them. Although the first products did not reach the market until the early 1980s, biotechnology caught hold of the national imagination; commercialization accelerated. A technology transfer system that gave strong incentives for universities to license their inventions to industry, an intellectual property protection regime favoring strong protection of biotechnology-related patents, and flexible regulatory approaches stimulated commercialization. The Federal government opened wider the tap of federal funding to NIH, which channeled most of it to universities, which used it to turn out more inventions and discoveries. Many of these inventions were patented and licensed to existing and newly formed companies; researchers themselves often formed companies to commercialize their findings. When firms needed assets they did not themselves possess, they found in big drug companies able and willing partners in drug development; drug companies in turn looked to biotechnology firms as external sources of knowledge assets that would boost their own competitive positions. The industry grew rapidly, building out to an equilibrium market structure of about 1,400 companies. It continues to generate almost as much excitement (and volatility!) among investors today as it did two decades ago.

Japan was a latecomer to the new field of biotechnology. Little, if any, of the core research leading to the invention of recombinant DNA and monoclonal antibodies was conducted in Japan. Nor did its drug firms have the scale economies in R&D and research-intensive drug development found in the US. By the time Japanese firms recognized the opportunities biotechnology had to offer, commercialization had already been under way in the US for several years. Lacking a domestic research base, firms found themselves forced to import the technology and license many of the first generation of products from foreign firms. Even after the government eased its regulation of academic research using recombinant DNA, few dedicated biotechnology companies appeared to commercialize the results; no technology transfer system was in place to induce universities to patent inventions and license them to industry. Rather large food, drug, and chemical companies led the commercial response. Although the government played a major role in galvanizing interest and inducing firms to initiate their own research programs, it contributed relatively little public funding; no single institution provided research funding or leadership in setting research directions comparable to that of America's NIH. Moreover, with as many as six ministries and agencies competing to offer their own biotechnology programs, the result has often been wasteful duplication of programs and an inability to forge a common vision. Finally, Japan historically has maintained a fairly rigid wall of separation between applied and basic R&D, the former being done mostly by private companies, the latter by academic scientists, most of whose funding comes from the Ministry of Education. The absence of mechanisms linking academic research, the origin of most innovations in biotechnology, to industry has made it difficult for Japanese firms to harness the scientific tools of biotechnology to develop innovative products that have global commercial appeal. For these reasons, Japan quickly fell behind the US, not only in conventional indicators of scientific output in the life sciences but in the fact that most products brought to market to date are licensed versions of ones previously developed in the US. Although biotechnology was designated two decades ago as a strategic technology, there is no evidence that Japan has even caught up with, let alone overtaken, the US in setting the pace of technological change. Why outcomes fell short of expectations is a major theme of this book.

National innovation systems and biotechnology

According to the Oxford English Dictionary (online version), innovation is "the introduction of novelties; the alteration of what is established by the introduction of new elements or forms." That is the first definition. The sixth definition applies the idea of novelty to business: innovation is "the action of introducing a new product into the market." These two simple definitions underscore the two difficult tasks involved in the act of innovating: generating novelty and translating that novelty into an asset that delivers more value than the asset that came before. Novelty implies the qualities of both newness and difference: something "novel" is, simply, something new and different. From whence does novelty originate? In the context of industrial innovation, the list of originators might include a corporate, academic, or public research laboratory; a user of an existing product or process; individuals or groups that make, test, or market an existing product; a competitor, a related firm, or a lone inventor. The answer depends in large measure on the artifact in question. In chemistry, new ideas tend to spring from the research laboratory; in automobiles, assembly workers, designers, and customers play a critical role. The point is that there is no single pathway to the generation of novelty. Rather different industries draw from different sources in different proportions. And even if there were a proliferation of novelty generators, a would-be innovator confronts the second challenge: converting the "new thing" into something that adds value to a would-be user. This is difficult and expensive. It entails finding and combining organizational, managerial, and other resources to develop, manufacture, test, and market the new gadget, which may need to be accompanied by other new or existing gadgets to be viable in the market.

In other words, 90 percent of the effort involved in innovation may be in novelty generation, but the other 10 percent will be finding a way of turning novelty into something that delivers added value to a user and, in the long run, added value to the firm!

Another aspect of technological innovation is its interdependence on space and context; innovation clearly does not occur in a vacuum. In a modern economy, the firm is the primary locus of innovative activity. Yet, as Chapter 2 will explain, firms themselves are part of a larger constellation of organizations that work together to promote and shape innovation. Building on the work of Nelson, Edquist, Freeman, and others, I use the concept of "national innovation system" (NIS) to describe the whole of a country's infrastructure involved in the management of technological innovation.[29] Steil, Victor, and Nelson pithily define the NIS as "the cluster of institutions, policies, and practices that determine an industry or nation's capacity to generate and apply innovations."[30] Within this cluster are the nation's research universities, public research institutes, legal framework for intellectual property protection, regulatory regimes, venture capital and other financial resources, and other supporting firms and industries. Governments, moreover, implement policies intended to direct technological advance toward fulfillment of broad social and national objectives. Taken together, these public goods, and the way in which they are provided, bend and shape the direction of technological change at the national level. Moreover, just as nations differ in their political and economic structures, so too do they differ in the composition and characteristics of their innovation systems. The most successful innovators in a given nation will most likely be in industrial sectors in which the processes of innovation – bear in mind the two steps discussed above – draw most heavily on the resources and capabilities found in relative abundance in the NIS.

The science and technology infrastructures in Japan and the US, as well as the respective social and political milieu in which they are situated, have focused technological innovation in different ways. Japanese firms have held historically strong positions in world markets for automobiles, consumer electronics, machine tools, and semiconductors largely on the basis of their exceptional capacity to innovate in those sectors. Yet in many other sectors, Japanese firms have long struggled to develop a global presence: rarely, for example, have Japan's chemical, pharmaceutical, financial services, construction, and software industries been celebrated as global standard bearers in technological innovation.[31] Why is Japan more successful at exporting electronic components than drugs, automobiles than fertilizer? Why has the pattern of government policies, industrial organization, and corporate strategies that created competitive advantage in machine tools and semiconductors exhibited only modest success when applied to biotechnology? Does the comparatively poor environment for basic research in Japan mean that the deck is stacked against its bid to be a global standard bearer in pharmaceuticals and biotechnology? Finally, what accounts for American industry's success in exploiting technological opportunities in science-intensive industries like biotechnology, despite well-known difficulties in maintaining globally competitive positions in other manufacturing sectors?

Japanese firms tend to excel in industries in which simple learning by doing and incremental technological advance constitute the primary method of innovation. As a late industrializing nation, Japan had no choice but to channel resources toward the creation of institutions and organizations that facilitated technological catch-up. Consequently, applied research and process innovation have received the most attention.[32] While the US pushed back technological frontiers, Japanese firms built on basic technologies that often originated elsewhere, effecting incremental quality and design improvements and adapting them to low-cost mass production.[33] However, the organization and incentive structures that created advantage for Japanese firms in consumer electronics, color televisions, commodity memory chips, and machine tools are not necessarily well suited to innovation in sectors at the scientific frontier. Now that Japan has achieved technological parity with the US, it confronts internal and external pressures to commit more resources to basic research and knowledge creation. Understanding how Japan is making that transition, as well as the factors governing it, is another major aim of this study.

This book is intended to make a contribution in two broad areas. First, it advances a novel theoretical approach to the problem of explaining national differences in technological innovation, relating those differences to institutional factors contained within the borders of the nation-state. In contrast with most of the literature on the comparative political economy of Japan in the 1980s and 1990s, it focuses on a sector of the economy in which industrial policy has had limited success and in which government policies have been anything but unified or consistent. In this sense, the book reveals a bureaucracy far less coherent and effective in its planning and execution of industrial policy than the image portrayed by, for example, Anchordoguy, in her study of high technology policy in the computer industry, or Johnson, in his work on the history of the Ministry of International Trade and Industry (MITI).[34] This study rather corroborates the findings of Okimoto, who found that "MITI's power is dependent on the political configurations that take shape within each policy domain,"[35] and of Callon, who found evidence enough in his study of high technology consortia organized by MITI of a "finely-tuned industrial policy machine that ran aground in the 1980's."[36]

In contrast with Japan, the US has generally been portrayed as a "weak state," penetrated and sometimes paralyzed by squabbling interest groups, where, outside the narrow scope of national security, the market determines which technologies get developed and which do not.[37] The extent to which the preferences of molecular biologists carried the day in the early debates over whether to permit experiments with recombinant DNA in the 1970s certainly confirms the openness of the policy process to organized interests, in this case the scientific community. At almost every turn in the debate about the release of genetically modified organisms, the views of the scientific community prevailed over those who called for caution. In this sense, the conventional view appears to be correct. On the other hand, government promotion of research in medicine and the life sciences is centralized within a single agency, the NIH; there is no organization remotely comparable to it in budget or influence in Japan. On this point, the US clearly comes across as more of a "strong state" than the political economy literature has typically acknowledged.

The book also contributes to the historiography of the biotechnology industry. It presents a detailed comparison of the emergence of commercial biotechnology in Japan and the US during the crucial decades of the 1970s and 80s, when the paths of commercial development from the laboratory bench were first becoming apparent. It also reaches back to the early history of molecular biology and microbiology in the two countries to gain insight into subsequent commercialization: the divergent trajectories of early commercial development in the US and Japan can only be understood in the context of this pre-commercial history. More than simply a recounting of discoveries and events, however, the approach here is to situate biotechnology in the broader context of the national innovation system, to consider how the processes of discovery and product development were shaped by national institutions, politics, and public policies; only through careful understanding of the institutional environment supporting technological advance can the development of an industry be fully appreciated.

Finally, the book sheds light on the politics and practice of science in the two countries. Here, it builds on and confirms the insights of Coleman, who found in his ethnographic research on the daily life of scientists in various life science institutes in Japan that recruitment practices and hierarchy, among other things, frustrate progress in basic research.[38] It also confirms the findings of Wright[39] and Greenberg[40] on the political influence of scientists in the US, especially their ability to maintain self-regulation and, when necessary, take their case to Congress when research funding is being threatened there, or to regulators when Congress is threatening their freedom of action. The novel element in my study is to connect the discourse in science policy to the broader discourse on political economy and industrial competitiveness. In this sense, it integrates strands of the literature from various disciplines and perspectives in an effort to explain differences in patterns of innovative performance.

The market for biotechnology products

In the most general sense, biotechnology is the use of living organisms and biological processes to do something useful. This definition, of course, encompasses a broad range of techniques, from brewing beer to making cheese; some have been around for thousands of years. In the US, "biotechnology" usually has a narrower meaning: the Biotechnology Industry Organization prefers to use the term "new biotechnology," which is "the use of cellular and molecular processes to solve problems or make products."[41] Using this definition, the category "biotechnology products" encompasses drugs, diagnostics, vaccines, enzymes, and crops made using recombinant DNA and monoclonal antibody techniques: gene chips and probes; genetically modified experimental animals; and environmental remediation systems that use genetically modified microbes. Japan defines the market more broadly, usually including products made using mass cell culture, as well as equipment and reagents used to support biotechnology research. Thus direct comparisons of the two markets can be misleading and should be considered with caution.

Commercial biotechnology arose from three clusters of advances in basic research in biochemistry, molecular biotechnology, and genetics. First was the identification of DNA (deoxyribonucleic acid) as the basic unit of heredity and carrier of genetic information. This itself was the result of no single discovery or experiment but the culmination of three decades of painstaking research, culminating in the elucidation of the structure of DNA by James Watson and Francis Crick in 1953.[42] Although Watson and Crick postulated a mechanism by which cells translate the genetic message in DNA into the synthesis of proteins, the choreographers of the molecular dance that makes all life possible, it would take another two decades of research to determine precisely how this is done. This second cluster of advances includes Arthur Kornberg's discovery in the late 1950s of DNA polymerase, the enzyme responsible for catalyzing synthesis of DNA; François Jacob's and Jacques Monod's elucidation of a molecular control system regulating the process by which genes express proteins; the discovery of messenger RNA (ribonucleic acid) as the transcriber of information contained in DNA and transporter of that information from the cell's nucleus to the point in the cell where proteins are made; and the working out of the genetic code in the 1960s. The final cluster of innovations came in the early 1970s and involved the actual cutting and splicing of DNA, and moving it from the genome of one organism to the genome of another, a process known as "recombinant DNA" or, "genetic engineering." This made possible the development of new drugs and new, more efficient processes for making existing drugs. More recently, and controversially, these techniques have been used to produce genetically modified seeds that yield herbicide-resistant soybeans, and pest-resistant corn and cotton, among other crops.

Later, other innovations were added to the basic recombinant DNA toolkit. These included the ability to produce monoclonal antibodies, immune cells that zero in on specific proteins in the body's cells and tissues, binding to them and disrupting their biological activity. These can be used both as diagnostic tools that test for the presence of disease, and as powerful therapeutic agents that attack cancer cells without harming normal tissue. More recent innovations include automated gene and protein sequencers, gene chips that allow simultaneous testing for the presence of thousands of genes in a tiny sample of blood or other biological materials, and a constellation of techniques that speed up drug discovery.

In the US, the market for "new" biotechnology products reached $20.7 billion in 2001.[43] A total of 1,457 firms (including 342 public companies), employing 191,000 people, comprised the industry. The industry has grown steadily since its inception in the late 1970s; sales picked up significantly after 1995 as the flow of new products onto the market began to accelerate. That year, sixteen new biotechnology drugs and vaccines were approved by the Food and Drug Administration (FDA) for marketing; the approvals rose to twenty in 1996, followed by nineteen in 1997, then twenty-one, twenty-two, thirty-two, and twenty-four, respectively, between 1997 and 2001. To date, 130 drugs and vaccines have been approved for marketing in the US, and 350 drugs are in various stages of clinical trials. In addition, twenty-four agricultural products are currently being marketed, including canola, carnations, corn, cotton, papaya, peanuts, rapeseed, soybeans, sunflowers, and milk from cows given a genetically engineered growth hormone. A striking characteristic of the industry is the weight of the sales of the top five first-generation companies – Amgen, Biogen, Chiron, Genentech, and Genzyme – in total sales. In 2001, they contributed about a third of the sector's total sales, leaving two-thirds to be shared among the remaining 337 public companies (Figure 1.1).

In Japan, the market for biotechnology products and services reached 1.3 trillion yen in 2001 ($10.7 billion), and is growing at an annual rate of about 10 percent.[44] The government boldly forecasts that this market will expand to 25 trillion yen ($208 billion at the current exchange rate) in 2010. Growth at the present rate would lift the market to 3.4 trillion yen in 2010; the government's forecast thus assumes that the growth rate will increase dramatically over the next few years.[45] Figure 1.2 shows how recent growth has been distributed across a range of products. The stagnation in the pharmaceutical component shows clearly the effect of the Ministry of Health, Labor, and Welfare's biennial revisions to its drug-pricing schedule in an effort to rein in soaring health care costs. As in the US, the drug EPO, which boosts red blood cell counts in patients receiving kidney dialysis treatment or chemotherapy, has been the perennial best-selling drug since it came on the market in the early 1990s, chalking up 116 billion yen ($955 million) in 2001, which is a little more than a fourth of the entire market. However, the top-selling biotechnology product for the past decade (150 billion yen in sales in 2001) has been laundry detergent containing an enzyme produced using a recombinant DNA process that enhances the enzyme's ability to break down grease, oils, and fats. Also on the list are genetically modified soybeans, corn, cotton, and rapeseed, all of which are imported; they collectively generated 20 billion yen in sales in

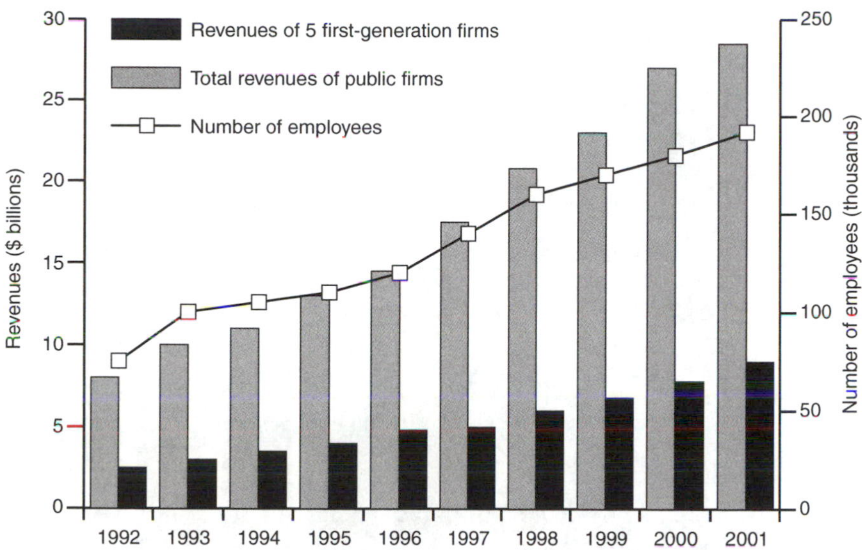

Figure 1.1 Trend in revenues and number of employees of US biotechnology firms

Sources: Adapted from industry metrics compiled by the Biotechnology Industry Organization (BIO).

Total revenues: http://www.bio.org/investor/signs/200210rva0.asp (accessed 24 January 2003).

Revenues of five first-generation firms: http://www.bio.org/investor/signs/200210rv5p.asp (accessed 24 January 2003).

Number of employees: http://www.bio.org/investor/signs/200210emp.asp (accessed 24 January 2003).

Note: The five first-generation firms include Amgen, Biogen, Chiron, Genentech, and Genzyme.

2001. Although imports rocketed after the MHLW issued approvals for their marketing in 1996, the introduction of mandatory labeling of foods containing genetically modified organisms in April 2001 brought sales growth to a halt. Opposition to genetically modified food in Japan remains significant, casting doubt on whether Japan will see much additional growth in this market segment.

On the surface, the size of the market for biotechnology products in Japan appears not to be abnormally low compared with the US when adjustments are made for population. The figures cited above for Japan, however, include several product categories not included in the American data. Japan's Patent Office recently published normalized market data that permits cross-national comparison. These are displayed in Table 1.1. Notice the widening of the gap between Japan and the US: in 2002, the size of the US market was expected to be six times larger than the size of Japan's market in 2002, while Europe's market was expected to be three times larger than Japan's. Thus, despite two decades of concerted effort by Japan's government and private sector to catch up in biotechnology, a formidable gap remains.

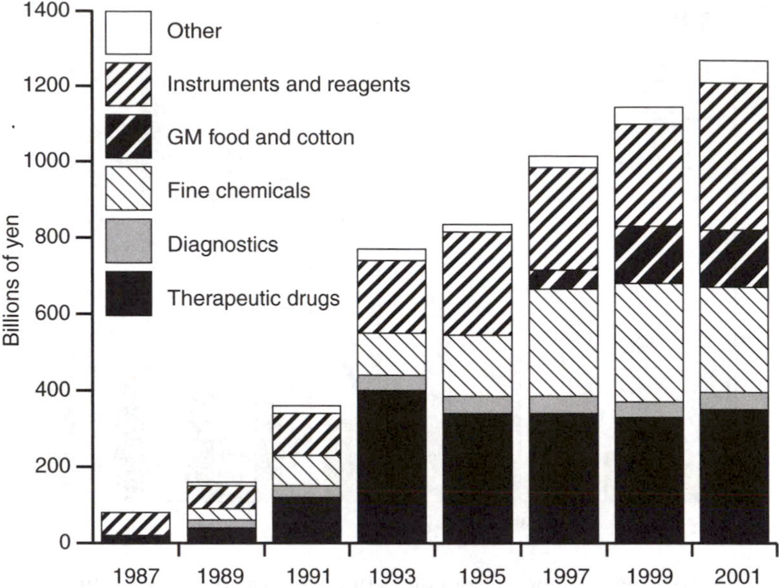

Figure 1.2 Biotechnology product sales in Japan by type of product

Sources: *Nikkei Baioteku*, various issues.

Table 1.1 Comparative market data for products incorporating biotechnology base technologies (in billions of yen)

	Japan			*United States*			*Europe*		
	1997	*1999*	*2002*	*1997*	*1999*	*2002*	*1997*	*1999*	*2002*
Pharmaceuticals	285	290	447	888	1,168	1,973	580	725	1,151
Chemicals	217	240	337	765	868	1,267	698	781	1,116
Food products	10	30	40	711	1,190	1,718	349	378	501
Agricultural products	66	164	195	554	1,500	1,645	88	265	313
Analytical equipment and reagents	78	104	224	310	425	714	175	219	387
Medical diagnostic	6	6	9	29	36	55	20	25	38
Total	662	834	1,252	3,257	5,187	7,372	1,910	2,393	3,506

Source: Adapted from Tokkyocho, Gijutsu chosaka, "Baiotekunoroji-kiban gijutsu ni kansuru gijutsu doko chosa" [Survey of Trends Concerning the Biotechnology Technology Base], 11 December 2002, Table 6, online, available HTTP: <http://www.jpo.go.jp/shiryou/toushin/chousa/pdf/bio.pdf> (last accessed 23 June 2003).

Notes: The biotechnology base technologies are recombinant DNA, DNA analysis, embryo engineering, protein engineering, carbohydrate engineering, and bioinformatics.

Data for 2002 are estimates.

A road map

The argument introduced and summarized above is developed in the following five chapters. Chapter 2 introduces the methodology used for comparing the history and success of technological innovation. Chapter 3 compares the national systems of innovation in Japan and the US, focusing on the role of firms, universities and research institutes, and science and technology policies. Chapters 4 and 5 round out the study with historical accounts and analysis of the emergence of biotechnology in the US and Japan, respectively. The concluding chapter pulls together the various strands of the argument.

2 Firms, technological regimes, and national innovation systems

Introduction

This chapter develops the conceptual framework for analyzing the emergence of commercial biotechnology in the United States and Japan. It begins from the premise that neither business organization and strategy nor research and industrial policies alone provide a satisfactory explanation of national variations in technological innovation. Rather we must examine the differences in the institutional, social, and political environments in which entrepreneurial agents and other organizations produce knowledge and apply it commercially. Nor is it sufficient merely to list institutions involved in scientific research and technological development and compare their characteristics across countries; different technologies and industries draw on different systems of institutions that form a subset of the larger national system. The relevant dependent variable is technological change in a particular industry, not technological change across the whole economy. Having identified and characterized a particular technology, we can thus proceed to isolate the relevant subset of institutions and examine their respective capacities to respond to the economic opportunities the new technology poses: their capacity, that is, to generate and maintain the relevant knowledge base, and translate that knowledge into products and services that create value in the market.

Two hypotheses underpin this analytical framework. First, cross-national differences in technological trajectories in biotechnology reflect variation in the institutional and organizational environment out of which new knowledge arises and through which innovative activities are filtered and focused. The second hypothesis rests on the argument that different technologies pose different kinds of problems, the solutions for which emerge from different kinds of institutions and innovation strategies. The United States has become home to the world's most innovative biotechnology firms because it has evolved institutions and organizations best equipped to exploit a technology for which commercial success turns on a strong science base and on efficiency in transforming new knowledge into innovative products. Examples include a world-class basic research system in the health sciences that is readily accessible to industry, a flexible industrial structure that permits ease of market entry and exit, powerfully competitive supporting industries, and science and regulatory policies that for decades have shone favorably on the human health care sector. Japan, though not as weak in biotechnology as is commonly assumed, was slow to develop appropriate regulatory policies and organizational mechanisms needed to match entrepreneurs with the new commercial opportunities arising from its own research laboratories. Japanese firms thus quickly fell behind their counterparts in the US and Europe in the early commercialization of new products based on recombinant DNA, especially in the human health care sector. That early gap has proved difficult to close as newer techniques such as those based on monoclonal antibodies and genomics have become important platforms underpinning drug discovery and new product development.

In this chapter, I introduce a set of general propositions about the relationship between entrepreneurial agents and the technologies they are trying to advance. The goal is to capture the influences of supporting institutions and organizations that form an integrated system in which innovators go about their business of generating novelty and translating it into marketable products. I begin at the simplest level: that of the single entrepreneurial agent, which in most cases is a firm, though lone inventors and professor-entrepreneurs may also initiate the innovative response. Development of the model moves outward from the firm to encompass the broader range of supporting institutions at the sectoral and finally the national levels. I conclude by integrating firm, sectoral, and national level variables into a comprehensive explanatory framework.

The firm as innovator

Building on insights already discussed, I construct a theory of innovation that is both historical and comparative across nations and industries. I derive it in three stages, moving from micro to macro levels of analysis. It begins at the level of the firm. I start there for two reasons. First, in capitalist systems it is the firm, not the state or larger society, that ultimately makes and executes the decisions necessary to transform knowledge into value.[1] Even in industries in which lone inventors supply the creative spark, the firm ultimately provides the physical, organizational, and managerial resources required to bring new ideas and inventions to market. Second, it is the firm that lies at the crucial interface between the stock of knowledge available to entrepreneurs (the supply side) and the market forces providing the incentives for entrepreneurs to transform that knowledge into new goods and services that add value to the economy (the demand side). Successful innovation generally depends on entrepreneurial agents "getting right" a sequence of bets that correctly interpret the often vague and rapidly changing streams of information provided by these demand- and supply-side factors.

To simplify matters, I initially assume that technological change is exogenous, bracketing for the moment the influence of public policy, capital markets, universities, and other contextual factors. Knowledge, moreover, is freely appropriable: once it becomes available to one firm, it is available to all. This leads to the following six propositions, upon which the remainder of the analysis is based:

1 Competitive advantage based on technological innovation ultimately depends on decisions firms make in response to perceived market signals and technological opportunities.
2 Innovation builds on a base of accumulated scientific or technical knowledge. Sources of knowledge may be internal or external to the firm. The ability effectively to link internal and external knowledge to create value greater than the sum of the value of the individual elements is itself an important source of competitive advantage.
3 Successful innovation requires the capacity to efficiently combine new knowledge with other factor inputs, as well as managerial and organizational resources necessary to produce and deliver a marketable good or service.
4 Accomplishing propositions 2 and 3 entails transaction costs.
5 A firm expands its organizational boundaries (through full or partial integration or by creating a new subsidiary, for example) to minimize transaction costs. Alternatively, it expands virtually through the creation of inter-organizational alliances with other firms, universities, or public research institutes.
6 Governing the firm's organizational response is a process of search and selection that reflects existing organization, technologies, and accumulated competencies, experiences, and resources.

Together, these propositions suggest certain conclusions. First, creating competitive advantage through technological innovation is difficult and costly; for every firm that succeeds, many will fail. Second, innovation is both a technical and an organizational problem. It is technical in the sense that scientific, engineering, marketing, and other resources have to be developed. It is organizational in the sense that a firm must choose whether to develop these capabilities internally, contract for them externally, or do something intermediate between the two. Third, success involves not only generating or appropriating new knowledge and embodying that knowledge in a final product. Innovating firms must also gain access to, or themselves produce, other inputs that it packages together with the final product, making it easier or more attractive for the consumer to use; competition to supply these "complementary assets" may be as heated and critical to the firm's competitive success as is competition to produce the original technological breakthrough.[2] Finally, the cumulative and collective nature of learning, which is central to the process of innovation, sets up a condition of path dependence. Given the uncertainty surrounding innovation, management will tend to build incrementally on existing capabilities, rather than investing in opening up radically new technological trajectories, especially if the firm has a major stake in the existing technology.[3] Consequently, exploiting a new technology will often require transformation of current business organization and strategy to permit the degree of coordination necessary to activate a new trajectory.

In some circumstances, path dependence may lock incumbents into existing practices and technologies, raising the threshold to adopting a new technology beyond that which would yield an innovative response in a perfectly competitive market. The larger the financial stake in the current technology, the more reluctant a potential innovator will be to make a decision that undermines the value of that technology or renders it obsolete. This creates opportunities for new firms willing to bear the risk of commercializing a new idea or invention that incumbents fail to exploit. It is precisely this dynamic that led to the creation of a dedicated biotechnology industry in the US, which emerged at least in part because of failure of incumbent pharmaceutical and chemical firms to exploit the new inventions and scientific knowledge flowing out of academic laboratories in the 1970s and 1980s.

The above propositions lead to a key hypothesis: given the appearance of a new technology, competitive advantage will accrue to the firm whose organizational resources and search routines permit a transaction cost-efficient "innovative response," resulting in delivery to the market of a product whose performance or costs or both surpasses that of rival goods. To the extent the firm is able to appropriate the returns to its investment in the innovative response – through patent protection, trade secrets, or faster cycle times, for example – its competitive advantage is likely to be sustained. In the event that market structure or lock-in from path dependence or both deters incumbents from responding to the appearance of a new technological opportunity, the door is open to new entrants, which may be start-up companies or existing firms entering the market from other sectors. In the case of biotechnology, in neither Japan nor the US did incumbents exploit the opportunities made possible by the invention of recombinant DNA processes. In the US, new firms dedicated to commercializing these inventions kicked off the commercial biotechnology revolution, while in Japan many of the early movers were existing firms diversifying into biotechnology from unrelated industries, such as cosmetics, fine chemicals, and textiles.

Although this hypothesis sheds light on innovation at the micro level, it says nothing about the influence of the social environment surrounding the firm, nor does it provide insight into why particular innovative responses succeed or fail. Through the 1980s, Japanese firms in one industry after another conquered world markets through their innovative prowess. Yet in many other industries, including pharmaceuticals, computer software, aerospace, and telecommunications, Japanese firms have not only met with limited successes at the global level, they have struggled to maintain positions in their domestic market. Likewise, in the US powerfully competitive global firms and industries coexist with ones that long ago ceded technological leadership to competitors in Asia or Europe. While differences in factor endowments may explain international patterns of comparative advantage in industries that make intensive use of natural and human resources unevenly distributed globally, they are less useful in explaining patterns of competitive advantage in high technology industries today. In these sectors, the abilities to create and use knowledge, to respond quickly to the emergence of new knowledge, to direct that knowledge to the points in the value chain where it can be most effectively used, and to apply problem-solving processes appropriate to the knowledge at hand ultimately separate innovators from followers and also-rans. Is it possible that certain technologies require certain organizational forms and institutions to enable their successful application? To what extent do capabilities and resources outside the firm and sector shape the innovative responses of firms? The remainder of the chapter modifies the model sketched to enable it to address these questions.

Technological regimes and trajectories

Modern macroeconomic growth theory underscores the importance of technological innovation in economic growth over the long run, especially in free-market economies.[4] Among the primary sources of technological change are the accumulation of knowledge and its interplay with other factor inputs.[5] At the level of the firm, therefore, successful management of knowledge – its creation, articulation, combination with existing knowledge, and conversion into different forms – is an increasingly important source of a competitive advantage.[6] Yet because different industries draw on different types and mixes of knowledge, management practices that succeed in one industry will not necessarily be applicable to others.[7] The institutional and organizational resources outside the firm, moreover, are apt to be specialized to the support of knowledge creation in certain industries while being irrelevant to others. Biotechnology, automobiles, and computer software differ substantially in terms of their dependence on basic scientific research, reliance on the accumulated knowledge of workers on the shop floor and production line, and the relationship between tacit knowledge (organizational and individualized knowledge that is difficult to articulate) and explicit knowledge (knowledge that is codifiable and easy to articulate). We would thus expect to find that approaches to knowledge management and engagement with external resources vary across these industries. How to capture this sectoral variation, and operationalize it as an independent variable, is the goal of this section.

The literature on the characteristics of technology has identified a number of dimensions along which different technologies differ. These include the attributes mentioned above, appropriability conditions (the extent to which the innovator, as opposed to competitors or society at large, captures the returns from investment in R&D), opportunity conditions (the probability that investment in R&D will deliver substantial returns to the firm), and the degree of cumulativeness (the extent to which technological advance progresses incrementally rather than in bursts).[8] The mix of characteristics intrinsic to a technology tends to shape the manner and pace of its advance. According to Nelson and Winter, technologies follow "natural trajectories" in which "advances seem to follow advances in a way that appears somewhat 'inevitable' and certainly not tuned to the changing demand and cost conditions."[9] They go on to argue that natural trajectories are specific to a particular "technological regime," which they conceive to be "a frontier of achievable capabilities, defined in the relevant economic dimensions, limited by physical, biological, and other constraints, given a broadly defined way of doing things."[10] Dosi offers a similar, though more concrete, formulation. Taking his cue from Thomas Kuhn, he argues for the existence of "technological paradigms":

> A "technological paradigm" defines contextually the needs that are meant to be filled, the scientific principles utilised for the task, the material technology to be used. In other words, a technological paradigm can be defined as a "pattern" for solution of selected techno-economic problems based on highly selected principles derived from the natural sciences.[11]

Because a technological regime or paradigm identifies the problems that have to be solved, it channels research efforts and search routines toward particular trajectories. Examples of such paradigms include microelectronics, aircraft, and petroleum-based technologies.[12]

Although the concept of paradigm has both intuitive and logical appeal, identifying those factors that distinguish among different paradigms is no simple affair. Scholars have suggested a number of strategies. Dosi argues that paradigms differ in terms of "(a) the opportunities of innovation that each paradigm entails; (b) the degrees to which firms can obtain economic returns to various kinds of innovation, that is the degree of appropriability of innovation; and (c) the patterns of demand that firms face."[13] Freeman, by contrast, emphasizes differences in the relationship between internal (or private) and external (or public) sources of knowledge.[14] Kitschelt, building on insights from transaction cost theory, classifies technologies along two dimensions – degree of coupling of specific assets and complexity.[15] Finally, Nelson distinguishes technologies based on the relative importance of "tacit" versus "latent public" sources of knowledge. In some industries, especially those in which chemical composition is a central aspect of design, knowledge is easily reproducible, and hence more of a public good. In other industries, especially those in which products take the form of complex systems, knowledge is localized, tacit, and thus transferable only at considerable cost. In the former, which include chemicals, pharmaceuticals, plastics, and synthetic fibers, patent protection and secrecy are important sources of advantage. In the latter, which include semiconductors, telecommunications, and aircraft, advantage lies more in exploiting a head start and upgrading one's earlier advantage once imitators emerge.[16]

To use technology as a variable, it must be operationalized in a way that accords with observed variability. Pavitt proposes four stylized sectors which relate the content of technological strategy to the processes through which they are developed and implemented.[17] Key parameters are the source of new knowledge and the institutional relationship between that source and the rest of the production process. At one extreme are "science-based" sectors. Here, innovation is coupled closely with basic scientific research; tacit knowledge imbedded in workers is relatively insignificant. The institutional challenge for the firm is to access complementary assets needed to deliver a new product to the marketplace. Examples include most segments of the chemical industry and advanced electronics. At the other extreme are "specialized supplier" sectors. Here, innovation depends on informal links between supplier and user. There is little formal R&D; potential to innovate depends on the accumulated skills and knowledge of workers. The institutional challenge is to absorb user experience and identify new product niches. Examples include mechanical engineering, precision instruments, and machinery sectors. Falling between these extremes are "scale-intensive" and "information-intensive" sectors. The former are similar to "specialized supplier" sectors except that economies of scale and high-asset specificity encourage vertical integration over subcontracting. Representative industries are automobiles, ferrous and non-ferrous metals, food products, and electrical equipment. Innovation in the latter also depends strongly on user–supplier relations, though scale economies are relatively insignificant, and incentives for integration vary widely. Retailing, financial services, and computer software are representative examples.

Working from a somewhat different angle, Kitschelt is concerned with linking sectors to appropriate innovation governance mechanisms on the basis of their corresponding "technology systems."[18] He employs a four-cell classification scheme in which sectors are grouped along two dimensions: complexity of the technology's causal structure (a cognitive variable) and the degree of coupling of co-specialized assets (a technical variable). Unlike Pavitt, however, Kitschelt pitches innovation not as a strategic challenge to the firm but as an institutional challenge to the nation as a whole. Japan, he reasons, excels in sectors whose technology systems are characterized by tight coupling but "linear causal structure," which include most mass-produced consumer goods. The US, by contrast, excels in sectors characterized by "complex interactive technology," whether they use tightly coupled systems (nuclear technology and aircraft) or loosely coupled ones (software, biotechnology, and pharmaceuticals). Put simply, Japanese institutions supporting technological change are adapted to innovating in sectors formerly associated with Fordist mass-production characteristics; they perform far less effectively in the newer science-based industries.

Both Pavitt and Kitschelt provide a useful means of operationalizing the concept of technological paradigm. Pavitt's model has the advantage of compactness and simplicity by virtue of its micro focus: a firm innovates successfully when its strategic response corresponds to the character of the technological system, or trajectory, the proxy for which is the source of technology. Kitschelt's model, in contrast, sacrifices rigor for the messiness of reality: a nation innovates successfully when its firms (or sectors; it is not clear precisely whom he casts in the role of innovator) adopt sectoral governance mechanisms that correspond to the properties of the technological system.[19] Taking the nation as the dependent variable is a crucial step to the extent that it directs attention beyond the firm to government policies, universities, and national research infrastructure that augment firms' own innovative efforts. I take that step in the next section.

Given the importance of regime characteristics of technology, it seems sensible to seek a middle ground between Pavitt and Kitschelt. A theory of innovation has to start from micro principles – the firm is the locus of innovative activity – while recognizing the shaping influence of contextual factors, the components of which comprise what Lynn has termed the "innovation community."[20] It needs to acknowledge that organizational routines and capabilities, both internal and external to the firm, that foster successful innovation in one type of technology might be neutral, or even counterproductive, when brought to bear on a different technology. Explaining innovative performance thus requires a model that takes into account differences in technologies and how they relate to the strategic behavior of the firm, while also recognizing that the firm itself is a product of the social context.[21]

Consider the case of biotechnology. First, the knowledge that flows out of biotechnology R&D tends to be codified in the form of product and process patents that, in the absence of a regime of strong intellectual property protection, would be readily appropriable by rivals. Compared to microelectronics or automobile manufacturing, tacit knowledge embodied in workers and networks has been less important as a source of competitive advantage than ownership of key enabling technologies. Second, biotechnology has commercial application in a wide range of industries, and the direction and pace of technological change is highly uncertain and unpredictable. It is thus reasonable to express the paradigmatic qualities of biotechnology along two taxonomic dimensions: tacitness of knowledge and breadth of application. As noted above, biotechnology as a technological regime is characterized by low tacitness and pervasive application. This combination of characteristics leads to a third quality: high uncertainty. Together, these attributes determine in a broad way the organizational and cognitive challenges firms face in exploiting the technological opportunities arising from research in biotechnology.

Consider the regime characteristics of biotechnology and their consequences for firms in more detail. Biotechnology relies strongly on basic R&D as a source of knowledge and opportunity. To the extent that scientific results are generally widely published, such knowledge is easily articulated; once generated, a finding becomes available to anyone who has access to scientific journals and conferences and the capacity to engage in reverse engineering. The process of recombinant DNA, for example, is well known and widely used, even in university undergraduate laboratories. The value of a new product, moreover, often lies in knowing the precise location and function of a particular sequence of genes known to produce a therapeutically valuable product. Although such knowledge is often the culmination of a decade of expensive R&D, once it is known, its application in the manufacture of a new product is, by comparison, relatively imitable.

This has several important consequences in terms of firms' strategic behavior. First, because new products often arise directly from basic research, with little or no intervening period of applied research or development, firms have to spend lavishly on high-risk R&D. In addition, the history of commercial development points to the crucial importance of universities and public research institutes that support the advancement of scientific knowledge in the biomedical and genetic sciences. American firms benefit mightily from their proximity to the National Institutes of Health (NIH) and an unrivaled system of research universities. These institutions contribute not only a solid scientific foundation but also scientists and engineers who often carry that knowledge with them to the private sector. A second consequence concerns the problem of appropriability. Securing private returns to innovation whose origins lie in an easily codifiable knowledge base depends on patent protection; uncertainty in the process of administering and enforcing patents in genetic engineering can act as a powerful deterrent to investment in R&D. Because the US government was the first to uphold patenting of genetically altered organisms, American companies enjoyed a substantial early advantage over their competitors.

The second dimension is the pervasiveness of biotechnology in terms of its influence across a wide range of industries. Over the past decade, genetic engineering has found application in industries as diverse as basic chemicals, food processing, agriculture, textiles, paper, cement, and pharmaceuticals. In pharmaceuticals, for example, combinatorial chemistry and high-throughput screening techniques challenge traditional, labor-intensive methods of screening large quantities of molecules. In food processing, mass cell culture has revolutionized older fermentation techniques in the production of enzymes, flavor enhancers, and other food additives. And in microelectronics, the fusion of semiconductor and biochemical techniques has led to the development of microarrays, tiny chips coated with short strands of DNA that can sense the presence of hundreds of thousands of discrete DNA sequences in a small sample.

The consequences of pervasiveness are equally profound. First, it extends the potential reward to innovation across a broad range of industries. Thus, while the US has evolved a distinctive "biotechnology industry," key players also hail from traditional research-intensive industries, especially pharmaceuticals and chemicals. In Japan, firms from industries as diverse as steel, dairy, paper, and agrochemicals have mounted commercial forays into biotechnology. Another consequence of pervasiveness is the extent to which cumulative development of the knowledge base has drawn on contributions from related industries. Indeed, as the case of the US bears out, an excellent pharmaceutical and chemical industry, on whose knowledge bases biotechnology overlaps, has been crucial to innovative success. By contrast, traditional strength in semiconductors has made Japanese firms world leaders in the development of biosensors and their application in novel electronic systems.

Finally, the combination of high pervasiveness and low tacitness of knowledge, coupled with ethical and safety concerns that are unique to biotechnology, create conditions of enormous risk and uncertainty. On this point, much is beyond the control of the individual firm; a coherent and predictable regulatory regime and availability of risk capital establish a threshold of certainty below which the rate of innovative activity would be sharply diminished. For many applications of biotechnology, moreover, the enormous sums of capital needed to conduct clinical trials and clear regulatory hurdles generates additional uncertainty. Consequently, competitive advantage accrues to firms able to forge strategic alliances or other efficient means of reducing transaction costs and exploiting synergies with other firms.[22] Under these conditions, a fluid industry structure, ease of entry and exit, and flexible options for forming alliances provide crucial hedges needed to sustain innovative success.

In sum, the biotechnology technology regime poses a unique set of organizational and technical challenges. Low tacitness of learning, pervasiveness of application, and extraordinary high risk and uncertainty present a set of problems far different than those associated with microelectronics or automobiles. Indeed, as history bears out, the complexity of the regime demands a marshaling of resources far beyond what any single firm can provide. Understanding the pattern of innovation in biotechnology thus requires situating the firm in its broader institutional context – what I call the national system of innovation. Before doing that, however, it is appropriate to add to the original set of propositions outlined earlier to reflect issues highlighted in this section. These are as follows:

7 Whether a firm moves successfully onto a new technological trajectory depends on the extent to which that firm's strategic response yields

organization structures that conform to the cognitive and technical characteristics of the technological regime.

7a By virtue of proposition 6, a firm's ability to effect the appropriate organizational response is constrained by its existing routines, experiences, and accumulated competencies.

Biotechnology and the national innovation system

A firm is not an isolated node of production whose actions are independent of its external environment. Rather, it is situated in a constellation of interlinked institutions whose activities augment and supplement its own. Examples include universities, public research institutes, regulatory agencies, policy-making bodies that promote scientific and technological development, and even social attitudes and values. By providing information and reducing uncertainty, these institutions raise incentives for productive entrepreneurship and channel innovative activities in socially desirable directions. Rosenberg aptly refers to these institutions as "focusing devices," which selectively raise the level of private returns to R&D beyond what would be available under free-market conditions. The catch, he writes, is that it is not possible to know precisely in advance which institutions will conduce to desired paths of innovation:

> The exact institutional arrangements which will make for success[ful innovation] will always be difficult to specify *a priori*. I would like to suggest that this is so mainly because success or failure always depends on the environment in which any particular institution is immersed – that is, on the complex of *other* institutions as well as widely shared values and traditions which critically affect its operation.[23]

Because firms prefer to minimize uncertainty and risk, they will place their bets on techniques for which institutional resources are comparatively abundant. In addition, the form in which they place those bets, and the likelihood of success, depends on the character and quality of those resources. The consequence for a theory of innovation is to shift attention from the firms and markets to the broader institutional context whose systemic features are manifest at the national level.

Capturing the complex relationships among firms and their institutional environment is the goal of an approach that in the past decade has gained currency among scholars of technological change. At its core is the concept "national innovation system" (henceforth, NIS), which is used to explain cross-national differences in patterns of innovative success.[24] According to Christopher Freeman, who appears to have coined the term, an NIS is "the network of institutions in the public and private sectors whose activities and interactions initiate, import, modify, and diffuse new technologies."[25]

In his description of the Japanese NIS, Freeman emphasizes four key components: government policy, the general structure of industry, systems of education and training, and corporate R&D.[26] Lynn, emphasizing the interaction among the various actors, conceives those actors as "forming a bounded structure encompassing a superstructure of coordinating organizations, a substructure of organizations producing key components of the commercialized technology, and linkages between the substructure and superstructure and among the various actors." For Lynn, in addition, this bounded structure "coevolves with the technology."[27] Other theorists have extended this approach to comparisons of a broad range of countries, emphasizing different components and interactions among them.[28] Despite disagreement over which institutions merit inclusion under the NIS umbrella, the core argument is the same: national patterns of technological innovation result from the combined influence of market selection and institutional focusing of the innovative activities of firms and entrepreneurs.

What institutions comprise an NIS in biotechnology? I find it useful to stylize the concept as a series of concentric spheres centered on the firm (Figure 2.1). At the center, the firm represents the point at which knowledge, information, and learning are completely private and localized at the site where value is being created. The outermost circle, where information and knowledge are completely social, represents the general policy environment. Here, legislators and public officials make decisions that influence innovative activity in biotechnology throughout the system. In between are institutions whose activities have both social and private components. Public research institutes and mission agencies generate a knowledge base that in most cases, though by no means always, is freely appropriable. Research universities, most of whose funding comes from mission agencies, generate knowledge that is mostly generic, but is occasionally licensed to,

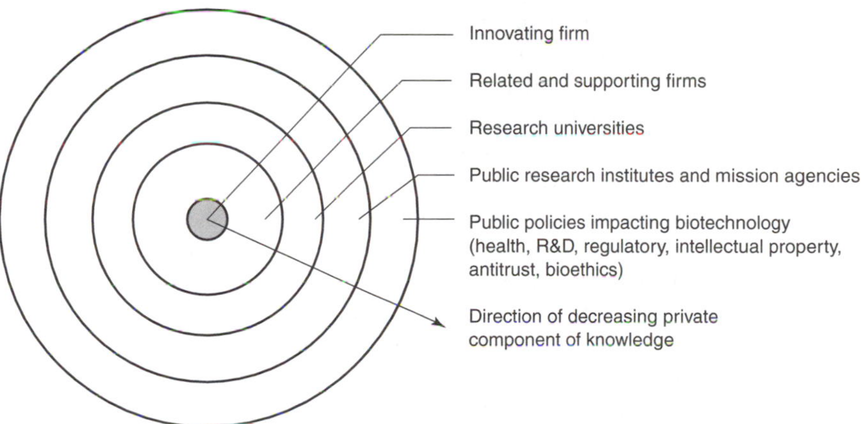

Figure 2.1 National innovation system in biotechnology

or done under sponsorship of, a private firm. Finally, surrounding the firm itself is the constellation of firms in related or supporting industries.[29] Among these are competitors and potential collaborators: depending on the circumstances, they may serve as potential research partners, providers of finance or technology licenses, or sources of complementary assets which the innovating firm needs to bring its new products to market.

In comparing Japanese and American NIS, variation in institutional structure and capabilities is striking at each level of the system. At the point closest to the boundary of the innovating firm, conditions in related and supporting industries have been especially crucial, both at the early and later stages of the product cycle. American biotechnology firms have benefited enormously from the ability to access diverse sources of capital, as well as to integrate partially or wholly with related firms as part of their strategic response. In Japan, membership in *keiretsu* and access to information through various inter-organizational networks and consortia have provided firms with a completely different range of strategic opportunities, albeit ones that appear to have worked less effectively given the characteristics of the biotechnology regime. The upshot of differences in this institutional sphere is that firms in the two countries face a markedly different set of constraints and opportunities for effecting transaction cost-efficient innovative strategies.

Differences are also plainly visible in the other institutional spheres. Universities, particularly those in the US, gave rise to most of the major discoveries that launched commercial biotechnology. Public research institutes, again especially in the US but also in Japan, have contributed powerfully to creating the knowledge base in molecular biology and medicine that supplements research done in universities. Finally, the policy environment in both countries has shaped the rate and direction of innovation. In the US, the crucially timed decision to extend patent protection to certain genetically modified organisms, in conjunction with issuing the world's first regulatory guidelines on recombinant DNA, helped to catapult American firms to the frontier of commercialization. In Japan, by contrast, delay in implementing a supportive regulatory regime and the fragmentation of regulatory and promotional authority across multiple agencies set back commercialization by several years.

To summarize, firms reside in a constellation of institutions that focus their innovative activities, skewing technological trajectories in certain directions. Like firms, these institutions are governed by their own routines and standard operating procedures, which may be likened to sets of "genes" whose development unfolds in evolutionary fashion. Capabilities distributed throughout the system add to the "stock" of cumulative knowledge and learning that, when accessible to innovating firms, can exert a powerful inducement effect. As I argued earlier, innovating firms reduce transaction costs by shifting their organizational boundaries; complementary institutions in the NIS provide the medium, so to speak, through which firms' boundaries continually move. Yet whether the resources available in that medium conduce to successful innovation depends on whether those resources are specialized to the technological regime associated with the field in which firms are attempting to innovate. Consequently, successful innovation that translates into enduring competitive advantage is most likely to be found in sectors embedded in an NIS whose resources and institutions are specialized to the problems and challenges posed by the particular technological regime associated with that sector.

I conclude this section with three final propositions that complete the model. These reflect the additional forces that impinge on firms' innovative strategies, yet lie outside their organizational boundaries:

8 The institutional environment in which the firm is embedded provides resources and capabilities that focus the firm's innovative activities.

9 These institutions as a whole evolve in accordance with the dynamics of path-dependence similar to that outlined in proposition 6.

10 Whether a firm lacking relevant resources and capabilities, which would permit a successful response under proposition 7, successfully moves onto a new technological trajectory depends on the extent to which it can access and internalize relevant knowledge and complementary assets that reside elsewhere in the NIS. The probability of success is greatest when the NIS contains resources and capabilities that are specialized to the combination of technical, cognitive, and risk characteristics associated with the technological regime in which the firm is attempting to innovate.

Putting it all together

I have attempted in the foregoing analysis to develop a general framework for comparing cross-national and cross-sectoral patterns of innovation. I started with the firm because of my belief that the firm, whether an incumbent or the result of an act of entrepreneurship in response to a new technological opportunity not being exploited by incumbents, plays the critical and final role in articulating the innovative response. In my model, moreover, the firm is not motivated necessarily to achieve short-term efficiency. There is nothing "efficient" about innovation; it is costly and risky, forcing firms to sacrifice short-term profits for highly uncertain future gains. Yet there are ways firms can hedge their bets: instead of betting the store on the next novelty that appears to have future promise, the firm may choose to in-license a technology from another firm, form a joint venture, take an equity position in a firm working in the area of interest, or other similar strategy. This is precisely how most large drug firms responded once they perceived the opportunity in biotechnology. Large Japanese firms also pursued alliance strategies, especially in the mid 1980s, when partnerships with American biotechnology firms were all the rage.

Micro-level analysis, however, leaves unanswered the question of what constitutes an appropriate organizational response to technical change and whether that response will ultimately succeed. Here, meso-level reasoning steps in. I argued that technologies have regime characteristics that establish broad criteria for problem solving with which innovating firms have to contend. This led to the conclusion that successful innovators are those whose organizational response to technical change solves the particular technical and cognitive problems intrinsic to the technological regime. I identified two variables – tacitness of knowledge and breadth of application – as having particular bearing on choice of organizational response. For biotechnology, I argued that relatively low tacitness of knowledge, high pervasiveness, and high uncertainty pose a special set of problems and opportunities for potential innovators. When biotechnology first emerged as a viable technological opportunity, Japanese and American firms responded in completely different ways, generating completely different results. While American firms forged ahead in riskier, more sophisticated applications in human health care, Japanese firms initially carved out niches in fine chemicals, electronics, consumer products, and other sectors in which Japan's firms had already achieved strong market positions at home, abroad, or both. In both countries, path dependence foreclosed some responses while opening the way to others. Most strikingly, in the US the availability of ample venture capital, prodigious public investment in biomedical research, ease of technology transfer from universities to industry, ease of market entry by academic researchers and other entrepreneurs starting up dedicated biotechnology firms, and unregulated prices of drugs, all but guaranteed that innovative efforts in the US would be focused heavily on pharmaceuticals. In Japan, by contrast, conditions in the NIS nearly opposite those mentioned above for the US provided far fewer incentives, and made innovative success less certain, in biopharmaceutical applications. Interestingly, policy decisions made in Japan during the 1990s have strengthened Japan's NIS in areas relevant to biotechnology applications in medicine and research. Consequently, new firms have been forming to exploit opportunities in these areas, and innovative activities in Japanese biotechnology are converging on those in the US.

Finally, despite the usefulness of the technological regime concept, to say that for each technological regime there is a uniquely optimal way of orchestrating the innovative response would be overly simplistic. I argued rather that firms do not innovate in a vacuum; the firm rather is one part of a national innovation system that works, as a system, to promote but also shape technological innovation within the country's borders. Universities, research institutes and, above all, government policies contribute capabilities and resources that favor certain technologies over others. Consequently, the rate and direction of technical change is as much the result of institutional capabilities external to the firm as it is the outcome of business strategy and market selection. In terms of biotechnology, when the core technologies emerged in the 1970s, the Japanese and American NIS could hardly have been more different.

The bottom line is that neither micro nor macro variables alone offer a complete explanation. Innovative success turns on the combined efforts of firms and supporting institutions to meet the challenges posed by technical change.

3 Biotechnology and national innovation systems in the US and Japan

The purpose of this chapter is to relate the differences in the commercial development of biotechnology in Japan and the US to the underlying characteristics of their national innovation systems as they were identified in the previous chapter. It is organized in the form of paired comparisons of the two countries for each of the major components of the innovation system as they relate to biotechnology: industry, universities and public research institutes, and public policies.

Industry

At the heart of the national system of innovation are the individual firms whose research and commercial development strategies represent the institutional locus of value creation. Here, labor and capital transform information and raw materials into finished goods and services. Technological innovation, whether in the form of new product or process, enables the creation of more value in output without a proportional increase in factor inputs. Successful innovation depends on the quality of the firm's internal knowledge base, its ability to perceive and react to the needs of consumers, and capacity for accessing, adapting, and internalizing know-how and other resources from outside the firm as the need arises. At times, organizational innovation, such as the creation of a new research joint venture, may be a prerequisite to the successful generation, appropriation, and development of new knowledge.

The United States

American companies active in biotechnology fall broadly into two major groups: small, relatively young start-up companies, and large, established pharmaceutical and chemical companies. Because firms in the first group focus exclusively on applying the tools of biotechnology to develop new products and services, this book refers to them as "dedicated biotechnology companies," or DBCs, a term used by the US Congress's Office of Technology Assessment (OTA) in its 1988 report on biotechnology.[1] Most of these companies are very small and privately held; none is more than thirty years old. The latter group comprises vertically integrated chemical and pharmaceutical companies that have undertaken major investments in biotechnology. They include not only American companies but also US sites of foreign multinationals that perform research and develop new technologies and products inside the American NIS. Although a handful of older DBCs have succeeded in becoming independent, fully integrated firms, most specialize in research and development, or they provide specialized products, technologies, and services to other firms. They often enter into strategic alliances with each other and with large drug firms; collaborating in this way enables firms to bring together complementary assets that complete the value chain needed to move products from the laboratory to the market.

Small companies

Commercial biotechnology is the culmination of decades of research in molecular biology and genetics that since the 1940s has identified DNA as the carrier of genetic information, characterized its molecular structure, and elucidated the biochemical mechanisms by which it expresses protein in cells. Academic scientists, funded mainly by research grants from the National Institutes of Health (NIH), Rockefeller Foundation, and a few other federal agencies and private organizations, performed the vast bulk of this research. Because most of this research was basic in nature, concerned as it was with understanding the biochemical basis of living systems and the diseases that afflict them, industrial laboratories paid little attention to it; no industrial sector was waiting in the wings to commercialize it. The pharmaceutical industry, for its part, was still profiting handsomely from new products developed from chemical synthesis, screening, and assaying techniques that had been around since the 1950s. Few drug firms, therefore, took notice when scientists in the early 1970s first spliced a segment of DNA from one organism into the DNA of another organism, thereby causing the latter to produce a protein it does not make in its natural state. Since many drugs are proteins, and therapeutic proteins are often difficult to synthesize using standard chemical techniques, this new technology offered the possibility of creating practically unlimited quantities of proteins that are difficult or impossible to make using basic chemistry. Being large organizations that for decades had relied on chemistry to develop new drugs, however, most pharmaceutical firms responded cautiously to this new biological approach. A window of opportunity thus opened up for newcomers willing to shoulder the risk of building a business model around the new technology.

A small number of venture capitalists and entrepreneurs, mostly based in the San Francisco Bay and Boston regions, decided to seize the moment. Convinced that biotechnology would lead to radically new therapies and cures for disease, they persuaded molecular biologists, biochemists, and geneticists to form companies dedicated to commercializing their research. Thus were born Genentech, Amgen, Genetic Systems, Biogen, and others in the first wave of DBCs, which appeared in the latter half of the 1970s.[2] By the early 1980s, these first DBCs had become darlings of Wall Street investors; money poured into the sector. By the end of the decade, hundreds of DBCs were developing products ranging from human insulin and growth hormone to vaccines and interferons used to treat cancer.

At the beginning of 2002, a quarter century after the first wave of firms had appeared, there were 1,457 biotechnology firms in the US, of which 342 were public companies.[3] For a decade, the number of firms had hovered in a narrow range between 1,250 and 1,350 before the excitement surrounding the sequencing of the human genome and technology boom of the late 1990s led to a spurt of new start-ups in 2000. The industry earned $27.6 billion in revenues in 2001, spent $15.6 billion on R&D, and employed 179,000 people. Because employment more than doubled between 1992 and 2001 while the number of companies grew only 18 percent, the average number of employees per firm nearly doubled, from 64 in 1992 to 123 in 2001. The industry has clearly developed beyond the embryonic stage.

To survive, DBCs must invest enormous sums in research and development, especially if they are developing products requiring clinical testing in humans. Recent studies peg the cost of bringing a drug to market at somewhere between $240 million and $802 million, depending on who is doing the tallying and whether opportunity costs are taken into account.[4] Moreover, because the path from lab to market can take a decade or more, firms must have the capacity to sustain a high-level investment over a long period; and they must do so knowing that only about one-fifth of compounds that enter the last phase of development – clinical trials in humans – end up being approved for sale as new drugs. For many smaller firms with only one or two products in development, failure of any single product in clinical trials can spell the end of their existence as independent entities.

DBCs thus face constant financial pressure, which manifests itself in three distinctive characteristics of the industry. First, it is awash in red ink: in 1999, the industry collectively lost $5.6 billion.[5] *Nature Biotechnology* reckons that only 74 of 440 public companies whose finances it tracks were profitable in 2001.[6] Second is the extent to which a handful of companies generate most of the revenue, and all the profits. The top ten public drug-based biotechnology companies, ranked by revenues, collectively earned $11.9 billion in revenues in 2001; put another way, just 3 percent of public companies earned 46 percent of the industry's total revenues.[7] Strikingly, the four industry leaders – Amgen, Genentech, Chiron, and Biogen – together earned more than a third of the industry's revenues. Finally, despite the formidable risks, investors have patiently continued pumping capital into the industry, albeit increasingly to a select few firms. Though down sharply from a peak of $32 billion in capital raised in 2000, when excitement over the completion of the first draft sequence of the human genome was driving investor sentiment, the industry still managed to attract $11 billion in 2001 and $10.4 billion in 2002, which were dismal years for US equity markets. However, a recent string of last-minute failures of products to clear regulatory approval, along with allegations of accounting irregularities and financial misdeeds at some firms, has delivered a stunning reminder to investors of the risks that still inhere in biotechnology investments. The industry was especially jolted by the FDA's decision in late 2001 not to grant approvable status to ImClone's much anticipated cancer drug Erbitux and subsequent allegations that the firm's chief executive sold shares of stock in the firm just before the FDA's decision was made public. This case underscores the sensitivity of the market values of biotechnology firms to regulatory decisions and the great uncertainty that entails.

Since biotechnology came of age in the 1970s, DBCs have played a pivotal role in its commercialization. They are, in a sense, transmission belts that convey commercially promising research in genetics, molecular biology, and related fields from universities to the marketplace. Because of the close relations most of them maintain with universities, the path from the lab bench, where the basic knowledge usually originates, to applied research, product development, and manufacturing is comparatively open and direct; inventors themselves often participate in the development of their ideas and share in the profits they generate. DBCs thus came to fill a technical and institutional void left open by established drug and chemical companies, which were slow to develop their own capabilities in new biotechnology.

Biotechnology firms have always valued ease of access to the latest academic research in biomedicine, genetics, and biology. The science infrastructure most in demand resides at a few large research universities located mainly on the east and west coasts. Consequently, the biotechnology industry is heavily concentrated on the two coasts, with lesser agglomerations of firms in the Midwest. During the industry's infancy in the 1980s and early 1990s, firms tended to cluster in regions characterized by the presence of excellent research universities but even more importantly of "star scientists," so named because of their exceptional research productivity.[8] Because of their comparatively large numbers of active stars, Boston, Washington, DC, the Philadelphia–New York corridor, the San Francisco Bay area, San Diego, Los Angeles, and Seattle quickly emerged as favored locations for new DBCs. The tendency to cluster has grown even more pronounced over time: the concentration of firms as a ratio of the concentration of population rose from 1.42 before 1980 to 2.03 in the 1990s.[9] At the same time, academic research funded by the National Institutes of Health (NIH) has become more widely distributed. Today, many firms seek not only proximity to excellent academic research but also access to venture capital and potential alliance partners. Because venture capital and research alliances are even more geographically concentrated than the science base, the effect has been to reinforce the tendency of biotechnology firms to cluster spatially.

Finally, DBCs engage in many types of collaborations with large companies. These usually involve the drug company providing up-front licensing fees, funds for R&D, milestone payments contingent on the partner's achieving a succession of goals on the path to commercialization of a product, and, less often, investment in the partner's stock. In return, the drug firm receives rights to use a technology and a guaranteed royalty on revenues from products brought to market under the agreement.[10] In some cases, the large company may use its global presence to introduce into foreign markets a drug developed by its partner. Between 1988 and 1996, drug companies and DBCs entered into 768 alliances.[11] The number of new collaborations has grown steadily, from 69 in 1993 to 425 in 2001.[12] Deals struck in 2001 were expected to reach $7 billion. Nearly a fourth of that amount comes from a single agreement: the spectacular $2 billion deal between Bristol-Myers Squibb and ImClone to co-develop and co-promote the latter's anticancer drug Erbitux for a period of 17 years.[13] In that deal, BMS agreed to pay $1 billion for a 20 percent stake in the company and 39 percent of the net sales of the product. Additional funding would come in the form of milestone payments paid at three points: at the time of signing, when the Product License Application (PLA) is filed with the FDA, and when the product is approved for marketing.

The peculiar economics of biotechnology compel many DBCs to seek partnerships with other companies. Three reasons stand out. First is to access complementary assets needed to bring products to market. Except for the largest biotechnology firms, few single companies have the capacity to combine all the elements of the value chain, from research and clinical development to manufacturing and marketing, under one corporate roof; management of human clinical trials is an especially formidable challenge for small firms. Since their strength typically is in their science, DBCs tend to focus on research to develop a product or technology to a point where it is ready to undergo clinical testing or be licensed to a firm that will use it as a tool in its own product development. Second, firms enter into partnerships to acquire new technologies.[14] Such partnerships have been especially important since the appearance of new drug-discovery tools based on genomics (use of information about genes to develop new drugs), bioinformatics (use of databases and computer analysis to interpret biological information), combinatorial chemistry (automated techniques for synthesizing very large numbers of related chemical compounds for testing against a target molecule), high throughput screening (high-speed processes for screening large numbers of candidate molecules against a drug target), and microarrays (tiny glass chips that test for the presence of certain genes); these techniques have become indispensable in the identification of new drug targets and the generation and screening of new compounds. Having developed most of these new techniques, DBCs now find themselves in a far better position to extract favorable terms from drug companies than they were in the past. They are also forging more partnerships among themselves. Finally, small firms often find that collaborations with a respected partner confer strategic benefits, such as validation of the firm's intellectual property and management expertise. Venture capitalists and public equity markets, for example, give higher valuations to firms that have forged alliances with drug companies, no doubt in part because products developed in cooperation with a drug company are more likely to proceed smoothly through the clinical trials process.[15] Thus, even though DBCs' weak bargaining positions often lead them to license their technology on terms highly favorable to their larger partner, they gain in the long run through improved access to capital and greater likelihood of bringing their products to market.

Large companies

Although established chemical and pharmaceutical companies have not been the major sources of biotechnology innovation, they have played a crucial role in its commercial development. When the science was still in its infancy in the early 1970s, they were among the first to realize its commercial potential. Later, they provided critical financial and organizational support to the newly formed DBCs, in return for which they obtained access to new products and approaches to drug discovery. By the early 1990s, more than 140 large companies had established significant R&D or product development programs in biotechnology.[16] In 1994, pharmaceutical companies were marketing six of the ten best-selling biotechnology drugs, all of which had been developed by DBCs; drug makers were still marketing, alone or in cooperation with DBCs, five of the top ten drugs in 2001.[17]

Among the first drug companies to test the waters in biotechnology was Eli Lilly, the world's largest supplier of human insulin. Inventor in the 1920s of the process of manufacturing human insulin from the pancreases of cattle, the Indiana-based company kicked off the biopharmaceutical boom in the late 1970s when it turned to Genentech, the first true DBC, for the techniques to make human insulin in bacteria using recombinant DNA.[18] Others followed, such as Schering-Plough, G.D. Searle, and Bristol-Myers, but few drug companies made aggressive investments, at least until the 1980s. Close on their heels were established chemical and petroleum companies. Rocked by the oil shocks of the 1970s, overcapacity in low-margin commodity chemicals, and diminishing returns to research, Dow Chemical, Monsanto, Allied Chemical, Chevron, and Dupont started building internal research capabilities in biotechnology, which they sought to use as leverage for gaining entry into higher value-added agricultural chemicals and pharmaceuticals.[19] Drug and chemical firms alike supplemented their relatively small research capabilities in biotechnology by entering into research contracts with universities and DBCs; sometimes they would take equity stakes in start-up companies in return for access to their research or a share of future profits from products resulting from that research or both.[20]

The propensity for drug and biotechnology firms to partner is driven in part by the vast difference in size between the two groups. Compared to the typical DBC, the average drug firm is a behemoth. Consider Merck & Co., America's second largest drug maker by market share. Its revenues alone in 2000 exceeded by more than 50 percent the combined revenues of all 1,379 public and private biotechnology firms.[21] Diversified health care and consumer products giant Johnson & Johnson markets two of the top-selling biotechnology drugs: Procrit for boosting red blood cell counts (developed by Amgen) and Remicade for rheumatoid arthritis (developed by Centocor, formerly a DBC, which was acquired by Johnson & Johnson in the early 1990s and made into one of its operating divisions). In 1999, it employed more than 90,000 people; the average biotechnology company employed 127.[22]

Not only are America's drug firms big, they also comprise one of the country's most enduringly competitive industries. Drug exports in 1998 topped $8.7 billion, 10 percent of world drug exports: though less than Germany's 16 percent, it was well ahead of Japan's 2 percent.[23] American drug firms that year sold nearly 33 percent of their output, and performed a fifth of their corporate R&D, in foreign markets.[24] They also dominated their home market, where imports supplied only a tenth of domestic demand; Germany's import penetration, in contrast, was 47.5 percent.[25]

At least three factors underpin the global competitiveness of American drug makers. First is the enormous size of the domestic market. Drug purchases by Americans exceeded $127 billion in the year ending September 2001. Demand, moreover, has grown rapidly: from 2000 to 2001, it surged by 16 percent, and since 1992 the share of US demand in total global demand has soared from 34 to 51 percent.[26] Between 1970 and 1998, per capita consumption of drugs rose at an average annual rate of 3.7 percent, considerably faster than the 2.2 percent average annual rate of growth of per capita GDP.[27] Second, American firms spend lavishly on R&D. In 1999, drug companies headquartered in the US performed $12.3 billion worth of R&D, three times the amount spent by second-place Japan and six times that of third-place Germany.[28] Finally, unlike governments in other industrialized countries, the US government does not regulate drug prices. Although health insurers use their purchasing power to influence demand and pricing, firms are generally free to set the price of a drug at its marginal cost plus an allowance to help offset the amount spent on research and development. In no other industrialized country do drug makers have a comparable degree of freedom in setting prices.

Japan

In the pattern of entry into biotechnology and evolution of market structure, Japan differed markedly from the US. Large established companies, sometimes lured by government incentives, led the way in Japan. Many of them came from the science-based chemical and pharmaceutical industries, which already had in place a research infrastructure in basic chemistry and biochemistry. Others came from the food and brewing industries, many of whose firms had decades, sometimes centuries, of experience with fermentation, microbiology, enzymology, and other traditional biotechnologies. Yet many others came from industries that had no obvious connection to biotechnology: several large textile firms, for example, took advantage of the biotechnology revolution to diversify into drugs and health care products, which offered far rosier prospects for growth than their existing markets. Research and product development were initially concentrated in fine chemicals, food processing, antibiotics, and industrial products, fields in which Japanese firms have traditionally held strong positions in their home market and, in the case of antibiotics, in foreign markets as well. Although therapeutic drugs, vaccines, diagnostic tools, and genomics became the favored targets of investment in the 1990s, many of the most active and innovative companies in these areas hail from outside the pharmaceutical industry. A striking example is Ajinomoto, best known for its processed foods and flavor-enhancing ingredients, which became the world's first private company to clone the important immune system regulator interleukin-2.

Unlike in the US, large companies in Japan had little competition from start-up firms created by entrepreneurs to commercialize academic research in molecular biology and genetics. Japan's innovation system begot no organizations comparable to America's DBCs. However, start-up companies, once rare, began to appear in growing numbers in the mid and late 1990s. Although it is too early to assess their contributions to Japan's competitiveness in biotechnology, their growing numbers, in conjunction with the easing of restrictions on academic entrepreneurship and greater availability of venture capital, could be indicative of major change in Japan's innovation system as it relates to biotechnology.

Commercial biotechnology in Japan began in the early 1980s when established firms from a broad range of industries diversified into the field. By 1985, chemical majors Mitsubishi Kasei, Mitsui Toatsu, Sumitomo Chemical, and Showa Denko had established significant research programs. Reeling from the twin oil shocks of the 1970s and soaring energy costs, chemical firms looked to biotechnology to help them diversify into higher value-added fine and specialty chemicals. Joining them were textile makers such as Toyobo and Toray, food processors Ajinomoto and Yamasa Shoyu, and brewers Suntory and Takara Shuzo, all of whom made investments in biotechnology as part of a strategic shift away from stagnant or maturing markets. Takeda, Chugai, Shionogi, Fujisawa, Kyowa Hakko, and other core pharmaceutical firms did the same for reasons not unlike those that motivated drug makers in the US. By 1988, of the 177 firms with active research programs in biotechnology, fifty-two were from the chemical industry, thirty-one were food and beverage firms, twenty-three were pharmaceutical companies, and the remainder were scattered across ten other industries, ranging from pulp and paper to steel and electronics.[29] Interest extended well beyond drugs and health care products, which had quickly emerged as the favored markets for applying biotechnology in the US. Indeed, according to a 1991 forecast of the size of the market for goods made using biotechnology in 2000, food products came in first place at 28 percent of total market value, followed by pharmaceuticals at 20 percent, basic and fine chemicals at 17 percent, energy at 14 percent, and agriculture at 13 percent.[30]

To be sure, in the US a similarly motley group of large industrial companies tested the waters in biotechnology, either by starting their own small research programs or by investing in the first wave of DBCs. Standard Oil, National Distillers, and Shell Oil invested in Cetus, the first company in America to devote a significant part of its business to biotechnology. Allied Chemical helped launch Amgen, now the world's largest biotechnology company; Monsanto, developer of genetically modified corn, soybeans, and other crops, was until the 1980s mainly a producer of basic chemicals. Except for Monsanto, however, none of these big industrial companies played a significant role in biotechnology's subsequent evolution.

In Japan today, large established firms are still a strong force behind commercial development. According to the Japan External Trade Organization (JETRO), of the 320 firms active in biotechnology in 2000, 260, or 81 percent, were "major corporations." By contrast, only 19 percent of firms active in biotechnology in the US, and 7 percent of firms in Europe, are similarly classified.[31] In a recent survey conducted by the Ministry of Economy, Trade, and Industry (METI, the successor to MITI), of firms known to be working in biotechnology broadly defined, 64 percent of the 946 responding companies had at least 100 employees; 40 percent had 300 or more. Nor are firms young, at least in comparison with biotechnology companies elsewhere: nine of ten respondents were more than five years old.[32]

While large firms continue to lead the development and commercialization of new products, the composition of the market for biotechnology products has shifted from food and fine chemicals to pharmaceuticals. According to the METI survey cited above, domestic manufacturers using recombinant DNA or cell fusion techniques shipped pharmaceuticals valued at slightly more than 741 billion yen in 2000, which amounted to 57.3 percent of the value of all "new biotechnology" goods shipped. Chemicals followed at 23.8 percent, and analytical instruments made up 9.8 percent. Significantly, and in sharp contrast with the US, respondents reported no significant domestic production of foods using "new biotechnology."[33] If imports are included with domestic production, pharmaceuticals made up 39.1 percent of the market for biotechnology products in 1998, double the weight analysts had predicted earlier in the decade.[34] Chemicals were second with a 27.4 percent share, followed by agricultural, forestry, and fishery products at 19.8 percent, and medical diagnostic products at 8.7 percent. Processed foods and ingredients made using biotechnology comprised 4.6 percent of the market, a mere fraction of what analysts had predicted.[35] A similar breakdown of the market in the US shows that therapeutic drugs accounted for 74.8 percent of sales in 1997, diagnostics 17.4 percent; in other words, health care products alone comprised an overwhelming 92 percent of the American market.

Three conclusions immediately follow. First, forecasts of future markets have limited utility in fields in which the technology is new and changing rapidly.[36] Second, although pharmaceutical and health care applications have come to play a greater role than had been previously forecast, the range of products that Japanese firms have brought to market has been remarkably diverse. Third, Japanese firms have clearly sought to integrate biotechnology into a broader range of industries and products than has been the case in the US.

The application of biotechnology across a broad range of industries in Japan was, this study contends, a natural outcome of the intersection of the technological regime with the specific character of Japan's national innovation system. In the first place, Japanese food and chemical firms have a long history working with fermentation, bioreactors, and the cultivation and handling of microbes used in fermentation processes. These technologies have long underpinned the production of fermented soy-based foods, which are staples of the traditional Japanese diet, sake and other beverages made by fermenting rice, and more recently of industrial enzymes and antibiotics. For firms, application of genetic engineering in fields close to traditional areas of expertise reflects a path-dependent institutional response to the appearance of a new technology. Second, the scattershot distribution of innovative activity unfolded partly by design. Since MITI first targeted the field for commercial development in the early 1980s, policy makers have repeatedly underscored the importance of biotechnology as a "base technology" (*kiban gijutsu*), whose pervasive application across the economy justified its special status. Indeed, reports in Japan often have portrayed biotechnology as the roots of the modern economy, whose branches represent different industries, the leaves new products. Early on, technology policies reinforced this conception by promoting research associations that drew together firms from different industries and by funding research at the intersection of different fields, such as biosensors (molecular biology and microelectronics), bioinformatics (molecular biology and information technology), and green biotechnology (molecular biology and environmental remediation). Policy makers and analysts refer to this integration of knowledge from two different fields to form a third hybrid field as "technology fusion" (*gijutsu yugo*); it is a term frequently encountered in Japan's technology policy discourse, and is discussed in more detail in Chapter 5.

Japan's innovation system has not been fertile soil for the establishment and growth of start-up companies. Established companies thus faced little domestic competition in the race to commercialize biotechnology. Large companies control the major marketing and distribution channels, especially in drugs and many types of fine chemicals. In addition, the manner in which the Ministry of Health, Labor, and Welfare regulates prices and distribution of pharmaceuticals makes it difficult enough for large companies to wring profits out of sales of individual drugs; small start-ups, which typically have few other sources of revenue, fare even worse. Until recently, moreover, there have been neither incentives nor means for university researchers in Japan to commercialize the results of their individual efforts through establishing or participating in a start-up venture. Start-ups in biotechnology have appeared, as they have in other industries, but they have usually been the result of a large parent company setting up its own new business unit, seeding it with its own funds, and sometimes spinning it off as a separate business once it has developed the capacity to survive on its own.[37] This situation is beginning to change in ways that could portend a major shift in biotechnology commercialization. As discussed further below, the government has recently made major policy initiatives aimed at promoting technology transfer from universities to industry, deregulating financial markets, and increasing the availability of start-up capital. At the same time, the rate of increase in formation of new biotechnology firms shot up in the late 1990s, as I will show in Chapter 5. Nonetheless, for the period covered in this study, commercial biotechnology in Japan has been overwhelmingly the preserve of established firms in mainline industries.

Finally, that traditional drug companies have not become significant global developers and marketers of biotechnology-based products is consistent with the overall global competitiveness of Japan's pharmaceutical industry. In contrast with automobiles, consumer electronics, video games, steel, machine tools, and semiconductors, Japan's pharmaceutical industry never has had a strong presence outside the domestic market. Its drug makers supply only 2 percent of world pharmaceutical exports, while US and German firms supply 10 and 16 percent, respectively.[38] The figures for Japan are especially striking in light of the fact that firms operating in Japan produce close to 15 percent of total world output of drugs, compared with 30 and 7 percent, respectively, for firms in the US and Germany. In addition, import penetration of Japan's domestic market for pharmaceuticals, 6.4 percent in 1998, is low even by the comparatively low standard of import penetration in manufacturing as a whole (8.6 percent). On the opposite end of the scale, imports in Germany that same year supplied 47.5

percent of domestic consumption of drugs. On the other hand, the domestic operations of foreign-owned firms are gaining greater influence in the domestic market, their share of drugs shipped domestically having grown from 16.9 in 1990 to 25.6 percent in 2000.[39]

Nor has Japan's pharmaceutical industry regularly been a major source of innovative drugs, at least in comparison with competitors in Europe and the US. One important qualitative measure of innovation is the number of drugs domestic firms introduce into their home market that go on to penetrate markets abroad. By this measure, 22 percent of so-called "new chemical entities" (NCEs), which are drugs based on completely novel chemical compounds, introduced by American companies in the US between 1985 and 1998, went on to be marketed in foreign markets. In contrast, only 6 percent of NCEs introduced by Japanese companies in Japan achieved similar status, while the comparable figure for Europe was 13 percent.[40] There are, of course, important exceptions: Sankyo's anti-cholesterol drug Pravastatin, marketed as Pravachol by Bristol-Myers Squibb, became a global blockbuster after its introduction in 1989. Eisai's Aricept, which treats dementia associated with Alzheimer's disease, racked up more than 42.5 billion yen ($363 million) in global sales in the six months ending in September 2001; and Takeda's Actos, which treats type 2 diabetes, earned $542 million in sales in the US over the same period.[41] Not surprisingly, even though Japan's drug sector has done comparatively well in recent years, the profits of firms aggressively expanding into foreign markets are growing much more quickly than those of companies more dependent on the domestic market.[42] This is likely to fuel the polarization of the industry into, on the one hand, a small elite of globally competitive firms that perform much of their drug development outside Japan, and on the other, a large group of weak firms mainly focused on the domestic market.

The peculiarities of Japan's drug industry – its home market is the world's second largest, and it combines a historically strong but weakening position at home with a relatively weak presence abroad – stem from several causes. On the positive side is an affluent population that devotes a sizable part of its health care budget to drugs. Japanese spend less per capita on drugs than Americans do: $301 on a purchasing power parity basis by Japanese versus $422 by Americans in 1998. However, drugs make up a higher share of total health care expenditures than they do in most other countries: 16.8 percent compared with 10.1 percent in the US and 12.7 percent in Germany in 1997/98.[43] Add in the rapidly growing share of elderly in the population and it is clear that the structure of demand strongly favors a robust drug industry. Several other factors, however, work against domestic drug makers. First, the market is highly fragmented; few firms have anything like the economies of scale in research and production of Pfizer or Merck, two American giants. Japan today has 1,396 drug manufacturers, the top ten of which garner 40 percent of the industry's sales.[44] Takeda, Japan's largest drug company by sales, only ranks fifteenth among the world's drug firms; Merck's revenues from product sales in 2000 exceeded that of Japan's top fifteen drug firms combined.[45] Second, spending on R&D is low by international standards. Pfizer, America's biggest performer of pharmaceutical research, spent more than $4.4 billion on R&D in 2000; Japan's Takeda spent $833 million.[46] Since the mid 1980s, Japanese drug makers have steadily boosted their spending on R&D as part of a strategy to develop more innovative products with global appeal. R&D spending per researcher has increased, even as the number of researchers has increased by half. The bigger problem, however, may be the way in which the funds are spent: in the words of one analyst, even though R&D spending has increased substantially, "the shift toward basic research that is essential for the development of innovative products has not yet occurred."[47]

Finally, public policy pulls the drug industry in two different directions. While the Ministry of Health, Labor, and Welfare has been promoting R&D as a means of boosting the industry's competitiveness, every two years it also cuts the reimbursement prices of listed drugs, which it sets under the country's national health insurance system.[48] In April 2000, it cut prices by 7 percent, slowing growth in drug company profits to 1.9 percent from the sizzling 12.9 percent growth of the previous year and keeping it well below growth rates of firms in Europe and the US. The government's price-setting formula actually endeavors to promote innovation by granting premium pricing to innovative drugs. On the other hand, by not permitting the price of older drugs to fall in line with the drop in manufacturing costs that usually occurs as companies gain experience in production, "old drugs thus probably offered the highest profit margins to many Japanese companies, further curtailing the incentive to innovate."[49]

To sum up, in the race to commercialize biotechnology, firms in America's national innovation system have faced a set of institutional constraints quite different from that of their counterparts in Japan. In the US, a ready supply of academic scientists-turned-entrepreneurs, a pool of risk capital willing to place large bets on a technology whose development was fraught with uncertainty, and strong supporting industries in pharmaceuticals and chemicals created a fertile environment for the rapid emergence of new firms. Japan, in contrast, lacked institutions capable of translating academic research into specialized start-up companies. Nor had it a pharmaceutical industry with the scale and global presence comparable to that of the US or Europe. On the other hand, strong capabilities in related industries such as food processing and fine chemicals, coupled with a market structure that enabled firms from these industries to diversify into biotechnology, have compensated to some degree for the weaknesses in the pharmaceutical sector. Even firms from sectors as distant from biotechnology as textiles, paper, and cement moved with remarkable speed to exploit the opportunities biotechnology offered to enhance existing technological capabilities and diversify away from maturing products. American entrepreneurs combined resources available to them within the US innovation system to create the DBC, a new institutional entity specialized to the task of commercializing academic research in biotechnology. Japanese firms, similarly responsive to the resources available to them, reacted instead by pushing existing corporate boundaries outward, bringing internal knowledge and capital to bear on the problem of commercializing biotechnology in a manner consistent with their existing organizational and technological capacities.

Research infrastructure

Outside the private sector, a variety of academic, public, and non-profit institutes form an infrastructure that supports technological innovation in biotechnology. These organizations perform research primarily geared to the generation and dissemination of knowledge that is both generic and public in nature. In the US, research performed in academic and public research institutes over many decades created the knowledge base out of which grew commercial biotechnology. Linking that knowledge to the marketplace were formal mechanisms of technology transfer that provided a legal framework for protecting intellectual property and reducing the transaction costs associated with its deployment to points within the innovation system where it could be most profitably used. Like the US, Japan also devotes considerable resources to an academic and public research infrastructure that supports innovation in biotechnology. Although that infrastructure turns out excellent science in many areas of biotechnology, its organization and management, in addition to the system for allocating funds to it, have limited its capacity to contribute to commercialization. Nor until recently have Japanese universities and public research institutes maintained formal institutional channels for transferring technology to private firms. As a result, commercial biotechnology in Japan has drawn more on knowledge generated within firms' own research laboratories and from technology in-licensed from abroad than it has in the US.

The United States

Although universities and public research institutes perform 22 percent of the nation's total R&D in dollar terms, they perform 60 percent of the country's research in the life sciences.[50] Since 1980, they have borne the added responsibility of managing intellectual property resulting from the research they support and undertake, and ensuring its broadest possible diffusion consistent with its development into useful products and services.

According to the most recent data from the National Science Board, from research obligations totaling $38.7 billion in 2001, the federal government allocated $18.25 billion to research in the life sciences. The

Department of Health and Human Services (HHS) received by far the largest share of that amount: $14.3 billion, or 78.4 percent. The Department of Agriculture (USDA) was a distant second at 7.3 percent, followed by the Department of Defense (DOD) and National Science Foundation (NSF) at 2.9 percent each, with the remaining 8.5 percent scattered across ten other agencies.[51]

As both a source of funds for academic research in the life sciences and a performer of research in its own laboratories, no agency rivals HHS. Housing the National Institutes of Health (NIH), Centers for Disease Control (CDC), and the Food and Drug Administration (FDA), its mission is to promote, protect, and improve human health. It had a total R&D budget in 2001 of $19.2 billion, second only to DOD. Of that amount, 57 percent was slated for academic research in the nation's universities and medical centers, while a quarter was to be allocated to intramural research. HHS is the largest source of federal research funds for universities (62 percent) and nonprofit organizations (71.6 percent).[52] While the NIH performs and supports biomedical research, the FDA regulates the introduction and manufacture of drugs and certain food products, a clear institutional separation being maintained between regulatory and promotional functions.

The NIH occupies a special position in the US innovation system as the institution most responsible for American leadership in biomedical research. It consists of twenty-seven separate and largely autonomous institutes and centers, most of which perform research on specific disorders or organ systems. Major areas of emphasis today include HIV/AIDS, cancer, diabetes, and bioterrorism. A public preoccupied with health and powerful friends in Congress have kept it flush with funds: its budget is expected to swell to $27 billion in 2003, fulfilling the promise Congress made in 1997 to double the budget over five years.[53] To underscore the size of this budget, it is more than a third larger than Japan's entire government budget for R&D in 1999!

The NIH supports biomedical research both within its own institutes and in external laboratories throughout the country. Most of its budget is devoted to extramural research proposed by researchers at universities, research centers, private firms, and nonprofit institutes throughout the US. In its budget for 2000, 56.8 percent of its funds were allocated to 35,000 investigator-initiated "Research Project Grants" proposed by individual investigators, 8.7 percent went to groups of investigators at research centers, and 6.4 percent supported research contracts with firms and nonprofit research institutes. Finally, 10 percent of its budget supports research performed internally within the various institutes.[54]

Research supported by the NIH has contributed to the development of many drugs and other biomedical products. Three of the top four biotechnology drugs on the market today – Epogen and Procrit for enhancing the number of red blood cells, and Neupogen for boosting white blood cells – were developed with support of the NIH.[55] In addition, research done within the NIH reportedly led to the commercialization of seven diagnostics, six therapeutic and vaccine products, and five research materials that had significant product sales in the mid 1990s.[56] Included among them are the powerful anticancer drug Taxol, two drugs that inhibit the replication of the HIV virus (ddI and ddC), and a vaccine for Hepatitis A. NIH research, in addition, opened up the field of gene therapy, which has the distinction of being the first technology commercialized jointly by NIH and the private sector.

Potentially valuable new drugs, devices, and therapies resulting from research sponsored by the NIH generally require lengthy and expensive development and clinical testing before they can be brought to market. Investment in such activity is beyond the scope of the NIH mission and contrary to the philosophy that has underpinned American science policy since the end of World War II: that while government should support generic and precommercial research, it should leave development and commercialization to the private sector. At the same time, few firms on their own, especially small ones, are willing to invest in the generic research in which federal labs specialize; though the potential returns may be high, the chance of failure is perceived to be even higher.

For these reasons, Congress in the early and mid 1980s passed a series of laws to facilitate the development and transfer of technology from federal laboratories and publicly funded nonfederal laboratories to the private sector where it would have the greatest chance of contributing to social welfare.[57] Among these, the Stevenson–Wydler Technology Innovation Act of 1980 required that each federal laboratory establish an "Office of Research and Technology Application" (ORTA) to facilitate licensing of federally owned technology. The Bayh–Dole University and Small Business Patent Act of 1980 (Public Law 96–517) allowed government agencies and non-government recipients of federal funding, including universities, to retain title to intellectual property resulting from federally funded research performed in their laboratories. Not until the Federal Technology Transfer Act of 1986 (Public Law 99–502), however, did individual federal laboratories obtain the authority to manage their own intellectual property and license it to private companies; just as important, it allowed federal labs to enter into Cooperative Research and Development Agreements (CRADAs) with nonfederal organizations. In a CRADA, federal and non-federal parties agree to share personnel, equipment, and other resources, though the federal party itself may not provide funds, in an endeavor to achieve a specific, highly focused scientific objective. Any federal agency conducting scientific research can participate in a CRADA. Under a CRADA, an invention made by federal scientists becomes the property of the laboratory that carried out the research; that laboratory may license it to the nonfederal partner for a reasonable royalty. For an invention made jointly by federal and private sector researchers, the private firm has the first rights to refuse to enter into an exclusive licensing agreement.

Within HHS, the FDA, CDC, and NIH all enter into CRADAs and participate in technology transfer activities. The Office of Technology Transfer of the NIH manages CRADAs and intellectual property for both NIH and FDA; CDC has its own Technology Transfer Office. The NIH has the most extensive portfolio of intellectual property and research collaborations. CRADAs executed by NIH may involve cooperative development of a product or process resulting from research performed within any of its institutes, collaboration on clinical trials of a drug candidate owned by the corporate partner, or the transfer from the private partner to NIH of proprietary materials without which NIH researchers could not pursue a particular line of research.[58] By participating in a CRADA, NIH researchers gain access to personnel, facilities, funding, and expertise of an external partner, as well as property rights to inventions that ensue from the collaboration. The external partner gains access to personnel, facilities, and expertise of the NIH, as well as the option to an exclusive or nonexclusive license of the intellectual property resulting from the collaboration.

Since the first agreement was executed in 1985, the NIH has through fiscal year 2002 entered into 1,110 CRADAs involving collaborative research and 566 material transfer CRADAs (the latter of which have been authorized only since 1996).[59] In 2000, the three laboratories of HHS together entered into 50 CRADAs while maintaining 244 active ones (not including material transfer CRADAs). The number of active CRADAs grew rapidly in the late 1980s, gradually through most of the 1990s, then surged by 50 percent between 1998 and 2000.[60]

Perhaps the best-known CRADA in the NIH portfolio involved development of the anticancer drug Taxol (trade name for paclitaxel).[61] Since the 1960s, scientists had known that paclitaxel, a substance found in exceedingly small quantities in the bark of the Pacific Yew, had a powerful therapeutic effect on certain tumors. The difficulty and expense of extracting it in meaningful quantities, however, limited its appeal as a potential new anticancer drug. Two separate CRADAs helped solve this problem. The first involved an agreement in 1990 between the Agricultural Research Service (ARS) of USDA and Phyton, Inc., a biotechnology start-up. ARS had developed a plant tissue cell culture technique for producing paclitaxel; in the agreement, Phyton received an exclusive license to adapt the ARS technique for producing the drug in commercial quantities. In the second, pharmaceutical giant Bristol-Myers Squibb entered into a CRADA with NIH to collaborate in the clinical development of the drug. NIH agreed to provide BMS with sufficient quantities of paclitaxel extract for testing and exclusive access to clinical data from NIH-supported research that BMS needed to gain regulatory approval of the drug as an anticancer treatment. BMS would develop technology to increase the yield of extracting paclitaxel from yew bark and provide support for research into a more efficient alternative to Phyton's plant tissue cell culture technology. It also provided NIH with additional quantities of the drug, which enabled NIH to expand clinical trials it was then conducting. In 1992, BMS received approval from the FDA to market paclitaxel under the trade name Taxol for treatment of advanced ovarian cancer; five of the six clinical studies whose data BMS filed with the FDA in support of the application were conducted or funded by the NIH. The drug later received approval for treating other cancers, and between 1993 and 2002, it brought BMS over $9 billion in worldwide sales.[62]

The technology transfer activities of NIH and the other HHS laboratories also generate large revenue streams from inventions licensed to external end-users. In 2001, HHS earned $41.3 million from the 1,007 active invention licenses it managed that year.[63] More than $36.6 million of that amount came in the form of earned royalty income, annual payments made by the licensee to the licensor based on the sales of products based on the licensed technology. This was nearly 70 percent of the total royalty income earned by all federal agencies combined. More than three-quarters of the active licenses maintained by NIH as of 1 October 1998 were nonexclusive; 52 percent of licensees were small businesses or individuals.[64] In 2001 NIH received eighty-eight patents, down significantly from the peak of 171 in 1998 in a trend that Guston attributes to an effort on the part of NIH to discourage "overpatenting."[65] Were NIH a university, it would rank fourth behind the University of Wisconsin in number of patents awarded to universities.

No other federal agency comes close to matching the funding and staffing levels of HHS. This is not surprising given the large and growing concentration of federal funding for non-defense research in the health sciences.[66] Nevertheless, important research related to biotechnology is also performed in other federal agencies. The USDA has profoundly influenced nearly every aspect of farming in the US. Like health care, agriculture is an industry in which direct government intervention and promotion has rarely been questioned. Most of this support, however, has been targeted not at generating knowledge internally but promoting adoption and adaptation of existing knowledge through its countrywide extension services.[67] Like HHS, USDA promotes collaborative research with external partners and technology transfer through its Agricultural Research Service, whose Office of Technology Transfer manages intellectual property and external relationships. In 2001, ARS maintained 219 active CRADAs and earned $2.6 million in total income from 255 active invention licenses.[68] Elsewhere, the Departments of Defense and Energy sponsor smaller amounts of research in biotechnology related to their respective missions.

Most of the extramural research supported by federal R&D agencies is performed in universities. Academic research in the US has long been closely associated with both government and industry.[69] Federal government support for university programs in agriculture dates from the Morrill Land Grant College Act of 1862. This law granted every state that remained in the Union 30,000 acres of public land for each member in its Congressional delegation. Proceeds from the sale of the land enabled the states to establish more than seventy new colleges where, according to the text of the law, "the leading object shall be, without excluding other scientific and classical studies and including military tactics, to teach such branches of learning as are related to agriculture and the mechanic arts."[70] Subsequent legislation, notably the Hatch Act (1887) and Adams Act (1906), set up and funded agriculture experiment stations and the cooperative extension service. Around the same time, the advent of mass-production technologies generated growing demand from industry for applied science and engineering expertise. The chemical industry, for example, developed in parallel with the new field of chemical engineering, which emerged as a separate subject of study and substantive field of research.[71] To meet these new needs, universities introduced a wealth of new educational and research programs before World War II. The goal, however, was not to advance the frontiers of knowledge but to provide American firms with the capacity for scientific and engineering "catch-up." In this, they were performing a function not unlike that of Japanese universities, against which they are so often contrasted.

World War II transformed the American research university in several ways. First, the federal component of funding for university research increased sharply, replacing state governments and industry as the primary source of funds. Second, the absolute level of funding rocketed: for the thirty-five years between 1953 and 1988, spending on university R&D grew 12 percent per year, or 7.3 percent in real terms, a faster rate of growth than in any other sector. Third, new research programs associated with the National Science Foundation and NIH provided large doses of support for academic research across a broad range of fields. Large increases in funds from mission agencies such as DOE and DOD also contributed to the overall increase. The combined effect of strengthening institutional support for university research and raising absolute funding levels vaulted American universities to the forefront of the world's major research institutions.[72]

Universities spent about $30 billion on R&D in 2000, 11 percent of the total R&D performed in the US. The federal government provided the majority (58 percent) of this funding; and of that amount, 60 percent, or $10 billion, came from the NIH.[73] That a third of all expenditures on academic research in the US comes from the federal agency most closely aligned with the advancement of biomedical knowledge is indicative of the strong and growing orientation of the nation's academic research toward biotechnology and the health sciences. Whereas the NIH provided only 35 percent of total federal obligations for academic R&D in 1970, it provided more than 60 percent in 2000.

In no field has the recent growth in spending on academic research had more impact than in biotechnology: in constant 1996 dollars, spending on academic research in the life sciences rose from $4.55 billion in 1973 to nearly $14.88 billion in 1999, or from 59 to 67 percent of total academic R&D in the sciences.[74] While much of that increase came from the massive expansion in the NIH's budget for extramural research, nonfederal sources increased their financial support at an even faster rate.[75] Industry sponsorship of academic research became increasingly common as biotechnology entered the commercialization phase. In the 1970s, research contracts with universities gave large corporations early exposure to the new technology with a minimal commitment of their own resources.[76] Enactment of the Bayh–Dole Act in 1980 created new incentives for universities to develop faculty inventions with an eye to commercialization, which often entails collaborative research between faculty inventors and actual or potential corporate licensees. By the mid 1990s, according to one survey, more than half of all life science companies conducting research in the US supported academic research; if consulting relationships are included, the proportion jumps to 90 percent.[77]

Funding alone, of course, does not necessarily lead to high-quality research. America's leadership in biotechnology depends in large measure on the extent to which that science base informs and drives commercial innovation, which in turn depends on the ability of the innovation system to translate the results of academic research into new knowledge, goods, and services that add value to the economy and improve productivity. This capability has become increasingly important as industrial innovation draws more and more from public science, as recent studies suggest it is doing.[78] According to one measure of the linkage of innovation to its underlying science, the number of citations in US patents to scientific and technical articles, that linkage has tightened dramatically over the past decade. From about 22,000 in 1985, the number of citations on US patents rose almost exponentially to 310,000 in 1998. In addition, the average number of citations per patent increased more than five-fold over the same period.[79] Driving this general increase were huge jumps in biomedical research and clinical medicine, whose numbers of citations rose from about 3,000 per year in 1987 to more than 60,000 by 2000 in biomedical research and more than 40,000 in clinical medicine. The share of biomedical research citations in the total rose from 24 to 45 percent.[80] The evidence suggests that while innovation in all fields is drawing more than ever before from the underlying science, that linkage is even tighter in biotechnology.

Among the vexing problems associated with the transfer of knowledge across organizational boundaries are the inventor's fear of missing out on future returns to the original investment, the buyer's fear that the inventor will share or sell the knowledge to another party, and both side's uncertainty over the drafting and enforcement of a contract. The federal government's solution to this transaction-cost problem through the creation of a legal framework governing technology transfer, which in essence created a national market for universities' intellectual property, is perhaps the most important part of the story of the development of the US innovation system in biotechnology. As explained above, the Bayh-Dole Act created a uniform patent policy among the federal agencies that fund scientific research in universities and other organizations. The motivation behind it is that firms need the guarantee of exclusive rights to a university invention to have incentive to commercialize it; such a right could only obtain if universities themselves managed their own intellectual property. Under the Bayh–Dole Act and subsequent related legislation, universities are permitted to retain title to the intellectual property that results from federally funded research. Researchers, for their part, are required to report inventions to the university's technology transfer office, which assesses each one for its patentability and commercial potential, then decides whether or not to file patents. If an invention has commercial potential but requires considerable additional investment, the university may opt to apply for a patent, which it could license exclusively or nonexclusively to a firm wishing to develop it. Collaborative research between the firm and the original researcher may facilitate development and commercialization. In the extreme case, the university may license the technology back to the inventor, who may then use it to start up a new company.

University patenting did not begin with the Bayh–Dole Act. Before 1980, universities received 250–350 patents annually; there was simply no common legal framework to manage it. There are even doubts about the extent to which the surge in university patenting after 1980 is attributable to it; the economy's shift to more knowledge-intensive production could also be a factor.[81] Whatever the reasons, surge it did: the number of patents awarded to academic institutions grew from 464 in 1982 to 3,151 in 1998.[82] Other indicators followed suit: invention disclosures rose from 4,880 in 1991 to 10,052 in 1999; new licenses and options from 1,079 to 3,295, and the number of licenses generating revenues from 2,210 to 6,663.[83] Consistent with the legislation's emphasis on helping small companies, two-thirds of new licenses and options drawn up in 2000 were with newly formed or small companies. That year, 454 new companies were formed around academic research, yielding a cumulative total of 3,376 new firms formed since 1980, 2,309 of which were still in business in 2000. Universities earned an adjusted gross income of $1.26 billion on 9,059 licenses/options, fifteen times the amount earned by federal agencies.

Biotechnology has been the primary beneficiary of this increase in university–industry interactions since 1980. Many of the core technologies and products trace their roots back to federally funded academic research. The technology that kicked off the biotechnology revolution in the 1970s, the Cohen–Boyer patents for producing recombinant DNA constructs in bacterial plasmids, netted Stanford University and the University of California roughly $200 million in licensing fees before the patents expired in 1998. For years, the biggest income earner in the University of Washington's license portfolio were the so-called Hall technologies for the recombinant expression of Hepatitis B vaccine in yeast. And Florida

State University licensed to Bristol-Myers Squibb a technique for synthesizing Taxol that did not require the use of bark from the rare Pacific Yew tree. In many cases, universities entered into licensing agreements with newly formed biotechnology companies to commercialize their inventions. UCLA, for example, licensed to Xoma, a DBC, monoclonal antibodies for treating septic shock; the State University of New York (SUNY) licensed to Cortech, also a DBC, elastase inhibitors.

Universities do not limit their technology transfer activities to the mere management and licensing of intellectual property. They also often leverage their intellectual property to build mutually beneficial collaborations with industry. These collaborations provide revenues for the university, funding for faculty research, and new ideas and inventions that form the basis for new products and processes for industry. Although research partnerships take a variety of institutional forms, they generally involve either a research contract between a university and a private company or a grant from a third party that has the specific intent of fostering university–industry collaborations. The third party may be a cooperative research center funded by state or private sources, or a federal agency that supports technology transfer from universities to small business through the Small Business Technology Transfer (STTR) Program.[84] In biotechnology, according to one study, more than 1,100 university research collaborations with industry were in progress in the mid 1990s: a sample of publicly filed agreements found that universities on average received $42,000 in upfront fees, $282,000 in milestone fees, and an additional $681,000 in payments for sponsored research.[85]

The presence of thriving academic research centers is a powerful predictor of whether or not a particular region has a strong biotechnology industry. The most successful firms tend to be located in close proximity to academic scientists who have been most productive in publishing highly cited articles in the biomedical literature; in particular, the number of collaborations with these so-called "star scientists" correlates strongly with a company's success in developing new products.[86] A recent study by the Brookings Institution of biotechnology in fifty-one metropolitan areas confirms this finding. What distinguishes the nine most successful regions are the presence of a top-ranked medical school, a high number of doctorates conferred annually in the life sciences, a large share of disbursement of research funds by the NIH, and a high number of biotechnology-related patents by organizations in the region.[87] In short, the geographic development of the industry has closely followed the geography of American biomedical academic research.

Japan

In 2000, Japan's public and academic research institutes together spent about 883 billion yen on R&D in the life sciences ($8.2 billion at the IMF exchange rate).[88] By contrast, federal obligations to research in the life sciences at the US HHS and Veterans Administration totaled about $15.9 billion in 1998. Japan's government spends far less on research in the life sciences than does its counterpart in the US, though the gap narrows when figures are adjusted to account for differences in population and size of the economy. Differences in budgeting practices render suspect any direct comparison in funding levels, especially expenditures on academic research; more meaningful are comparisons of trends in expenditures and changes in funding priorities. Yet meaningful or not, much of the policy analysis of biotechnology in Japan makes a point of underscoring the magnitude of the difference in public commitment to R&D and the negative impact it has had on the development of Japan's biotechnology industry

Although public research institutes and universities perform 29 percent of the nation's total R&D in yen terms, they perform 50 percent of research in the life sciences.[89] This is somewhat less than the 60 percent supported by universities and public research institutes in the US, reflecting the greater weight of Japanese industry in the performance of research in the life sciences, which is consistent with the pattern observed in other fields. Until recently, neither government research institutes nor universities have participated in technology transfer activities under a unified legal framework. Although many academic researchers in the sciences and engineering fields engage in collaborative research with industry and even transfer intellectual property rights over to their industrial partners, the processes governing such interactions have been informal, and universities themselves rarely retain ownership to intellectual property resulting from research performed by their faculty. This situation began to change in the late 1990s: many public universities that had in the past shied away from patenting and transferring technology to industry are now promoting it vigorously, and policy makers are deploying a growing array of incentives to support it. This recasting of the university as an instrument for reviving Japan's flagging economy through the creation of new firms and industries adds a new twist to Japan's postwar science policy, and while it is still early to assess the precise economic impacts, the effects are already being felt in the biotechnology industry.

Japan's public research institutes spent 221 billion yen ($2.1 billion) on R&D in the life sciences in 2000. Most of this research has been carried out in laboratories associated with four ministries and agencies of the central government: the former Ministry of International Trade and Industry (from 2001, the Ministry of Economy, Trade, and Industry); Ministry of Agriculture, Forestry, and Fisheries; the former Ministry of Health and Welfare (now Health, Labor, and Welfare); the former Ministry of Education; and the former Science and Technology Agency (these last two now combined into the Ministry of Education, Culture, Sports Science, and Technology). Although Japan fields several national research laboratories concerned with health-related R&D, there is no vanguard organization comparable to America's NIH for spearheading a national biomedical research agenda. Nor has the government supported mission-oriented academic research related to health or biotechnology through extramural programs; academic researchers receive most – until recently nearly all – their funding through the Ministry of Education, Culture, Sports, Science, and Technology (MEXT). Indicative of the difference in the magnitude of funds supporting research in national laboratories, America's HHS spent about $4.6 billion on intramural research in 2001, more than double the combined amount spent by all public research institutes in Japan on life sciences R&D.

Japan's government disperses its R&D funds across a remarkably broad spectrum of research institutes attached to both central and regional governments and including a wide range of special corporations that derive a large share of their funds from the central government. Especially complicating direct comparison is the large number of regional research institutes that support local agriculture and industry; these are mostly funded by regional governments but also receive significant subsidy from the central government. This vast network of regional and local research institutions has a long and often overlooked history, dating back to the Maeda Report of the early 1880s, which drew attention to the importance of supporting local entrepreneurship in small-scale craft industry.[90] Also defying comparison with the US are the large numbers of foundations (*zaidan hojin*) and special corporations (*tokushu hojin*) that support research at both the national and local levels, often mediating in communication and flow of funding between the central government and funding recipients in regional research institutes.

The largest and most important public research institute conducting research in biotechnology is the Institute of Chemical and Physical Research (Riken). A special public corporation, it receives most of its funding from MEXT. Established in 1917 and reorganized after World War II, it is one of Japan's oldest research facilities. It draws together the most diverse collection of researchers of any institute: on top of its present permanent staff of 663 researchers is a constantly rotating staff of 3,000 visiting scientists, contract researchers, and students.

Historically focused on chemistry and physics, Riken began working in earnest on biotechnology in 1985, when the Science and Technology Agency (STA) transferred its fledgling program to develop a high-speed automated gene-sequencing machine to Riken's Tsukuba Institute. In 1991, researchers there developed a technique for sequencing DNA at the rate of 100,000 bases per day, a blistering pace at that time.[91] Later in the decade, Riken joined hands with Shimadzu Corporation and the government-affiliated Japan Science and Technology Corporation to develop the world's fastest DNA sequencer, the RISA 384; using a laser to read DNA base sequences, it increased the speed of sequencing by a factor of four. Riken scientists went on to make a small contribution to the Human Genome

Project, the preliminary results of which were announced in June 2000; in particular, Riken produced about half the sequence data for human chromosomes 21 and 22.[92] However, few in Japan were pleased with this relatively minor role, especially considering that Riken was the world's first public research institute to mount a sustained effort to develop DNA sequencing technology beginning in the mid 1980s. Consequently, well before the announcement of the completion of the draft sequence, policy makers were positioning Riken to lead the way in the next phase of research: making sense of the vast amount of data generated by the Human Genome Project.

In 1998 the Science and Technology Agency and Riken launched the country's biggest genomics initiative to date: the Biomolecular Research Program. The goal is to combine genome sequence analysis with the study of protein structure and function. At their disposal is the giant Super Photon Ring accelerator (Spring-8) located in Hyogo Prefecture, whose eight billion electron-volt X-ray beam-line generator is the world's most powerful of its kind.[93] By shooting these X-ray beams at crystals of protein, researchers at Riken aim to solve the three-dimensional structures of 1,500 human proteins, knowledge of which is expected to enable scientists to design more powerful drugs that produce fewer side effects.[94] To house its genomics initiative, Riken built the Genomic Science Center, which opened in Yokohama in late 2000. Its centerpiece is the Nuclear Magnetic Resonance Facility, equipped with ten 600 megahertz and six 800 megahertz magnets for use in protein structure analysis, the latter of which are the world's most powerful. (NMR analysis enables the determination of the three-dimensional structures of proteins that cannot readily be formed into crystals as required in X-ray analysis.) Co-located with the Genomic Science Center are the Plant Science Center, Research Center for Allergy and Immunology, and SNP Research Center. The latter has already identified in the Japanese population more than 90,000 single-nucleotide-polymorphisms (SNPs), single-base variations in human DNA that are associated with certain diseases like cancer. Greatly facilitating this effort is the RISA 384 gene sequencer mentioned above; using this equipment, scientists can process 384,000 samples of DNA per day using much smaller samples of blood than conventional equipment. Scientists at the SNP Research Center claim to have discovered SNPs associated with asthma and diabetes.[95] The center aims to commercialize its findings through collaborative research with industry. One such project is with Mochida Pharmaceuticals, whereby Riken provides Mochida with the three-dimensional structure of proteins associated with disease, which Mochida then uses as targets for drug screening.

At the level of local and regional governments, various types of research institutes support prefectural and regional economies. The so-called *kosetsushi* (public research facility) and *shikenjo* (experiment stations) are similar to America's agricultural experiment stations and manufacturing extension partnerships, though in Japan they are better funded, older, and far more integrated into regional economies than their counterparts are in the US. There were 164 such institutes in 1997, employing 6,907 people.[96] Although they are organs of prefectural and local governments, they derive a significant share of their research funds from national R&D subsidies. Many work alongside or in collaboration with regional offices of the Ministry of Economy, Trade, and Industry (METI) and the Ministry of Agriculture, Forestry, and Fisheries (MAFF); some collaborate on R&D related to regional industry with local universities.

Regional agricultural research institutes, often in collaboration with universities, have played an especially important role in applying biotechnology to improving crops and livestock grown and raised locally. A surprising demonstration of their scientific capabilities came in summer 1998, when the Ishikawa Prefectural Center for Animal Husbandry and Research, in cooperation with researchers at Kinki University, produced the world's first cattle cloned from an adult somatic cell.[97] According to the Ministry of Agriculture, Forestry, and Fisheries, between July 1998 and November 2002, forty research institutes produced 318 calves using somatic cell nuclear transfer, in addition to twenty-two goats and two pigs. Most of these animals either were stillborn or died shortly after birth; only around 45 percent have survived for use in experimental studies.[98]

A cabinet resolution, passed in 1995 on the heels of the Diet's passage of the new Basic Law on Science and Technology, designated promotion of regional science and technology as a national priority, emphasizing support for university–industry relations and creation of regional industry clusters. In response, the Science and Technology Agency launched a number of initiatives aimed at encouraging regional research partnerships, including programs to establish local centers of excellence and regional industry clusters. Under the Second Basic Plan for Science and Technology, the government added "regional knowledge clusters" to its list of regional technology promotion initiatives, among which several are to target biotechnology. The main point behind these programs is to provide incentives for individual firms, universities, and research institutes to form partnerships around the development of technologies that best exploit each region's comparative advantage.

Japan's universities, like those in the US, perform the bulk of the country's basic research, especially in the life sciences. Universities perform 13.4 percent of Japan's R&D in the natural sciences but a much higher 37 percent of R&D in the life sciences.[99] Expenditures on academic research in the natural sciences approached 2 trillion yen in 2000 ($18.4 billion at the IMF exchange rate), which is actually higher on a per capita basis than the $27.5 billion spent in the US.[100]

Universities clearly have been an important component in Japan's national innovation system. Their role, however, has been quite different from that of universities in the US, the practical effects of which are especially pronounced in biotechnology and other industries characterized by rapid technological change. Japan's innovation system has lacked a component comparable to the institutionalized, public policy-driven technology transfer system responsible for commercializing academic inventions and renewing the corporate landscape in the US with a continual stream of new innovations and start-up businesses. In 2000 alone, inventions licensed from universities contributed to the formation of 454 start-up companies in the US, more than four times the 105 start-ups associated with academic research in Japan in 2001, which was a banner year. Through August 2002, the cumulative total of university-based start-ups still in operation in Japan stood at 424, compared to 2,309 in the US.[101] Perhaps in no sector is the effect of this difference so profoundly clear than in biotechnology: as of early 2003, Japan's universities had produced only two dedicated biotechnology companies to have successfully completed a public offering of stock (Anges MG and Transgenic), compared with hundreds that have done so in the US.[102]

An abundance of reasons account for this relatively low level of formal technology transfer and small number of DBCs associated with academic research. First, available indicators suggest that the linkage between basic science and commercial innovation has not been as tight in Japan as it has in the US. For example, between 1990 and 1997, universities and public research institutes filed 53 percent of the patent applications submitted to the US Patent Office by American applicants in the six categories associated with the foundation technologies of biotechnology. By contrast, Japanese universities and public research institutes filed only 13 percent of applications made by Japanese applicants to the Japanese Patent Office in the same six categories.[103] Second, relatively little of Japan's academic research funding comes from industry: only 2.3 percent in 1999, compared with 6.3 percent in the US and 11.3 percent in Germany, according to the OECD.[104] Japanese firms in fact have been investing more R&D funds in universities and research institutes overseas than in universities at home: in 1995, while firms were supporting R&D in universities in Japan to the tune of 67 billion yen, they were sending 94 billion yen to universities and other research organizations abroad.[105] Finally, until the late 1990s Japan had no legal framework for technology transfer comparable to that in the US under the Bayh–Dole Act; with few exceptions, academic researchers simply have had no legal obligation to disclose inventions or turn over decisions regarding their handling as intellectual property to their universities. This lack of policy and legal congruence between the two systems calls for caution: it is misleading to apply the same standards of comparison and benchmarks for assessment to both systems. In particular, nothing can reasonably be said about which system is "better" or more successful than the other; we can say only that they are different.

Nor have universities been spared criticism in their performance of basic research. On a quantitative basis, Japan's academic scientists are no slouches: they produced 9 percent of the world's scientific papers in 1999; though less than a third of the American total, it was more than that of any other country.[106] On the other hand, Japan's scientific papers deliver far less impact than their numbers suggest. Between 1993 and 1997, more than 44 percent of papers written by Japanese scientists merited not a single citation in papers written by other scientists, compared with 35 and 37 percent written by American and British scientists, respectively.[107] The relative citation index is a measure of the impact of a country's scientific papers based on the extent to which other authors cite them. An index above 1 means that the country's papers are cited by other papers more often than is indicated by the country's share of articles in that field. By this measure, scientists in Switzerland, whose relative citation index across all fields in 1999 was 1.37, produce papers with the greatest impact. In second place was the US with an index of 1.35. Japan's index of 0.83 ranked it a distant sixteenth.[108] More tellingly, the gap between Japan and the US is widest in biomedical research and clinical medicine, two of the major fields underpinning biotechnology; it is narrowest in engineering and technology, where Japan has traditionally been strong.

Tradition, or, more precisely, history, matters in this analysis because Japan's academic research system evolved to accommodate societal demands quite unlike those faced by universities in the US. It is natural, therefore, that the environment and character of academic research in the two countries would be different at any given point in time.[109] In the early postwar period, rebuilding and retooling the industrial base took precedence over pushing back frontiers of science. Firms imported and adapted advanced technology from abroad, a role that universities had played during the war. Universities, for their part, fed industry's insatiable demand for engineers and technicians, while faculty, mindful of the wartime role of university–industry collaboration in fueling the country's militarism, maintained a critical stance toward renewed university–government–industry collaboration. Preoccupied with the task of integrating and adding value to foreign technology, firms had little need for the basic research performed in universities. On the other hand, they competed fiercely with each other to hire the brightest students from the best universities. Channels of communication opened up between engineering faculty and the firms that hired their graduates. Professors at top-tier universities sought to place their best students in positions at top-tier companies. Having done so, they often maintained close relationships with their former students, sometimes collaborating in research and even in joint publication of the results.[110] The personal and generally informal links between individual faculty and corporate researchers are an often-overlooked feature of Japan's national innovation system, and they continue to be important today.

Universities underwent vast expansion during the 1960s and 1970s as they responded to soaring demand for higher education, fueled by the rapid growth of industry, the baby boom, and growing perceptions of the importance of an undergraduate degree as preparation for a successful career.[111] Academic research and graduate studies languished, however, as resources had to be concentrated on accommodating societal demands for undergraduate education. Nor was the aversion to formal collaboration with industry slow to dissipate. Many faculties saw themselves as frontline defenders of Japan's postwar democracy, a disposition that made it difficult for a truly competitive, merit-driven system of research of the type practiced in the US to develop; fairness and equality took precedence over merit in the allocation of research funds. This process is seen most clearly in the bureaucratic process for distributing research funding. The Ministry of Education traditionally has distributed funds uniformly across individual instructional units, or *koza*, rather than allocating them to individual researchers on a competitive basis.[112] This has produced a research system that has been, in the words of Brendan Barker, "dominated by small, narrowly focused projects, with funds awarded on the basis of seniority and with a preference for orthodoxy, linked to an institution rather than an individual, and watched over closely by the funding agency."[113] Moreover, the system of recruitment and promotion tends to freeze faculties in their current positions. Promotion within the *koza* depends on a vacancy at the next higher position. All individuals within it are tenured, making it exceptionally difficult to remove unproductive faculties. The resulting low levels of labor mobility and performance-based promotion produce what Samuel Coleman describes as stagnation within the "credit cycle" of academic research: relatively low levels of output of high-quality research leading to low levels of competitive grants that in turn further limits the output of high-quality research.[114] Even though the drawbacks to this system have long been acknowledged and discussed, the mindset behind it is deeply entrenched; it has proved stubbornly resistant to change.

By the 1980s, opportunities for growth through incremental innovation based on importation and adaptation of foreign technology had largely been exhausted. Industry began looking more seriously at universities as sources of new knowledge. At the same time, trade friction with the US and Europe evoked demands in those countries that Japan reduce its free-riding on the scientific knowledge of other countries. Japan's Ministry of Education responded by expanding opportunities for faculties to engage in joint research with industry and building new off-campus research institutes to accommodate new forms of industry–university collaborative research. With the Ministry of Finance maintaining a tight rein on government budgets through the 1980s, however, little new funding was available to improve the research infrastructure; conditions in academic laboratories dedicated to basic research continued to deteriorate. By the early 1990s, conditions had reached a point where the departing president of Tokyo University felt compelled to describe conditions in his own physics department, Japan's most prestigious, as "miserable and utterly unacceptable."[115] Facilities at half of the national universities were more than twenty years old, while 64 percent had equipment that had aged beyond its useful life.[116] Meanwhile, with universities in the US spinning out patents, industry licenses, and new DBCs in rapid succession, it was hard to envision how Japan's science infrastructure could even slow the widening of the science gap with the US, let alone close it.

By the mid 1990s, a strong political consensus had formed around the need for radical improvement of the domestic environment for scientific research. Citing the growing intensity of international competition, the challenges associated with an aging society, the hollowing out of industry, declining living standards, and loss of social vigor, the government in 1996 passed by a cabinet resolution the first Science and Technology Basic Plan. Mandated by the Science and Technology Basic Law that the Diet had passed a year earlier, the Basic Plan provided a five-year strategy for overhauling the national R&D system. Its most ambitious goal was to boost the government's budget for science and technology by an average of 11 percent for each of the five years from 1996 to 2001, bringing the nation's total expenditure on R&D to 17 trillion yen. For universities, the plan promised to expand the number of postdoctoral researchers to ten thousand, increase the number of competitive grants, promote collaboration between universities and industry, make it easier for faculty researchers to consult for and conduct research at private companies, and provide greater incentives for researchers to transfer technology to industry.[117] In short, it called for universities to move closer to the American model in the administration of basic research, handling of intellectual property, and technology transfer.[118]

Japan's universities took a significant step in this direction when the Diet passed the University Technology Transfer Promotion Law in August 1998. This law authorizes universities to establish Technology Licensing Organizations (TLOs) to manage intellectual property for faculties and facilitate its transfer to industry. Approved TLOs are eligible to receive subsidies covering two-thirds of the costs needed to establish them up to a maximum of 20 million yen over a five-year period. This law was followed in October 1999 by the Special Measures Law for the Revitalization of Industry, which permits recipients of central government funding for commissioned research (*itakukenkyu*) to retain 100 percent ownership of patents to the inventions they make using government funds; it also slashes by half the cost to TLOs of filing patents. A third law that came into force in April 2000, the Law to Strengthen Industrial Technology, eases regulations on the outside work of a faculty, permitting them to work directly with companies on developing the transferred technology. Finally, in 2002 the Ministry of Education, hoping to spur formation of spin-off companies, revised university regulations to permit researchers to use university equipment and facilities for starting up a company based on a faculty member's research.

TLOs perform many of the same functions as technology licensing offices in the US: receiving and evaluating invention disclosures from researchers, identifying potential commercial opportunities, filing patents, negotiating licenses, and administering licensing fees. The differences, however, are significant. Unlike its American counterpart, a TLO at a national university is not part of the organization of the university; rather it is a separate entity, set up either as a limited liability company or a foundation. In addition, a faculty whose research is funded by the government has no legal obligation to disclose inventions. Finally, in most cases, intellectual property rights to an invention arrived at through research funded by the government revert to the individual researcher, not the university or the government; this is true for both public and private universities. Income from licensing, however, is shared among the TLO, the individual researcher, and the university.

By the middle of 2002, twenty-seven TLOs had been established. Together, they had filed for 2,635 domestic patents and been awarded fifty-seven. They were also managing 517 licensing agreements, of which 371 were royalty-bearing, generating to date an income of 687 million yen.[119] All these figures have been rising at an accelerating pace, suggesting that these policies are not only bearing fruit but doing so far sooner after their passage than was the case with the Bayh–Dole Act in the US.

Yet even before the TLO law came into force, individual faculty inventors were regularly transferring rights to their inventions to corporate partners, exploiting the same informal channels mentioned earlier in the context of recruiting of graduates and joint research. For example, if a researcher who has had a long-term research partnership with a firm, or been sponsored in some way by it, invents something related to that firm's business, the researcher may offer the invention to the firm for patenting. If the company is interested, it will apply for patents, bearing the full cost of filing and maintenance. Such patents seldom are used – mostly, companies file them to keep the professor's invention out of the hands of competitors. Yet if they do end up generating revenues, the company will return a small part to the inventor in the form of a well-timed "donation" (*kifukin*), not tied to a specific purpose, often totaling about a million yen.[120] The amount of a million yen is common because that is the upper limit of what most companies can donate without the approval of the director of research. (Miyata refers to the timing of this donation using the expression "*a-un no kokyu*," which is commonly used to describe the emotional harmony between two individuals who understand each other without need of resort to the spoken word.)[121] The inventor's name often appears on the issued patent, a benefit for the researcher.

Informal technology transfer along these lines is no rare occurrence in Japan. In biotechnology, Kneller cites a study by the Japan Bioindustry Association of patent applications in the field of genetic engineering over a ten-year period ending in 1997. During that time, an average of 874 patents were filed each year; 40 percent of these patents listed a university faculty member as the inventor.[122] Exemplifying this reliance on companies to do the patenting is Keio University's Nobuyoshi Shimizu, a leader of Japan's contribution to the sequencing of the human genome. Since 1993, his research has yielded fifty patent applications, forty-eight of which were filed by corporate sponsors.[123] To sum up, while universities themselves rarely file patents, academic researchers do contribute to a significant share of the patenting that does occur in Japan, which belies the stereotype of academic scientists disconnected from the needs of industry.

Public policy

Public policies in both countries have played a fundamental role in shaping institutional development of the respective national innovation systems. In the US, although the government has never formally targeted commercial biotechnology as a matter of industrial policy, support of the basic research underpinning it, especially in agriculture and medicine, has long been a national priority. The close connection between basic research and commercial success in biotechnology has meant that policies promoting basic research have also profoundly influenced commercial development. In Japan, the government has never been a provider of research funds for biotechnology on a scale comparable to that of the US government, though public funding has accelerated since the mid 1990s. On the other hand, government sponsorship of research related to industrial applications played an important part in stimulating private sector interest in the new technologies and encouraging market entry. In both countries, regulatory policies have had enormous influence on the pace and direction of innovative activity.

The United States

Government policies promoting science and technology in the US, though extensive, have been highly selective. Until recently, science policy has been governed by the postwar paradigm, which holds that direct government promotion should be limited to generic scientific research, whose social returns are believed to be high but whose private returns are insufficient to warrant socially desired levels of private investment.[124] The federal government has mostly avoided supporting projects favoring particular firms or industries, except when justified by overriding national interest, as in defense, health, agriculture, and nuclear power.[125] Consequently, the bulk of federal funding has been allocated to universities or government research institutes through the various mission agencies of the federal government, especially the Departments of Defense, Energy, Health and Human Services, and NASA.

Promotion policies in biotechnology have followed the general pattern of the postwar paradigm, meaning that they have mostly focused on supporting basic research in the biological and medical sciences (for the purpose of advancing knowledge) and applied research in agriculture and medicine (which relate directly to national prosperity and well-being and hence qualify as targets for mission research). Twelve federal agencies have been funding R&D related to biotechnology, primarily through extramural research programs; the vast bulk of it is obligated to HHS and USDA, with lesser amounts going to NSF (which supports mostly basic research in biology and other life sciences) and DOE (which has played a significant role in the Human Genome Project). In 1991, the US government spent $3.4 billion on biotechnology, which, though dwarfing the $630 million the Japanese government spent on biotechnology that year, looks meager in comparison with the $38 billion and $6.4 billion allocated to defense and space, respectively.[126] Today, the federal government does not list a separate budget for biotechnology, nor does it coordinate investments in the field. Instead, it allocates funding to the life sciences to support the broader mission of each of the relevant federal agencies, the most important of which are HHS, NSF, and USDA. Federal obligations grew rapidly over the past decade, rising in real terms from about $9 billion in 1985 to $15.4 billion in 1998 (both figures in constant 1996 dollars). By contrast, total federal R&D expenditures actually shrank in real terms over the same period, from $71.6 billion to $64.7 billion.

The federal budget for biotechnology R&D is striking in at least two key respects. First, government expenditures on biotechnology R&D were 70 percent of industry's. Although this may not be surprising in light of the small size of most American DBC's, the figure is astonishingly high for a country traditionally suspicious of government's visible hand in the market. In addition, it is far higher than the proportion spent by Japan's government. Even in 1998, after the industry had grown considerably, the government funded 50 percent of all life science research in the US, compared to 35 percent in Japan.

Second, funds are overwhelmingly concentrated in the budget of NIH, most of which funds research in human health. During the Clinton Administration, which compiled a separate biotechnology budget, HHS absorbed nearly 80 percent of that budget. Over the past two decades, federal R&D investment in health has grown faster than that of any other R&D budget function, rising in constant 1996 dollars from $6.6 billion in 1980 to $17.2 billion in 2001. Not surprisingly, because spending had stagnated in most other areas in the 1990s, health's share in total federal R&D obligations soared from 12.4 to 23 percent. By 2003, as the NIH budget reached $27 billion, the commitment made by the Clinton White House to double the budget of NIH in five years had been fulfilled.[127] For all the government's rhetoric against picking winners in the marketplace, this massive infusion of funds into health-related research could be interpreted as a *de facto* industrial policy for commercial biotechnology. As Daniel Greenberg observes, "Ideological objections to funneling government research money through NIH were nil, because NIH focused on basic research conducted in nonprofit universities and hospitals. But the boundaries between fundamental knowledge and the market were blurred." To support the point, Greenberg goes on to cite evidence showing that NIH annually spends $1 billion, a quarter of its budget for applied research, on pre-clinical and clinical development of specific drug products.[128]

Several factors explain the surge in health-related R&D over the past several decades. First, a consensus has existed as far back as the Bush and Steelman Reports in the early postwar era that promotion of research on health is an appropriate objective of federal research policy. President Nixon deepened that commitment in 1971 with his War on Cancer, which opened the taps of federal dollars to cancer research and turned NIH into the research powerhouse it is today.[129] The commercial biotechnology boom of the late 1970s and the mobilization to search for the cause of, and treatments for, AIDS in the 1980s kept new federal dollars flowing in. For a time, the Clinton Administration had tried to shift the emphasis in health policy to cost containment and preventive care; his proposal for national health insurance sent shockwaves through the drug and biotechnology industries in 1994. That effort failed, stymied by the powerful political opposition of health insurers and the pharmaceutical industry. Instead, the Republican-controlled Congress began the 1995 term determined to eliminate the federal deficit by reining in spending, and health was to be no exception. It appeared that NIH had few friends in either Congress or the White House. That was before the scientific community itself unleashed its fully lobbying energies on the Congress. The NIH succeeded in the ensuing battle in not only regaining the annual increases in appropriations to which it had grown accustomed – including a staggering 15 percent increase in 1999 – it won a bipartisan commitment to double the budget over the next five years.[130] It must be underscored here that the political influence of the scientific community in the US, its ability to project its voice into the arena of Congressional politics, and the centralization of biomedical research into a single, massive federal agency have no real counterparts in Japan.

Congressional interest in and support for the biotechnology industry has grown since the 1980s. The image of an infant industry under attack by a unified "Japan, Inc," which was described in the first paragraphs of this book, did much to draw the attention of legislators, as is discussed in detail in Chapter 4. Some even proposed legislation that would promote biotechnology in much the same way as the Japanese government was targeting it.[131] In July 1991, a group of Senators and Representatives formed the congressional Biotechnology Caucus, which committed itself to expediting legislation favorable to the industry. Eventually the caucus included twenty-two Senators and sixty-nine Representatives; Senators Frank Lautenberg and Hank Brown joined Representatives Tom McMillen and Tom Bliley in chairing it.[132] The caucus participated in several conferences and field trips, and it provided an informal channel of communication between industry and Congress.[133] In addition the

Biotechnology Science Policy Forum brought together biotechnology enthusiasts from industry, academia, and health organizations to educate members of Congress on the benefits of new technology.[134]

The biotechnology industry today has many more resources at its disposal to influence public policy. Its representative in Washington, the Biotechnology Industry Organization (BIO), has grown over the past decade from seventeen employees representing 500 companies to seventy employees representing roughly 1,000 companies. It made $81,000 in donations to political parties and individual candidates in the 2001–2 election cycle, and it spends $2 million annually on lobbying.[135] Recently it deployed its powers of persuasion to convince the FDA and Congress to extend the Prescription Drug User Fee Act, which, though requiring firms to pay a fee to the FDA for each new drug application, helps the FDA employ resources needed to expedite reviews. Joining BIO in making the case for biotechnology in Washington is the much larger Pharmaceutical Research and Manufacturers Association (PhRMA), which spent $11.2 million on lobbying in 2001.[136] Collectively, drug firms spent $235.7 million on Congressional lobbying between 1997 and 1999, going as far as to hire 297 lobbyists to defeat a proposal to add a prescription drug benefit to Medicare in 2000.[137] According to *Public Citizen*, twenty-three of the industry's 623 lobbyists in the US are former members of Congress.[138] Schering-Plough alone spent $12 million over a three-year period in the late 1990s to lobby Congress for legislation extending patent protection on its blockbuster drug Claritin.[139]

All of which points to a powerful political coalition committed to sustaining the institutional underpinnings of the competitiveness of America's biotechnology and pharmaceutical industries. Again, no comparable coalition exists in Japan or anywhere else in the world for that matter. And though criticism abounds of an unholy alliance between politicians and drug companies that feeds health care inflation and corrupts the political process, penetration of that process by organized interests is certainly not unique to the US. In Japan, the construction industry often comes in for similar criticism. Judged solely by its impact on the technological capacities of a nation, a political system concerned more with the competitiveness of its biotechnology and health care industries is probably doing more to secure future rises in living standards than is one more beholden to traditional industries like construction, where the rate of productivity increase is slow.

While R&D policies have contributed strongly to the formation of a science base, patent policies have more directly influenced commercial activity. Commercial biotechnology would never have emerged without incorporation of genetically engineered organisms and processes under existing patent law. Patent protection is especially critical in biotechnology because of the lengthy and costly process involved in demonstrating safety (for food, agricultural and drug products) and efficacy (for drugs) of new products.[140] Firms simply could not afford to undertake the risk of investing in product development in the absence of such protection. Living microorganisms were determined to be patentable subject matter in the Supreme Court's 1980 landmark ruling on *Diamond v. Chakrabarty*. Transgenic plants and animals were subsequently determined to be patentable. In addition, linear molecules such as proteins and DNA sequences have been generally accepted as patentable.[141] Although controversy presently swirls around whether isolated human genes should be patentable, the US has been at the forefront in accommodating biotechnology within the patent system.[142] Indeed, it was action on the patent front in the US which shocked the Japanese government into ramping up its support of biotechnology in the early 1980s; similarly, America's permissive patent regime in the 1990s has been used by advocates of patent reform in Japan to push for a revision to that country's patent law.

On the regulatory front, too, America set the standard that was later followed in other countries, including Japan. Oversight of biotechnology is a highly complex and decentralized process. The consensus among scientists and regulatory agencies has been that risks associated with genetically engineered organisms are similar to those associated with organisms modified by traditional means. Consequently, oversight of new products employing biotechnology resides in whichever agency would handle the product if it were made using a traditional process. Various efforts have been made to coordinate regulatory activities, most of which have met with failure (see Chapter 4). Although agencies today regularly exchange information and ideas, regulation, like promotion, remains a highly decentralized affair; the present Bush Administration, unlike the Clinton Administration before it, appears unconcerned with this decentralized structure. Uniting all the regulatory agencies, however, is the philosophy that regulation should be grounded in science, not in a precautionary approach that anticipates potential harms not substantiated by rigorous scientific research.

Japan

Japan's public policies supporting biotechnology innovation have been strikingly different from those in the US. In the US, apart from the Human Genome Project and, more recently, programs aimed at countering bioterrorism, most public funding has gone toward supporting investigator-initiated academic research under the sponsorship of the NIH; there is no "grand strategy" to develop a commercial biotechnology industry. In Japan, too, no single grand strategy has provided a framework for unified innovation policy in biotechnology, at least until very recently. The similarity, however, ends there. Unlike in the US, in Japan no single agency dominates the funding and regulation of biotechnology research as does America's NIH. Rather many ministries and agencies have sought to promote and regulate those aspects of biotechnology that come under their respective jurisdictions. This was especially true at the beginning of commercialization in the 1980s and early 1990s. Although the government under current Prime Minister Junichiro Koizumi has drawn up what is billed as a grand strategy, and has mandated that the Council for Science and Technology Policy (CSTP) implement it, it is by no means clear that the decentralized pattern of policy making will yield to a more coherent and centralized approach.

Promotion of biotechnology has taken on growing importance since passage of the Science and Technology Basic Law in 1995. This law provides the legal foundation for the implementation of science and technology policy in accordance with a five-year Basic Plan, as was discussed above. By the time it expired in 2000, the first Basic Plan had achieved its objective of doubling the government's investment in R&D over the level of 1992, in part because of large increases in funding for genome research and research in basic biology.

While the legislative framework for science and technology policy was being revamped, Prime Minister Keizo Obuchi, following the recommendations of his predecessor Ryutaro Hashimoto, prevailed upon the Diet to pass legislation reorganizing and streamlining the organs of the central government. Eighteen ministries became twelve, one result of which was the merging of the Science and Technology Agency with the Ministry of Education to create MEXT, a super-ministry of science, responsible for 70 percent of the government's science and technology budget. The notoriously difficult task of coordinating science and technology policy making among ministries that jealously guard their respective turfs was made easier by the reconstitution of the former Council for Science and Technology into the CSTP within the Cabinet Office and creation of the post of Minister of State for Science and Technology Policy. The CSTP, which is supposed to meet once a month – the old CST met on average once or twice a year – is charged with setting priorities for science and technology, coordinating policy making across the government, and evaluating the results of its handiwork; it also renders opinions on policy and gives advice to the Prime Minister when asked to do so.

The new CSTP came on the scene just in time to oversee implementation of the second five-year Basic Plan. In effect from 2001 to 2005, it is even more ambitious than the first: it sets its sights on making Japan home to thirty Nobel Laureates over the next fifty years. To get there, it will increase the government's total investment in R&D and related activities from the 17 trillion-yen-level achieved at the end of the first Basic Plan to 24 trillion yen, or 1 percent of GDP, assuming an annual rate of growth in GDP of 3.5 percent.[143] More important perhaps is the goal of doubling the absolute amount of R&D funding awarded competitively: researchers in Japan today compete for only one-tenth of total R&D funds the government disburses; one-third of funds are disbursed competitively in the US.[144] Finally, the new plan designates four fields as strategic priorities for future development: life sciences (to cope with food problems and the health needs of an aging population), information technology (to prepare industry and citizens for life in the information society), environmental science (to promote health and preserve environmental resources), and nanotechnology (to sustain the country's long-standing leadership in materials engineering).[145]

For all the attention lavished upon it by Japan's government, public funding for the life sciences to date has been modest, at least in comparison with the US. According to a Japanese government strategy report, Japan's government in 1998 spent about 500 billion yen ($3.8 billion) on life science-related research, while the figure in the US was $18 billion.[146] Even after adjusting for differences in the size of the two economies, the US government still outspends Japan's by a ratio of 2 to 1. The report goes on to indicate that while the US government funds half of all life science research performed domestically, Japan's government funds only 35 percent. Partly as a result, whereas 58 percent of all government-funded academic research in the US is in the life sciences, the comparable figure in Japan is only 40 percent.[147] An exception is research related to sequencing and analyzing the human genome: public spending has more than quadrupled since 1998, reaching levels well in excess of the US government's annual budget for the Human Genome Project.

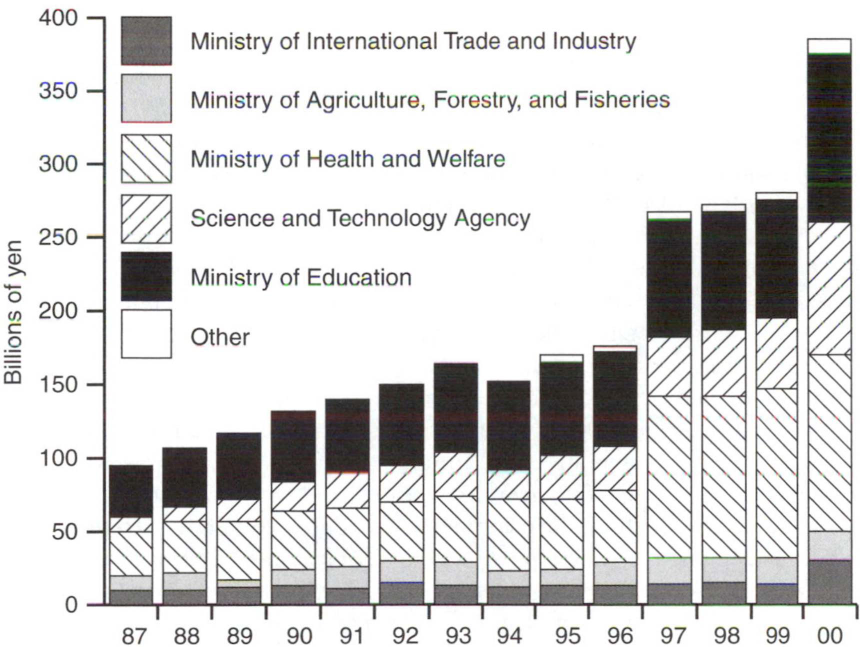

Figure 3.1 Japanese government budget for biotechnology (by Ministry)

Sources: For 1987–95, *Nikkei Baioteku* (various issues); for 1996–2000, Okasan Shoken, *Baio idenshi bijinesu* (Tokyo: Toyo Keizai Shimposha, 2000), p. 60.

In addition to its modest size, two other characteristics of public funding are noteworthy. First, it has grown steadily and at times even dramatically, as can be seen in Figure 3.1. Allocations leapt in 2000 with the inauguration of the Millennium Project, which provided a new framework for strategic planning and sustained funding of multi-year research projects in fields that, like biotechnology, span the jurisdictions of many ministries. Introduced as a plan to "welcome a new century filled with dreams and vitality," the Millennium Project harnesses university–industry collaboration to the task of shoring up the country's capacity to deal with the spread of information technology (*johoka*), aging of the population (*koreika*), and environmental issues (*kankyo taio*).[148] Of the 120.6 billion yen budgeted for the project for the five-year period beginning in fiscal year 2000, more than half, 64 billion yen, went to biotechnology, and most of that to research related to the human genome. The overarching goal is captured in the phrase "realization of the aging society in which people can live in good health and peace of mind." Targeted fields are new "tailor-made drugs" customized to the genetic constitution of the individual patient, regenerative medicine, functional foods (especially rice that lowers blood pressure and allergy-free crops), and disease- and pest-resistant crops. Although the Mori Cabinet changed the name to the "Special Framework for Japan's Renewal," the momentum achieved under the Millennium Project has endured into the new millennium.

The Millennium Project sought to not only ramp up spending on biotechnology research, but also to unify the separate programs of multiple ministries, eliminate duplication of efforts, and coordinate policy making. The fragmentation of projects across the government is another hallmark of Japan's public policy in biotechnology, and considerable efforts have been made to solve this problem. As the significance of biotechnology dawned on policy makers in the early 1980s, every ministry engaged in promotion of science and technology wanted to get into the act. The need to pay off massive debts accrued during the 1970s, however, made the budgets of the 1980s and early 1990s especially lean. Thus, not only turf wars but also pitched battles for new funds ensued. Among policy planners, this austere climate instilled what one official called a "scrap and build" mentality: getting funds for new programs required dismantling existing ones.[149]

Reinforcing fragmentation and competition is the vertical organization of policy networks connecting firms to the ministries that have jurisdiction over the industry in which the firm competes. Chemical companies, for example, come under the jurisdiction of METI (MITI until 2001), which both regulates and promotes the industry. Similarly, pharmaceutical companies come under the Ministry of Health, Labor, and Welfare, and food companies under the Ministry of Agriculture, Forestry, and Fisheries. Also associated with each ministry are special corporations, foundations, and industry organizations that mediate between firms and the corresponding ministry, forming a nexus of relationships that advocate on behalf of the industry; the practice of *amakudari*, by which a ministry sends retiring officials to posts in private or third-sector organizations associated with the ministry, reinforces the ties among them. Masahiko Aoki and Masahiro Okuno coined the term "partitioned pluralism" (*shikirareta tagenshu*) to describe the system that results when individual ministries compete in the annual budget process as proxies for the interests they represent.[150]

Compounding the problem of coordination is an unusual characteristic of the typical Japanese biotechnology firm that makes it quite different from its counterpart in the US: it is a big company, doing research and making products in several different industries. Kirin, for example, is both a beer and biopharmaceutical company; Takara Shuzo makes sake (rice wine), DNA chips, and gene amplification systems; Japan Tobacco is also a developer of biopharmaceuticals; Nippon Paper Industries, Japan's top maker of printing and writing paper, is also developing genetically engineered high-protein rice; Ajinomoto makes drugs to combat AIDS and diabetes while also supplying a third of the world's demand for monosodium glutamate. Firms like these cultivate close relations with multiple ministries. This has proved at times troublesome, especially in the 1980s, when the government sought to entice firms to enter biotechnology by first joining a research association. Problems arose when firms were asked to participate in research associations under different ministries. Similarly, ministries were often reluctant to see key clients cavorting with other ministries.[151] Some industry observers had rather harsh words about the forms of manipulation used to recruit favored firms into research association and processes by which participants were selected.[152]

Until their merger in 2001, the Ministry of Education, and Science and Technology Agency vigorously promoted biotechnology within universities and national laboratories, respectively. Although they shared the goal of promoting scientific research, they had very different histories, organizational cultures, and constituencies; friction between them was frequent. In principle, the Council for Science and Technology (CST) had the task of setting broad policy objectives in accordance with the Science and Technology Basic Plan; in practice, it lacked the authority to do so effectively. Nakamura and Odagiri give three reasons: (a) Except for the heads of the Science and Technology Agency and Ministry of Education, no other ministries promoting biotechnology had permanent members on the committee; (b) its authority did not extend to determining budget distributions but was limited to the setting of broad policy objectives; and (c) its thinking tended toward basic research rather than the more practical problems in which industry was interested.[153] Tanaka and Hirasawa add that the policy-making system in the CST "puts priority on the 'logic of the creators' and the organization finds it difficult to adapt the 'logic of the beneficiaries.'"[154] Reducing sectionalism in decision making and aligning the interests of creators and beneficiaries was to be a major focus of legislative activity in the second half of the 1990s.

The merging of the Science and Technology Agency and Ministry of Education at the start of 2001, along with the creation of the Council for Science and Technology Policy, is supposed to alleviate the inter-bureaucratic wrangling and fragmentation that in the past has dogged science and technology policy. This broader principle of policy coordination was also transferred downward to policy making in specific priority fields, including biotechnology. In July 1999, the five (soon to become four) ministries with jurisdiction over biotechnology – STA, Ministry of Education, MHW, MAFF, and MITI – released the "Basic Strategy for Creating a Biotechnology Industry."[155] Acknowledging the critical importance of cross-ministry collaboration at the administrative level (*jitsumu men de no renkei*), the new strategy called for the establishment of a liaison committee (*renrakukai*) to improve coordination and increase efficiency, though with due consideration to the autonomy of participating agencies. However, few details were given on how coordination is to be carried out in practice.

Despite the organizational changes and formal declarations of commitment to project coordination, there is little evidence to date of changes in actual practice. According to Nakamura and Odagiri, coordination and collaboration at the planning stage have not extended to actual implementation: single projects are simply passed out to individual ministries for execution, even when it would be more efficient to do so within a single agency.[156] Worse, the various implementing agencies sometimes outsource research to the same institute, and even to the same university professor; the result is loss of operational efficiency without the benefit of a rational, well-coordinated subdivision of tasks. Even the Millennium Project failed to change old habits. As the *Shukan Daiyamondo* recently put it, "The baneful influences of the old vertical administration structures remain."[157] MITI and Riken, for example, proceeded to build new research institutes for regenerative medicine in Amagasaki and Kobe, respectively, at points less than ten kilometers apart.

One thing that has changed over the past decade is the role of politicians in science and technology policy. Until recently, science has rarely been the stuff of political drama: politicians have had far more to gain by throwing their weight behind issues dearer to the hearts of constituents on whose generosity they depend for campaign funds and votes, namely, agriculture, public works and construction, and postal and telecommunications services. Such is the turf of the Liberal Democratic Party's famous *zoku*, or policy tribes, through which politicians gain policy expertise while nurturing a political base in their rise to influence within the party. Officials in MITI and STA, with whom I spoke in the early 1990s, could not recall any instances in which Diet members had contributed to science policy conception or implementation. For their part, legislators conceded that such technical issues are best left in the hands of the ministries.[158] Occasionally, however, matters of science and technology happen to intersect with other, more politically charged issues. This happened during the debate over deregulation of telecommunications in the 1980s, when the Ministry of Posts and Telecommunications, supported by the LDP's influential telecommunications *zoku*, successfully repelled MITI's effort to extend its jurisdiction into new information technologies.[159] It happened again in the early 1990s, when the administration of President George H. Bush turned up the heat on reluctant Japanese lawmakers to contribute $1.5 billion toward construction of the Superconducting Supercollider (SSC).[160] Around that time, former Director General of the STA Yohei Kono stressed to me in an interview that science and technology policy had now to be considered in the broader context of Japan's foreign relations: let others know, he said, that Japan is serious about fulfilling its international obligations.[161] Finally, the hollowing out of Japanese industry that began in the first half of the 1990s, coupled with the political instability surrounding the LDP's temporary loss of power in the mid 1990s, provided an unprecedented opportunity for political entrepreneurship, one result of which was the Diet-led restructuring of the science and technology policy-making system under the new Basic Law.[162]

At the time when the government was fashioning the first biotechnology policies in the 1980s and early 1990s, the LDP's Science and Technology subcommittee of the Policy Affairs Research Council reviewed all budgetary requests concerning science and technology issues. In addition, a score of Diet caucuses promoted various issue areas, including ocean and space development, energy, and the global environment. In biotechnology, the late Michio Watanabe headed one such caucus, though it rarely convened and appeared to have had little direct influence on government policy. Perhaps best known for lobbying on behalf of science and technology issues in general was the Nakamura *Chosakai* (study group), led by former Construction Minister Kishiro Nakamura. The Nakamura group played a key role in lobbying the Finance Ministry to boost government expenditures on R&D in the early 1990s, kicking off the political process leading to the restructuring of the science policy-making framework a few years later. The political muscle required to pull this off was great indeed: the Ministry of Finance, determined to restrain spending, simply would not be budged. As for the LDP's inability to budge the Finance Ministry, in spite of the numerous caucuses addressing the issue, one member summed it up with a well-known Japanese maxim: "*Abu hara torazu*!" (If you run after two hares, you will catch neither.)[163]

Efforts to increase spending on science may have come to naught had it not been for the political turmoil into which the government was subsequently plunged.[164] In summer 1993, a vote of no confidence resulted in the ousting of the cabinet of Kiichi Miyazawa, bringing down the curtain on thirty-eight years of continuous LDP rule. Although the party returned to power a year later as part of a coalition government, the shock to the system forced an adjustment in relations between the bureaucracy and legislature and facilitated the emergence of new leaders within the LDP.

After a year in opposition, the LDP returned to share power as junior partner in a coalition government, becoming the coalition leader after the Lower House election in 1996. LDP Prime Minister Ryutaro Hashimoto hardly had time to savor the LDP's comeback before the economy slid back into recession in 1997. Against the backdrop of economic stagnation, a few leaders within the LDP, most notably Koji Omi and Koichi Kato, perceived the importance of technological innovation as a means of kick-starting the economy and advocated on behalf of a stronger, more centralized policy framework. These efforts bore fruit in the form of the Science and Technology Basic Law and the five-year plans that followed, culminating in the establishment of the position of Minister of Science and Technology (*kagaku gijutsu tanto daijin*) in 2001. Never before in Japan's history has Japan's Diet asserted such determined leadership over science and technology policy, the result of which has been to give it its own political advocate in the Cabinet and a prominent place on the Cabinet's policy agenda.

If the government's role in promoting biotechnology has been fragmented and *ad hoc*, so too have its regulatory policies. In this case, however, the differences with the US are perhaps not as great. Where Japan clearly differed was in the speed of the government's response to the emergence of the new technology.

During the period in the mid 1970s when the US government was rolling back restrictions on research using genetically modified organisms, Japanese regulators remained on the sideline. Only in 1979 did the Ministry of Education move to permit such research in national universities, though only after four years of concerted lobbying by university researchers and scientific associations. Within months, the STA released a similar set of guidelines covering public research institutes under its jurisdiction. After the commercial boom began in the early 1980s, each concerned ministry issued its own guidelines: MITI's guidelines were aimed at industrial R&D, MAFF's at applications in agriculture, and MHW's at the drug industry. The result is a highly decentralized regulatory policy framework that mirrors the situation on the promotion side.

To summarize, despite the accepted legitimacy of close government–business relations and an institutional structure that facilitates such relations, scarcity of funds, absence of a strong political commitment to funding basic biomedical research, and bureaucratic sectionalism have hampered the effectiveness of public policies. Inter-ministry competition, while potentially increasing the variety of programs and alternate sources of funding, may have dulled incentives for firms to participate in joint projects during the early stages of commercialization. Moreover, unlike telecommunications and other politically sensitive issue areas, powerful politicians rarely took the initiative to champion biotechnology, though the role of politicians has clearly changed since the mid 1990s. The result is that the number of policy instruments at the government's disposal has been limited.

Conclusions

Differences in the organizational endowments and institutional characteristics of the national innovation systems in Japan and the US have produced important differences in the emergence and commercial development of biotechnology in the two systems. For firms in both countries, biotechnology posed a common set of challenges: the need to develop and access core scientific knowledge, opportunities to apply that knowledge across a broad range of industries, long lead times and high uncertainty of outcomes, and uncertainty concerning appropriate regulatory and promotion policies. How firms responded to those problems hinged on the combination of market opportunities and the presence and accessibility of assets and resources available to firms in the NIS.

In the US, large, internationally competitive pharmaceutical and chemical firms initiated the first commercial responses. The huge and growing market for human therapeutic products provided early demand stimulus. The bigger story, however, centers on the DBC as an organization specialized to the task of transforming the inventions and knowledge of academic science into novel products and processes. DBCs have flourished because of a combination of distinctive characteristics of the American NIS. These include the availability of risk capital, a flexible market structure permitting ease of entry and exit, high mobility of scientific labor, and public policies that have been largely stimulatory but that have also channeled innovative activity into the human health care sector. Rarely, however, have DBCs on their own completed the chain of steps needed to bring a product to market. Rather they more often have relied on partnerships with large companies.

Characteristics elsewhere in the national system support firms' efforts in two important ways. First, the system of academic research has served up a rich harvest of basic science. High mobility of scientists, strong patent protection, and a unified technology transfer system have fostered entrepreneurship, giving strong incentives to individuals and firms to commercialize the fruits of academic research. Second, public policies have for decades favored academic research in the health sciences, the effect of which has been to skew the pattern of innovation toward medical applications. Indeed, aggressive commercial pursuit of health care applications of biotechnology is a distinctive characteristic of the national system.

In Japan, by contrast, supporting institutions in the public sphere have played a far less crucial role than in the US. Lack of accessible stocks of scientific knowledge, scarcity of venture capital, and low levels of public funding for basic research made it necessary for firms to develop equivalent capabilities on their own. This is made easier in some cases by the dense web of interfirm linkages that lower the transaction costs of innovative activity. The practical effect, however, has been to limit market entry to larger firms endowed with internal research laboratories, manufacturing, and marketing capabilities, as well as the capital base to sustain them.

Outside the firm, the contributions of academic and other publicly funded research to commercial development, though important in some areas, have been modest. This is the result, first, of public policies aimed not at basic biomedical and molecular biology research but at technologies needed for technological catch-up on a national level. The second factor has been the institutional isolation of academic research from industry, at least in the formal legal sense. Bureaucratic sectionalism, austere budgets, and lack of policy coordination hampered the government's ability to promote the industry until the reorganization of science and technology policy making in the 1990s. Before that time, the government's use of research associations to stimulate market entry probably reinforced the tendency for innovative activities to concentrate in large firms in the chemical and food industries.

The Japanese government's belated efforts to promote biotechnology research and reduce the barriers to commercialization has had two important consequences. First, by failing to reduce uncertainty, it delayed firms' entry into biotechnology until well after American firms had begun to develop the first products; industry has been trying to catch up ever since. Second, firms that began commercial efforts pursued technological trajectories closest to those in which they already had accumulated expertise. These included industrial products and applications that fuse biotechnology with technologies from unrelated sectors, such as fibers, foods and beverages, and microelectronics. As a result, commercial biotechnology has advanced across a far broader range of products and sectors than it has in the US.

National innovation systems are not static entities; as institutions, their present character owes much to history. Commercial biotechnology in the two countries evolved in a pattern consistent with the characteristics of the respective innovation systems as this chapter has described them. The next two chapters recount the story of this evolution.

4 The emergence of commercial biotechnology in the US

Introduction

As the last chapter makes clear, America's leadership in biotechnology derives from the strength of its institutional underpinnings, at both the level of the firm and the broader national innovation system (NIS). At the heart of this success are the institutionalized linkages between university and industry, small start-up firm and large corporation. These linkages have propelled America's biotechnology sector to the forefront of innovation by uniting the forces of science push with market pull in an organizational context conducive to the joining of complementary functions in a value chain running from laboratory to clinical and product development to manufacturing and, finally, to the global market. Although these functions sometimes came together under one corporate roof, more often they were linked together through strategic alliances, research agreements, and other contractual relationships among firms and between firms and universities. In short, the institutional nexus among government, science, and industry has rendered America's NIS uniquely tuned to the opportunities provided by the new technology regime.

The discussion so far has focused on the interdependence of technological and institutional factors in shaping the pattern and direction of innovative performance in the American NIS, as well as the characteristics of the NIS itself. In this chapter, the emphasis shifts to the historical development of commercial biotechnology within the US national system. Recall from Chapter 2 the argument that technological advance is a cumulative process: winners and losers, successes and failures, are revealed through the interplay of search, selection, and learning processes which are heavily dependent on past capabilities and accumulated expertise. Thus, to understand the present conditions of biotechnology in the US, and how they differ from those in Japan, requires not only an understanding of the present institutional context but also how that context has evolved since the emergence of the new technological regime. This is the focus of the discussion which follows.

I find it useful to distinguish three phases in the emergence of commercial biotechnology in the US. The first phase, which lasted from the 1930s until the formation of the first DBC in 1976, marked the emergence of biotechnology's scientific foundation, molecular biology, as an independent field and gradual development of the core technologies of genetic engineering. Toward the end of this period, the university–industry nexus coalesced, opening a channel through which knowledge could flow between the molecular biology community and the marketplace. A few visionary scientists foresaw the scientific and medical possibilities of recombinant DNA; through their efforts, a regulatory regime began to take form, and the US became the first country to not only allow but also promote research with genetically modified organisms. Unable to rule out genetic engineering as an answer to their own problems, a small number of large chemical companies hedged their risks by making small investments in biotechnology research. In this first phase, the major sources of new knowledge were academic scientists and, to a lesser degree, large corporate research laboratories.

In the second phase, which lasted from 1976 until 1983, emphasis shifted from knowledge creation to knowledge enhancement and product development as new companies appeared to develop the new technology. Heralding the transition into this phase was the appearance of the dedicated biotechnology company (DBC), whose role would be to link the new science base with commercial possibilities. Regulations on research with genetically modified organisms were further eased, and the enactment of the Bayh–Dole Act vastly increased the attractiveness to corporations of partnerships with universities. The first experimental drugs made using recombinant DNA techniques entered clinical trials, and the first product, human insulin, cleared regulatory review and was brought to market. This phase also saw the first strategic alliances between DBCs and large drug companies; these would become the primary organizational vehicles for moving experimental drugs and technologies from the laboratory into the product development pipeline.

The third phase began in 1983 and continued to the end of the 1990s, culminating in the completion of the draft sequence of the human genome in 2000. During this period, biotechnology came of age. The commercialization of drugs and agricultural products based on first-generation technologies – recombinant DNA, monoclonal antibodies, and mass cell culture – began in earnest; the flow of new products onto the market reached a steady-state pace, then accelerated in the 1990s. In the past decade came a new generation of technologies, including genomics, combinatorial chemistry, and high-speed DNA sequencing systems. Firms combined these with the older techniques to create new products; in some cases, complementary technologies were harnessed into technological platforms for drug discovery that could be sold to big pharmaceutical companies. The main concerns for firms in this phase are financial and organizational: assembling the requisite complementary assets into a value chain, and obtaining enough capital to sustain their operations. For DBCs, institutional adaptation has most commonly taken the form of strategic alliances and joint ventures, as opposed to vertical integration or short-term contracts.

In all three phases, but especially the first two, strategies and processes of commercialization in the US have been far different from those of Japan. In Japan's case, the difficulty of transferring technology from universities to industry made that channel relatively ineffective as a generator of new companies. That left early commercialization to large firms, many of which could bring themselves to test the waters only after the government formed research consortia aimed at stimulating market entry. Given the qualities of pervasiveness, low tacitness, and high uncertainty which characterize the technology regime, the more flexible response of American firms, in conjunction with their proximity to the core knowledge base, has proved a source of enduring advantage over Japanese rivals.

Institutional formation and knowledge creation (1930s–1976)

Central to the emergence of commercial biotechnology were the development of the underlying science base and the establishment of regulatory and intellectual property protection regimes. Gradually, a distinct collection of institutions specializing in the promotion of biomedical research crystallized within the NIS. Before World War II, large drug firms and universities were the center of action; academic research was mostly funded internally or by private foundations and firms. After the war, generous infusions of federal dollars flowed into biomedical research, premised on the notion that today's heavy investment in basic research yielded tomorrow's improved living standards and cures for deadly diseases. Surging investment in academic research in the life sciences accelerated progress along a new scientific trajectory that had opened up before the war: molecular biology, which together with genetics would provide powerful new insights into the biology of living organisms and lead, ultimately, to the development of recombinant DNA and other techniques. The drug industry remained cautious, however, mostly content to reap the bountiful returns still coming from earlier investments in research. That left an opening for new competitors, often started up and run by the academic scientists who had done the original research. This period thus ends with the appearance of these new firms and the filling out of the regulatory and intellectual property protection regimes that would govern and shape their development.

The players

Commercial biotechnology rose on a foundation of basic research in the life sciences that in the first half of the twentieth century transformed our understanding of biological processes. The story begins with two sets of actors working at the interface of biology, chemistry, and medicine but from different directions. They would not find each other until the end of the period, but when they did so, commercial biotechnology as we know it today was born.

The first group consisted of large pharmaceutical companies and the universities on which they relied for research support. At the turn of the century, most American drug companies were still developing drugs through trial and error. Quackery was rampant. Many drugs were unsafe, ineffective, or both, until the federal government in 1902 passed the Pure Food and Drug Act, its first foray into regulating safety and marketing of drugs.[1] Firms responded by beefing up their quality-control practices; a small number built their own research laboratories, following the lead of their more advanced peers in Europe by harnessing the powers of modern chemistry to drug discovery. Parke-Davis was first to do so in 1902, followed later by Abbot Laboratories and Eli Lilly. Though originally focused on the chemistry of vitamins and development of processes to manufacture them, Merck established its Central Research Laboratory in 1933; it was one of the first corporate research facilities that encouraged academic-style publishing, and the first laboratory of any kind to be fully equipped with the most modern instruments of analytical chemistry. Strongly supporting and complementing the corporate research efforts were a handful of universities that had developed strong research programs in medicine, biology, and chemistry, including Johns Hopkins, Washington University, Harvard, Columbia, and University of Wisconsin. Drug companies often sought out the resources of these universities, giving rise to one of the most distinctive institutions in the American NIS: the university–industry partnership. Among drug companies, Parke-Davis forged close relations with the Mayo Clinic, University of Michigan, University of Wisconsin, and Washington University, each of whose faculties contributed ideas for the company's early research-based products. Abbot Laboratories nurtured a long relationship with University of Illinois, from which it drew many of its corporate leaders.

The appearance of the central pharmaceutical research laboratory and coalescence of university–industry collaboration paved the way for the institutionalization of drug discovery and development based on chemistry, pharmacology, and microbiology. Yet this alone would likely not have propelled the US drug industry into the forefront of innovation. By ending European dominance of the pharmaceutical industry while creating massive demand for antibiotics, World War II gave a large boost to American drug makers. It also brought the full commitment of the federal government to bear on funding and organizing scientific research. While one part of the wartime Office of Scientific Research and Development was secretly developing the atomic bomb, another of its divisions prevailed upon four of the largest drug makers to cooperate in scaling up the production of penicillin to meet wartime needs. To ensure the drug worked as expected in patients, it also pumped $2.7 million into clinical development at fifty-eight academic and industrial research laboratories. With a successful manufacturing process in hand, the government went on to provide twenty-two companies with the materials needed to build plants capable of meeting military and civilian needs for penicillin, as well as production facilities of its own. In this way, penicillin, a product of British science, became the lever that catapulted the American drug industry to a position of global leadership. Former niche players Pfizer, Merck, Upjohn, and Squibb used the experience and profits from penicillin to become America's most formidable drug firms. Penicillin was not an American innovation: Howard Florey and Ernst Chain, scientists at Britain's Oxford University, were first to demonstrate its clinical effectiveness in a famous 1940 paper. Rather it was the financial, organizational, and engineering resources the US government brought to bear on the problem of scaling up its production that made mass production of penicillin a reality.[2] Like the Manhattan Project, the scale-up of penicillin demonstrated the capacity of the federal government to mobilize scientific resources on a national scale for the pursuit of a technological objective not likely to be achievable by the private sector alone. It was a lesson not lost on the architects of America's postwar science policy.

A research-centered drug industry tied closely to federally funded academic research provided the institutional framework for the postwar expansion of the pharmaceutical industry; decades later, it would also be applied to biotechnology. However, as is true for most revolutionary innovations, the fundamental scientific discoveries behind biotechnology came from points far removed from the industry they were most likely to transform. For more than a century, research in the drug industry has been rooted in analytical and organic chemistry. In the words of Jürgen Drews, a former research head at Swiss drug maker Hoffmann-La Roche:

> At its core, pharmaceutical research is still chemical. It rests on experience and also on the assumption, later theoretically and experimentally supported, that vital processes can be described in chemical categories and that diseases can be described as measurable deviations from "normal" chemical processes.[3]

This paradigm is being challenged by a new approach that frames the study of living organisms in genetic terms: it views disease not as a chemical imbalance but the consequence of an "incompatibility" between the organism's genes and its environment.[4] This approach originated eighty years ago in the work of the second group of actors in our story. They are the physicists and chemists who first applied the analytical techniques of their respective disciplines to the study of living organisms. Their work gave rise to a new field of research, which forms the foundation of biotechnology: molecular biology.

The framing of biology in terms of physics and chemistry was prompted by two scientific trends of the first half of the twentieth century. First, although geneticists had described what genes do and their role in inheritance, their chemical structure and mechanism of action remained unknown.[5] For their part, geneticists were mainly content to accept the gene as a given and focus their energies on modeling its replication and understanding patterns of inheritance. Second, physicists and chemists were riding a wave of success following the development of quantum mechanics and elucidation of the ways in which molecules in living systems interact with each other. Unleashing the powerful new tools of electron microscopy, spectroscopy, ultracentrifugation, and X-ray crystallography, scientists in this group – which included Linus Pauling, Salvador Luria, Max Delbruck, and George Gamow – set about answering the questions geneticists had passed over: namely, what is the chemical structure of the gene, and by what mechanism does it direct the production of proteins and its own reproduction?

Although laboratories across Europe and the US participated in the founding of molecular biology, its most influential sponsor was the US-based Rockefeller Foundation. In fact, it was the head of the natural science division of the Rockefeller Foundation, Warren Weaver, who coined the term "molecular biology" to describe this union of biology with physics and chemistry.[6] The Rockefeller Foundation played an important role as a source both of ideas and funding in the development of molecular biology. Created in 1913 by the industrialist John Rockefeller, it initially devoted most of its resources to public health and education. The onset of the Great Depression prompted reconsideration of how the Foundation could best put its resources to use. The decision to shift its energies into funding research at the intersection of physics, biochemistry, and genetics was grounded in its diagnosis of the causes of the Great Depression. As Morange puts it:

> The scale of the slump implied a profound, noncontingent cause. For the Rockefeller administrators, the origin of the crisis lay in the gulf between humankind's understanding of the productive forces, which had grown continuously in the previous period, and its understanding of itself, which had not progressed.[7]

In other words, prevention of future depressions hinged on closing the gap between our knowledge of the physical world and knowledge of human biology; expanding knowledge of the latter meant applying the tools and ways of thinking of the former: in short, reducing living processes to their constituent molecules. Between 1932 and 1959, the Rockefeller Foundation provided an estimated $25 million to fund research in molecular biology. In particular, it generously supported the work of the so-called "phage group," a group of scientists led by Max Delbruck who between 1940 and 1960 studied biological processes at the molecular level using bacteriophages (viruses that infect bacteria) as a model organism. It also played a key role in the development of laboratory equipment such as centrifuges and electrophoresis systems, which became the essential tools of molecular biology research.

The reframing of life science research from the 1930s not only opened up new space for scientific inquiry, it also changed the political context in which public policy about scientific research in general, and the life sciences in particular, would be debated. Gottweis speaks of the emergence at this time of a "policy narrative" in molecular biology that "connected the various sites of the emerging governability regime by relating the new understanding of life phenomena in the discourse of molecular biology to central national political goals, institutional structures, and socio-economic contexts."[8] That the US, the rising hegemonic power of the postwar era, would be especially well positioned to profit from this new policy narrative is suggested in a revealing statement by Jürgen Drews:

> In contrast to chemistry, molecular biology stems from a primarily democratic, liberal, indeed libertarian, social order, in which formal hierarchies play a much smaller role, while on the other hand, personal development and freedom are more important than in the society of a century ago.[9]

Yet by no means were the effects limited to the US: significant amounts of the Rockefeller Foundation's funding went to European researchers, including Howard Florey, who used a Rockefeller grant to isolate and purify penicillin, Max Delbruck, who used a Rockefeller grant to come to the US prior to the start of his phage research, and Jacques Monod, a researcher at France's Pasteur Institute and co-discoverer of messenger RNA (ribonucleic acid). Although scholars debate the extent of the Rockefeller Foundation's influence on scientific research, its linking of grant funding to the achievement of broader political and economic objectives was a novel idea before World War II; it set a precedent that the federal government followed after the war.

World War II brought about a permanent shift in the federal government's science and technology policy. Before the war, the vast proportion of total investment in scientific research came from the private sector. In the 1930s, the federal government funded only between 12 and 20 percent of total research expenditures.[10] Generous federal support for agricultural experiment stations was the only exception to this pattern. Although the National Institutes of Health (NIH) had been established in 1930, it remained a small organization until the end of the war. At that time, the Office of Scientific Research and Development transferred its medical programs to NIH, substantially boosting the latter's budget. Although nothing so dramatic as the OSRD's penicillin program would be on the postwar agenda, Congress's inability to follow through on the recommendation of Vannevar Bush to create a National Research Foundation to manage federally funded research enabled NIH to gain a near total monopoly on biomedical research. Both the Bush and Steelman reports on science and public policy stressed the special importance of federal funding of health research; the arguments articulated then continue to be widely accepted today.[11]

By the 1950s, a powerful political coalition had formed to ensure that health research remained a high priority on the legislative agenda. Influential patrons in Congress, notably Lester Hill in the Senate and John Fogarty in the House, advocated strongly on its behalf, while on the outside, philanthropists Florence Stephenson Mahoney and Mary Lasker lobbied tirelessly for federal support of medical research.[12] The result was a win-win situation for legislators: as Kenney points out: "Politicians learned that voting for increased health appropriations would never lose them votes."[13] Predictably, the NIH's budget ballooned in the early postwar period, from $2.8 million in 1945 to over $1 billion in 1968.[14]

By 1975, the NIH budget for R&D had reached $1.6 billion, a four-fold increase in real terms over the level of 1960. As a percentage of total federal R&D, the NIH's contribution tripled from 3 to 9 percent over the period. But the best was yet to come. Although growth stagnated over the next decade, it took off again after 1985, nearly tripling in real terms by 2002 (Figure 4.1). The growth in the R&D budget for the NIH looks even more

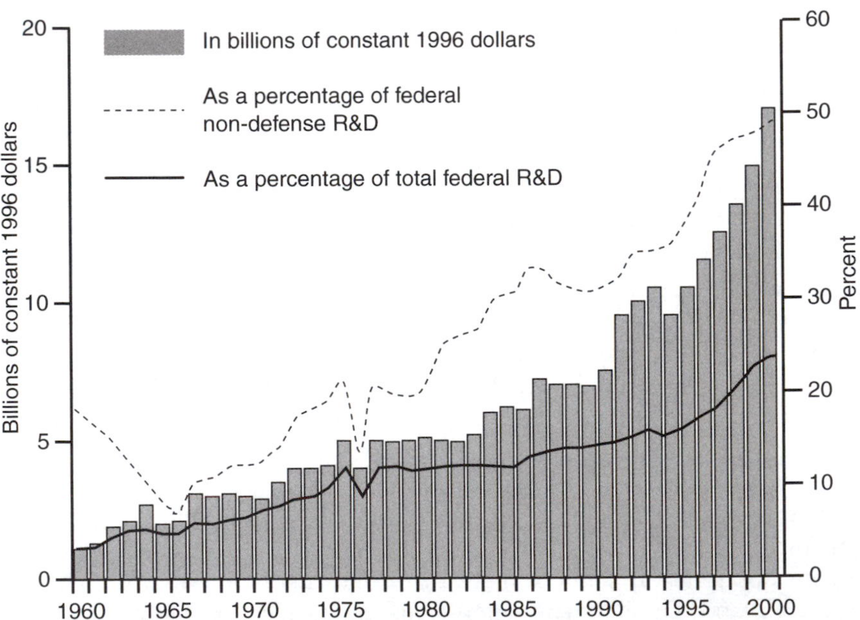

Figure 4.1 Trend in federal outlays for the conduct of research and development at the National Institutes of Health

Source: Office of Management and Budget, *Budget of the United States Government, Fiscal Year 2004, Historical Tables, Table 9.8*. Online, available HTTP: <http://w3.access.gpo.gov/usbudget/fy2004/hist.html>.

striking when compared with growth in other agencies for which R&D funding is a major mission (Figure 4.2). The R&D budget for the National Aeronautics and Space Administration in 2002 was 3.5 times the level of 1960 in real terms, while that of the Department of Defense had increased by only 60 percent. Contrast that with the NIH, whose R&D budget in 2002 was nearly sixteen times its level of 1960, with most of that increase coming since 1990. Because NIH is the largest source of funds for academic research, to which it allocates more than two-thirds of its budget, academic research in medicine and the life sciences fared especially well during this period.

In the 1970s, NIH began to face growing political pressures to demonstrate the utility of the research it was supporting. Such expectations filtered down to the academic biomedical research community, whose scientists felt increasingly obliged to justify their requests for NIH funding in the context of treating or curing disease.[15] The Nixon Administration's launching of the "war on cancer" fuelled rising expectations that the scourge of cancer could be made to yield to biomedical research if only

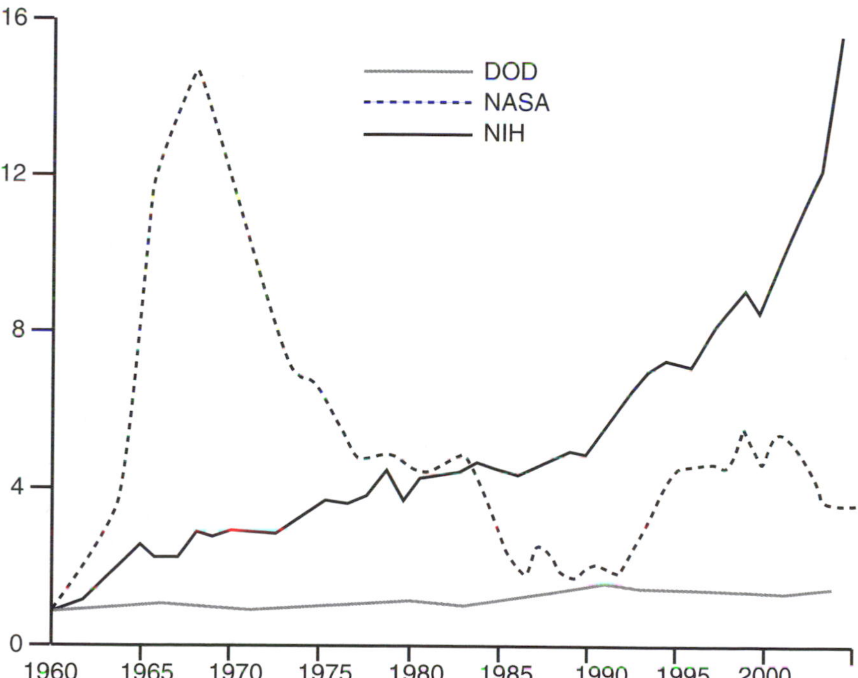

Figure 4.2 Trend in growth of R&D budgets for the National Institutes of Health, Department of Defense, and National Aeronautics and Space Administration (inflation-adjusted, relative to base year 1960)

Source: Office of Management and Budget, *Budget of the United States Government, Fiscal Year 2004, Historical Tables, Table 9.8*. Online, available HTTP: <http://w3.access.gpo.gov/usbudget/fy2004/hist.html>.

sufficient funds could be mobilized. The NIH's National Cancer Institute (NCI) became the focal point for the country's assault on cancer, as did twenty-two designated cancer research centers tapped to lead the effort. The influence of such policies was tremendous, both in terms of shaping subsequent technological trajectories and in transforming the research environments at institutions receiving NIH funds. As one analyst put it, "Biology in general responded like a plant to the shining sun of NCI's largesse."[16]

Through the 1960s and 1970s, universities grew increasingly concerned with maintaining the infusions of cash to which they had grown accustomed. As the growth rate of federal funding began to level off, universities turned to large pharmaceutical and chemical companies to diversify and supplement their sources of funding.[17] Large firms, for their part, recognized that the rapid pace of research in molecular biology made it imperative to keep abreast of new developments. In addition, funding university research gave firms exposure to the new science without having to invest heavily in new facilities and personnel.[18] As a result, the arm's-length character of industry–university relations that had prevailed in the 1960s gave way in the 1970s to a greater openness toward collaboration. For molecular biology and the life sciences, it became increasingly acceptable for researchers to justify their work on social and economic as well as scientific merits.

Before the mid 1970s, only the biggest pharmaceutical firms bothered with such abstruse fields as molecular biology. Chemists, not molecular biologists, ran the labs. Although development of new drugs was ostensibly linked to advances in basic research, for the most part drug discovery still depended on painstaking screening of libraries of compounds in search for ones that did something therapeutically interesting in a test tube or tissue sample; serendipitous discoveries were still common. Candidate compounds would then be tinkered with and tested more extensively in mice; toxicity and effectiveness would be fully characterized. If the compound passed muster in animal testing, human trials would follow. The process was long and expensive, which accounts for the large size of successful companies. Though not elegant, drug development the old fashioned way still proved to be a source of riches for American firms. In 1981, eleven of the world's top twenty drug makers were American; together they accounted for 60 percent of the total pharmaceutical sales of the top twenty firms. Japan's lone entry, Takeda, ranked a distant sixteenth.[19] Nonetheless, the rate of innovation was clearly slowing, and US shares of global drug R&D and exports were falling. Traditional methods of drug discovery, while still turning out the occasional winning product, appeared to have reached a point of diminishing returns. New techniques coming out of molecular biology offered the promise of a revolution in drug innovation. Because most of the action was taking place in universities, the major drug companies once again turned their attention to the ivory tower.

Building the knowledge base

The idea that foreign genes could be inserted into host cells to induce them to produce a specific protein was the culmination of more than three decades of research, extending back to the 1940s.[20] The problem, as noted above, centered on characterizing the nature of the gene and the molecular processes by which it orchestrates cellular functions. A remarkable succession of experiments from the early 1940s established the "one-gene–one-enzyme" hypothesis (that the synthesis of enzymes, which are a subset of proteins, is somehow controlled by genes, one gene for each enzyme). Other important findings from this period revealed that the specificity of proteins rests in their unique sequence of amino acids, that the sequence of amino acids must somehow correspond to a coding sequence in genes, and that DNA (deoxyribonucleic acid) is the stuff of which genes are made.

The stage was thus set for James Watson and Francis Crick at the Cavendish Laboratory of Cambridge University to solve the structure of the DNA molecule, which they did using X-ray crystallography pictures provided by Rosalind Franklin and Maurice Wilkins.[21] Watson and Crick went on to reason that DNA's structure – a double helix composed of two complementary strands, each a lengthy linear sequence of four nitrogenous bases (usually written as A, G, C, and T, the first letters of their respective chemical names) – enabled it not only to encode a protein but also to replicate itself within the cell.

How the information encoded by the sequence of four bases was translated into the production of proteins was worked out over the course of the next decade. The puzzle was completed in the late 1960s when researchers, with the NIH at the forefront, finally cracked the genetic code, which relates the sequence of amino acids in protein to the sequence of bases in DNA. Along the way, Arthur Kornberg at Washington University worked out the biochemistry of DNA replication, discovering the enzyme DNA polymerase that kicks off the replication process, as well as devising a way of synthesizing DNA in a test tube. François Jacob and Jacques Monod at France's Pasteur Institute discovered a mechanism by which genes control the expression of protein. Both the capacity to make DNA in the laboratory to one's heart's content and the ability to switch genes on and off to yield desired quantities of protein would become essential tools in the genetic engineer's toolkit. Consequently, by 1970, not only had molecular biologists worked out the precise chemistry of the gene, they were on their way to fashioning tools that would permit them to manipulate those genes in ways that would prove to be of extraordinary commercial value.

By this point, some molecular biologists had begun to perceive they were on to something big. But the burgeoning science base did more than simply swell egos. It portended the emergence of a new technological regime that, in Schumpeterian terms, challenged existing production paradigms and created a new economic space of opportunities and possibilities for entrepreneurship. That scientists were recasting their own roles in this process is reflected in the new models and motivations driving the research agenda. Reflecting back on the restlessness among molecular biologists at the dawn of the biotechnology revolution in the 1970s, James Watson writes:

> But all we had been doing so far was observing; we were molecular naturalists for whom the rain forest was the cell – all we could do was describe what was there. The time had come to become proactive. Enough observation: we were beckoned by the prospect of intervention, of manipulating living things. The advent of recombinant DNA technologies, and with them the ability to tailor DNA molecules, would make all this possible.[22]

Whether participants thought of themselves as architects of a new technological regime as well as a new scientific paradigm is difficult to prove in hindsight. Perhaps it does not matter; as Wright contends, "new forms of technology were inherent in the very constructs of molecular biology; this was recognized by practitioners in the 1950s and 1960s."[23] Yet it would be only a few years before many of these same scientists would sit on corporate boards as pioneers of a budding new industry.

Humanity quietly entered the genetic engineering age in 1971, only three years after the genetic code had been completely deciphered. With funding from the NIH, Paul Berg of Stanford University Medical School and two postdoctoral fellows David Jackson and Robert Symons demonstrated that fragments of DNA from different organisms, in this case the simian virus SV 40 and a bacteriophage (a virus that infects bacteria), could be joined to form a circular DNA molecule containing DNA from both the SV 40 and bacteriophage. The tools that made DNA splicing possible were "restriction enzymes," which permit very precise cutting of DNA molecules, and DNA ligase, which makes possible the annealing of cut strands into a composite DNA molecule in an equivalently precise fashion. The article reporting their results, which Morange asserts "has the same founding value as Watson and Crick's 1953 article [reporting the structure of DNA],"[24] drew out the full implications of their findings: that genes from one organism could be introduced into another organism of a different species, and bacteria could be used as a host cell for amplifying the resulting recombinant DNA constructs. Berg and his students stood on the shoulders of many colleagues in carrying out this work, most notably those who had discovered the restriction enzymes, ligase, and other tools that made it possible to manipulate DNA; even the concept of recombinant DNA had been articulated several years earlier by Joshua Lederberg. Berg's contribution was to bring together all the tools that made genetic engineering possible, demonstrate that it could be done successfully, and suggest to the world the enormous implications.

Two years later Stanley Cohen and Herbert Boyer of the University of California, San Francisco, carried the technique even further using bacterial plasmids. Plasmids are circular DNA molecules bacteria possess in addition to their genomic DNA. In the 1960s it was found that plasmids sometimes carry antibiotic resistance genes and that bacteria can acquire plasmids from other bacteria, after which they replicate the plasmid when they reproduce. Stanley Cohen had earlier found a way to induce bacteria to take up plasmids from their surrounding media in a process called "transformation." Following on the heels of Berg's experiment, Cohen and Boyer demonstrated that plasmids from different bacteria could be spliced together to form a hybrid plasmid, which could then be transplanted into bacteria using Cohen's "transformation" technique. The bacteria would then treat the transplanted hybrid as though it were its own, expressing the proteins coded for by the plasmid genes and reproducing the plasmids each time they underwent cell division. A year later, they conducted an even more dramatic experiment, this time splicing a gene from an African clawed toad into a bacterial plasmid and successfully transplanting it into bacteria. The Cohen–Boyer technique, subsequently patented, became the foundational technology for the biotechnology industry. By 1974, it was clear that genes from one organism could be spliced into another organism, causing the latter organism to express a protein it would not otherwise make in nature. The prospect of bacterial factories churning out large quantities of commercially valuable protein was about to become reality.

A second breakthrough, this one in Britain, opened another key technological trajectory, though with considerably less fanfare. In 1975, Georges Kohler and Cesar Milstein fused antibody producing *Beta*-lymphocytes with malignant cancer cells, yielding a hybrid (sometimes referred to as a "hybridoma") capable of expressing both the lymphocytes' specific antibody and the cancer cell's property of rapid proliferation. Perceived as simply a clever laboratory trick at the time, the technique, known as cell fusion, is used today to produce monoclonal antibodies used to diagnose a wide range of medical conditions, from pregnancy to the presence of the HIV virus. More recently, biotechnology firms have begun to introduce therapeutic monoclonal antibodies that treat cancers, rheumatoid arthritis, and other disorders.

The emergence of a new knowledge base grounded in genetic engineering and cell fusion techniques quickly caught the attention of both government and the academic research community. The NIH's response was immediate: it expanded its sponsorship of recombinant DNA projects from two in 1975 to 123 in 1976, 349 in 1977, and 546 in 1978.[25] Research breakthroughs continued apace, among the most important being the development of techniques for determining the base sequence of DNA in 1975 and 1976 by Fred Sanger at Britain's Cambridge University and Walter Gilbert at Harvard. Though initially slow and labor-intensive, these techniques were later automated, becoming the core technologies for the sequencing of the human and other genomes in the 1990s. The technique of molecular hybridization was also introduced, which made possible the identification of particular genes of interest within bacterial libraries containing many genes, or on single strands of chromosomal DNA. This technique is often combined with the polymerase chain reaction (PCR), discovered a few years later in 1983. PCR permits the amplification of even a tiny sample of DNA to the point where experimentally useful quantities are obtained. A year later came the development of pulsed-field gel electrophoresis, which permits mixtures of very long strands of DNA to be separated on the basis of their length.[26] Armed with restriction enzymes and the techniques of gel electrophoresis, molecular hybridization, gene sequencing, and PCR, scientists could not only search for and characterize almost any gene of interest but could map genes to locations on their respective chromosomes and even identify individuals on the basis of minute differences in their DNA.

Industry's response, however, was more cautious. According to a survey by the Pharmaceutical Manufacturers' Association, only six major companies were actively involved with genetic engineering in the mid 1970s – Upjohn, Hoffmann-La Roche, Eli Lilly, SmithKline and French, Merck, and Miles Laboratory.[27] New firms were beginning to appear at a rate of about fifteen a year between 1970 and 1977.[28] However, only Cetus Corporation, founded in 1971 near Berkeley, California, was working at the cutting edge of molecular biology. Funded in part by investments from Standard Oil, National Distillers, and Shell Oil, Cetus sought to make alcohol, vaccines, and therapeutic proteins using the new technique of recombinant DNA.[29] Led by Kary Mullis, a group of scientists at Cetus invented and patented the PCR technique, which the firm later sold to Swiss drug giant Hoffmann-La Roche. Cetus also had the distinction of being the first biotechnology company to attract the interest of venture capital companies in the Bay Area, notably Kleiner & Perkins (later, Kleiner, Perkins, Caulfield & Byers), for whom investment in Cetus was the first of many deals that would make the venture firm a key force in the subsequent California biotechnology boom.

New knowledge is a necessary but insufficient condition for commercial application. Firms need both an incentive to switch from existing ways and the physical and human resources to support it. Because of the complex, uncertain, and multidisciplinary nature of the new technological regime, the long time horizons required for large-scale research, and the lack of organizational and technical competence, the private sector needed time to test the waters and establish linkages to the new knowledge base. The major drug firms, many of which were ramping up funding of academic research, were perhaps best positioned to exploit the new techniques; after all, they already had well-endowed research facilities, elaborate marketing networks, and other complementary assets needed to internalize the new technology and incorporate it profitably into new products. However, firms' search routines and research culture were still largely rooted in chemistry, and so they remained cautious. Potential new entrants, though unburdened by old ways of doing things and often major contributors to the new knowledge base, lacked access to capital, management expertise, and other complementary assets; unlike in computers and software, getting in required more than a tinkering mindset, a few cheap tools, and a garage.

Regulation: the final hurdle

A major deterrent to market entry was the uncertainty surrounding public acceptance and federal oversight of the new techniques. As early as 1968, Congress had debated the implications of genetic engineering and property rights of human tissues. In February of that year, Senator Walter Mondale, acting on behalf of a group of Senators that included Edward Kennedy, Robert Kennedy, and Robert Byrd, introduced a joint resolution to establish a Commission on Health Science and Society that would examine ethical and social consequences of genetic engineering. At that time, as throughout the 1970s and even today, opponents of biotechnology invoked images of Huxley's *Brave New World*, while scientists blamed opponents for sensationalizing scientific research and deceiving the public with false claims of the technology's capabilities.[30] Immediately after Cohen and Boyer demonstrated the recombinant DNA process in 1973, voices inside and outside the scientific community, while acknowledging the scientific merits, also warned of the possible hazards. The broader discussion revolved around three issues: the ethical implications of tampering with genomes, potential hazards associated with releasing genetically modified organisms into the environment, and potential social impacts.[31] In fact, the ensuing debate within the scientific community all but excluded ethical and social considerations.

For Paul Berg and other pioneers of recombinant DNA, the most immediate concern was that their experiments might unleash cancer-causing genes into the environment. Following up on his demonstration of the feasibility of gene splicing, Berg proposed to transplant a hybrid SV 40/phage DNA construct into mammalian cells, proving, he hoped, that cells of higher animals could be genetically modified. The proposal worried some colleagues; at the time, the SV 40 virus was thought to be a potential cause of cancer, and there were genuine fears that SV 40 DNA could somehow find its way into *E. coli*, a species of bacteria present in large quantities in the human gut, changing it into a cancer-causing pathogen. Honoring the concerns of his colleagues, Berg postponed his experiment. In summer 1973, a group of prominent scientists convened a conference in New Hampshire to discuss how to deal with the risks posed by this powerful new technique. The conference ended with a vote in which a majority decided in favor of asking the National Academy of Sciences to investigate the matter and issue recommendations. The NAS formed a committee, chaired by Paul Berg, which reported its results the following year. It called for a worldwide moratorium on all research using recombinant DNA until potential risks could be evaluated or methods developed to prevent the spread of genetically modified material into the environment.[32]

Finally, in February 1975, 140 biologists convened in Pacific Grove, California, at what came to be known as the Asilomar Conference. The NAS, NIH, and National Science Foundation provided financial support to ensure broad worldwide participation.[33] After four days of presentations and discussion, the participants agreed to allow research to progress but under conditions of physical and biological containment. Physical containment would vary depending on the type of organisms being used: bacteria, which frequently exchange DNA in nature, would require the least; more complex eukaryotic cells (cells that contain a nucleus) would require the strictest containment. Biological containment would require that researchers modify genetically modified organisms to prevent their survival outside the laboratory. Strictly banned was research on pathogenic bacteria and genes that code for toxins.[34]

The Asilomar recommendations were quickly assimilated into a set of NIH guidelines issued in June 1976. Through these, the US became the first country to develop a formal regulatory framework governing use of the new technology. Even before Asilomar, in October 1974, the NIH had created an institutional body to draw up regulations, the Recombinant DNA Advisory Committee (RAC), which in its initial form was comprised almost exclusively of scientists from the academic biomedical research community.[35] After Asilomar, the RAC advised that the Asilomar recommendations be put into force pending development of more specific regulations. The NIH's risk philosophy was based, as Gottweis has shown, on "a mixture of facts and assumptions," but solidly grounded in the conviction that the potential contribution of recombinant DNA research to medicine and the advancement of science outweighed the potential hazards, the latter of which were based mainly on speculation and not grounded in quantifiable evidence.[36] This strong utilitarian flavor imbuing the approach to regulation is captured by James Watson's explanation of his opposition to the earlier moratorium:

> I now felt that it was more irresponsible to defer research on the basis of unknown and unquantified dangers. There were desperately sick people out there, people with cancer or cystic fibrosis – what gave us the right to deny them perhaps their only hope?[37]

Following Asilomar, the NIH guidelines embraced the idea of physical and biological containment: NIH-funded experiments with recombinant DNA could proceed so long as they were done within contained facilities and used organisms rendered incapable of survival outside the laboratory. In addition, handling or storing cultures of recombinant organisms exceeding ten liters was prohibited without a full review and approval by the RAC. Four levels of containment were specified, depending on the type of experiments being performed and the type of host organism and DNA vectors being used. Implementation of the guidelines involved the principal investigator proposing a particular experiment in a grant application and the NIH review committee that evaluated the application. The committee was charged with both assessing the scientific merits of the proposal and determining whether the proposed containment measures were in compliance with the NIH guidelines; difficult cases were referred to the RAC.

Issuance of the NIH guidelines was a great triumph for the scientists who wished to push forward on research with minimal constraints; they were, as Krimsky aptly describes them, "written by scientists for the general use of scientists."[38] The vast majority of experiments were exempt from the containment stipulation. But there was a hitch: the regulations applied only to researchers receiving NIH funding, which in effect meant academic scientists; they made no explicit mention of industry. As it turned out, most firms pledged voluntary compliance with the NIH guidelines; the alternative was more restrictive legislation, which was concurrently being debated in Congress.[39] To be sure, not everyone was pleased with the default arrangement that left NIH as *de facto* regulator of recombinant DNA in firms for whom compliance with the rules was optional. Some states and localities, including New York and Maryland, actually passed ordinances compelling firms to abide by the NIH guidelines.[40] Nonetheless, the guidelines not only provided a threshold of risk reduction that enabled subsequent commercial development, they became a model regulatory regime for other nations, including Japan, to emulate.

Looking back on the NIH regulatory regime, two things stand out: first, it put in place no requirements for systematic assessment of the risks associated with using recombinant DNA or genetically modified organisms. It rather assumed that such risks were low enough relative to the benefits to justify allowing research to progress: unless there were clear instances of harm to researchers or the surrounding environment, the research would be assumed to be safe. Second was the extent to which the policy debate excluded broader considerations of ethics and social implications. The matter was dealt with almost entirely in technocratic terms. In the words of Susan Wright, "the genetic engineering 'problem' was reprojected almost exclusively in terms of producing safety precautions to contain hazards. In other words, it was reduced and redefined in terms that made it susceptible to a technical solution."[41] This manner of narrowing a problem is familiar to students of Japanese politics, who often contrast it with the messier process in the US whereby the broadest possible range of constituencies tend to weigh in on policy debates. Yet in this instance, Japan proceeded with far more caution, delaying commercial response by several years.

Knowledge enhancement (1976–1983)

By 1976, both the knowledge base and institutional structures in the American NIS had developed to the point where commercialization could begin in earnest. Uncertainties remained, especially on the regulatory front.

Could NIH credibly wear two hats, one of promoter of research, the other of regulator of industry? And how could regulators resolve the uncertainty over the long-term health and environmental effects of releasing genetically engineered cells into the environment?

The NIS made ready

Two powerful scientific developments in the second half of the 1970s had the effect of undercutting the arguments of those advocating tougher federal oversight. First was the discovery that in higher organisms many genes contain long stretches of DNA having no known function; though this DNA is transcribed into messenger RNA along with the coding sequences, it is excised from the messenger RNA molecule before the production of protein. The significance of this finding lay in the implication that the simple transfer of an intact human gene into a bacterium would not result in that gene being expressed; only a human host cell has the biochemical components needed to express a human gene containing these non-coding regions.[42] The second concerns the excitement surrounding Genentech, the first dedicated biotechnology company, which was started in 1976. Under a contract with Genentech to demonstrate the "proof of concept" of genetic engineering, Keichi Itakura and Herbert Boyer at University of California, San Francisco, in fall 1977, succeeded in inducing bacteria to make the human hormone somatostatin. The somatostatin gene used in the experiment was not cut from human DNA but synthesized artificially in the laboratory to ensure it could be expressed by the molecular machinery of the bacteria host.[43] The experiment was the first demonstration that recombinant DNA could be made to express a protein coded for by a foreign gene. The economic implications were immediately clear; in Washington, announcement of the results of this breakthrough effectively laid to rest legislative efforts to impose a uniform, mandatory regulatory regime on all recombinant DNA research.[44]

From this point, the public policy focus shifted from managing risks to promoting the international competitiveness of the industry. In this, biotechnology received a boost from the changing political and economic climate of the late 1970s and early 1980s. The American economy had been buffeted by an oil crisis and high inflation; whole sectors of manufacturing that had been mainstays of the economy were staggering under the weight of rising costs and cheap imports. Accused of saddling industry with high costs, regulatory institutions came under attack, and important sectors of the economy, including trucking and the commercial airline industry, were deregulated. Structural adjustment was in full swing, and it appeared prudent to many lawmakers to help the process along, or at least not to thwart it with burdensome new regulations.

Thus the return to the default position: any regulation of industry would come under the purview of NIH. In January 1980, the NIH incorporated into its guidelines a mechanism for industry's voluntary compliance. Firms, in effect, were invited to submit proposals for recombinant DNA experiments to a review process that paralleled that required of NIH grant recipients but with one important exception: when it evaluated a proposal from industry, the RAC met in a closed session in an effort to avoid exposing industry secrets.[45] In 1982, the problem of secrecy was resolved by transferring the responsibility of review to local "institutional biosafety committees" (IBCs).[46] Though compliance was voluntary, firms have generally supported it because of the legitimacy a stamp of approval from NIH confers upon them. By 1991, the Office of Technology Assessment reckoned that about half of all firms engaged in recombinant DNA research had registered their IBCs with the NIH.[47] By the mid 1980s, virtually all the earlier limitations blocking or limiting commercial use of recombinant DNA had been eased; in 1983, *Business Week* could report that "federal regulatory agencies now treat gene splicing much as they handle other industries that fall under their regulatory umbrellas."[48] Emphasis now shifted to unifying regulations being implemented across different federal agencies into a coordinated framework and writing rules for the deliberate release of genetically modified organisms.

Not only had the regulatory climate shifted strongly in favor of commercialization. The broader economic and political climate was also turning in favor of greater acceptance of new technology and an accommodation to the growing linkages between science and technology. In particular, industry and academia considered each other with renewed interest as tough economic conditions forced both to turn outward in search of new sources of growth and income. (The context of public policy on this subject in Japan at the time of writing is startlingly similar to that which took place in the US in the late 1970s and early 1980s.) In 1980, as we saw in the last chapter, Congress passed the Bayh–Dole Act, allowing universities to retain ownership of intellectual property created through the use of government funds and to profit by licensing it to industry.

To facilitate the formation and growth of new firms that could exploit new technologies, a wide range of tax incentives and new financial tools were made available. Venture investment received a major boost through several policy innovations. In 1979, the Department of Labor reinterpreted a law that had previously prevented pension funds investing in venture capital. Two years later, in the Economic Recovery Act of 1981, the long-term capital gains tax for individuals was dropped from 49 to 20 percent. The pool of venture capital swelled from between \$3.5 and 4 billion in 1979 to \$7.5 billion by the end of 1982.[49] The budding biotechnology sector found itself awash in venture capital as the amount raised by firms doubled each year, from \$43 million in 1980 to \$140 million in 1981, \$210 million in 1982, and \$542 million in 1983.[50] Another popular investment vehicle was the Research and Development Limited Partnership (RDLP), by which individual or corporate investors could invest in firms' R&D as limited partners, writing it off as an expense; investors would then receive a royalty, taxed as capital gains, on future sales of products, and the option of buying stock at a discounted price. RDLPs were especially popular among the first wave of biotechnology firms in the early 1980s as vehicles for financing clinical trials and manufacturing scale-up.[51] Although they fell out of favor after the Tax Reform Act of 1986 eliminated most of the favorable tax treatment that made them attractive to individual investors, they had until then supplied a quarter of firms' financing needs.

The birth of the DBC

With scientific feasibility having been proved, a regulatory regime in place, universities eager to market their inventions, and investors willing to place bets on the new technology, all the groundwork was in place for commercialization to begin. Although one could possibly imagine a scenario in which large pharmaceutical and chemical companies would seize the moment, they did not do so, at least in the US. Rather there appeared a new kind of corporate entity, one born of the institutional linkage between science and business, university and industry, that can only be understood in the context of the interaction of biomedical science with the peculiar political and economic environment of the US in the late 1970s. That entity I have already referred to as the "dedicated biotechnology company," or DBC. Neither willed into being by industrial policy, nor spun out from big companies whose focus was elsewhere, the DBC rather came about through the spontaneous intermingling of complementary resources – human, knowledge, and financial – within the fluid social environment of the NIS; as the economic opportunities offered by the new technological regime became clear, these resources found each other, coalescing into the organizational units soon to dot the landscape as DBCs. That they could do so is testimony to the extraordinary number of opportunities these resources had to interface, a willingness on the part of scientists and entrepreneurs to take risks, patience to wait years for the expected returns to investment, and mobility of resources to move across organizational boundaries within the NIS. None of these characteristics were present in Japan at that time or anywhere else in the world. The DBC was a unique product of the American NIS, uniquely suited to the challenges presented by the new technological regime.

The prototype of this new institution was Genentech. Formed as a partnership between venture capitalist Robert Swanson and Herbert Boyer, co-inventor of the original recombinant DNA process, Genentech was the first company formed by academic scientists for the singular purpose of commercializing recombinant DNA. Other biotechnology companies had come before: Cetus, Collaborative Research, and Bioresponse, for example, had been formed even before the discovery of recombinant DNA.[52] Many firms, like Cetus, were funded by big oil and chemical companies interested in exploiting microbes and biomass as a source of industrial chemicals; Cetus later began work on drugs made using recombinant DNA. Genentech, however, set a precedent as the first company for which products from recombinant DNA were its sole commercial focus.

The story of Genentech's founding is worth recounting, if only because it illustrates so powerfully crucial differences between the American and Japanese NIS.[53] It begins in early 1976 with Robert Swanson, a young Harvard MBA who had been employed at Kleiner and Perkins. Convinced of biotechnology's promise, Swanson first tried his hand as an investor at Cetus, which at the time was one of the only operating biotechnology companies. Frustrated by its unfocused management strategy, he decided to start up his own business. To do that he needed scientific talent. In the course of approaching various scientists, he made a call to Herbert Boyer, whose central role in genetic engineering was not known to Swanson at the time. Though skeptical, Boyer agreed to meet Swanson in his laboratory. After only ten minutes, the two men opted to continue the discussion over beer at a well-known San Francisco pub. Boyer explained the potential of recombinant DNA as a means of genetically programming bacteria to produce in mass quantity fragile proteins hitherto impossible to isolate, let alone manufacture. The implications for making new drug products seemed enormous. In that same meeting, Swanson persuaded Boyer to set up Genentech. Boyer and Swanson each chipped in $500; Swanson's firm Kleiner and Perkins followed with $100,000. Later, in another move that would become standard fare in the formation of DBCs, Swanson persuaded a seasoned manager, Kirk Raab of Abbot Laboratories, to head the new firm, rounding out the corporate line-up.

In 1977, Boyer's team of scientists cloned the brain hormone somatostatin in bacteria (meaning that the human gene encoding somatostatin was inserted into the genome of a bacterium, which then multiplied to produce large numbers of daughter cells, each containing the human gene), proving the technique's commercial potential. But the real breakthrough came a year later, when Genentech scientists cloned human insulin. The cloning of insulin also led to a watershed event in commercial biotechnology: the signing of the first partnership between a biotechnology and pharmaceutical firm for the development and marketing of a product. In this case, the drug firm was Eli Lilly, owner of 85 percent of the US market for insulin. The trouble was that its insulin was derived from pigs; slightly different from the human form, porcine insulin sometimes provokes allergic reactions in patients. Demand, moreover, was growing so fast, the company feared that it would soon not have the capacity to keep up. Therefore, it was eager to work with any biotechnology firm capable of mass-producing insulin using recombinant DNA. Initially, it appeared that Biogen, another newly formed DBC, would win the race, using a different version of the technology. In the end, Genentech barely squeaked by, and in August 1978, it signed the history-making deal with Eli Lilly: Lilly would receive exclusive world-wide manufacturing and marketing rights and the know-how from Genentech, in return for which Genentech would receive payments for research and royalties on future sales. Lilly went on to invest $100 million on clinical trials and production scale-up, and in 1982, insulin became the first biotechnology product to clear FDA approval for marketing. Genentech went on to develop human growth hormone (HGH) in 1979; in 1986 it would become the first recombinant DNA product to be developed, manufactured, and sold by a DBC on its own. Not only did Genentech provide an institutional model, its string of products embodying the new techniques established recombinant therapeutics as the dominant technological trajectory.

Genentech's success catalyzed a boom in the formation of DBCs. From around twenty or so a year in the mid 1970s, the list of biotechnology start-ups grew by 32 in 1978, 42 in 1979, 52 in 1980, and 100 in 1981, the peak year for new company formation in this first investment cycle.[54] The boom was fed by intense publicity, mostly favorable, which built to a fever pitch in the early 1980s. Close on Genentech's heels were Genex, Biogen, Amgen, Genetic Systems, and Centocor, each of which was a variation on the Genentech model. As in Genentech's case, an entrepreneur or venture capitalist usually sought out the scientist; most scientists, though by no means all, were still wary of moving too close to business.[55] In the case of Genetic Systems, formed in 1980, two twenty-something stockbrokers, David and Isaac Blech, snared Robert Nowinski, an eminent molecular biologist at Seattle's Fred Hutchinson Cancer Research Center and the University of Washington; the company pioneered the use of monoclonal antibodies in diagnostic and therapeutic applications until it was acquired by Bristol Myers and then sold to the French firm Sanofi.[56] Hybritech, another pioneer in the developing monoclonal antibody-based diagnostics, was started by Brook Byers of Kleiner, Perkins, Caulfield & Byers in partnership with Ivor Royston and Norman Birndorf, researchers at University of California, San Diego; the firm was later acquired by Eli Lilly. Similarly, Genex was born in 1977 when venture capitalist Robert Johnson teamed with biochemist Leslie Glick; it was acquired by Enzon Pharmaceuticals in 1991.

In 1980, the industry moved toward its first climax, or rather several climaxes. It began in January, when Biogen announced the cloning of alpha-interferon. Interferon belongs to a class of immune system proteins that trigger the body's immune system to attack cancer cells and viruses; cells produce it naturally in response to infection, though in quantities far too small to be of clinical use. Its scarcity, coupled with its suspected value as a breakthrough therapeutic, prompted one researcher to comment that "if it were possible to make a pound of pure interferon, the price would be $22 billion."[57] Once it had yielded to the tools of genetic engineering, alpha-interferon could be produced in sufficient quantity to allow clinical development to begin. Although the trials showed promise in animals, in humans the drug produced serious side effects, knocking it out of contention as a treatment for all but a few rare cancers. Hepatitis B and C, and genital warts – significant markets to be sure, but far short of earlier expectations. In the mid 1990s, Biogen succeeded in bringing to market a closely related protein, beta-interferon, which has become an important treatment for multiple sclerosis.

Five months after Biogen's announcement, another pivotal event rocked the industry. The US Supreme Court, reversing an earlier Patent Office ruling, decided in *Diamond v. Chakrabarty* that a living organism – in this case a bacterium altered to increase its capacity to degrade oil – could be patented if it could be shown to meet the standard requirements of usefulness, novelty, and non-obviousness. The ruling guaranteed that inventors would be eligible to receive patent protection not only on biological processes used in the development of a product but also on the product itself, as well as on any intermediate biological materials used in its creation. Inventors, whether firms or universities, thus gained the ability to surround their inventions in a thicket of patents. While a strong patent protection regime no doubt spurred investment in research, it also invited frequent litigation as firms invariably found themselves intruding on intellectual property claimed by others.

Finally, in October 1980 biotechnology made a fittingly dramatic debut on Wall Street. Floating a million shares at $35 each, Genentech stunned the financial world when, twenty minutes after its offering, the share price soared to $89, shattering the record for an initial public offering (IPO).[58] Close on its heels was Cetus, which went public in March 1981 at $23 a share. Three other companies went public in 1981, followed by eight in 1982, and twenty-two in 1983, after which the IPO window for biotechnology firms all but closed for the remainder of the decade, except for a brief period in 1986.[59] In this first cohort of public offerings were firms that today form the core of the biotechnology sector: Biogen, Amgen, Chiron, and Applied Biosystems, all of which went public in 1983.

The case of Amgen, the largest biotechnology firm today and the only one to have entered the ranks of the Fortune 500, illustrates the importance of serendipity and flexibility in the biotechnology sector. Founded in 1980 by venture investors William Bowes and Sam Wohlstadter, the company attracted a strikingly large private round of financing ($19 million) just four months after opening its doors; investors included Abbot Laboratories, the former employer of Amgen's CEO George Rathmann, Rothschild, and the oil-shale company Tosco, which looked to the firm for biological approaches to extracting oil from shale.[60] Like Cetus, not to mention most Japanese companies then working in biotechnology, Amgen tried at first to be all things to all people, maintaining research programs in human therapeutics and diagnostics, animal health care, and specialty chemicals. Among its early accomplishments was the cloning of a chicken growth hormone that sped the growth of chickens by 15 percent; the company hoped to market it to chicken producers as a means of reducing costs associated with quartering chickens.[61] This, and a few other smaller programs, was enough to enable the company to mount a successful IPO in 1983. As it turned out, the winner for Amgen was erythropoietin (EPO), a growth factor protein found in trace amounts in urine that stimulates production of red blood cells. Amgen sequenced the gene that expresses it, cloned it in mammalian cells, and then developed a process for mass producing it in the form of a drug to treat anemia in patients receiving kidney dialysis treatment, for which anemia is a common side effect. Just as importantly, the company encased the process and related products in an impenetrable wall of patents that have successfully staved off competitors. The FDA approved EPO for marketing in June 1989, and it went on to become the world's biggest-selling biotechnology product.

The DBC and the American NIS

What factors account for the sudden and dramatic emergence of the biotechnology sector? The maturing of the knowledge base certainly provided sufficient science push; molecular biology by the late 1970s had delivered a wealth of techniques and know-how ripe for commercialization. Yet science alone means little if it cannot be articulated with market demand; knowledge and tacit expertise of academic scientists had to be transferred into a suitable commercial context. The DBC was an institutional solution to that transfer problem. Two factors made possible its emergence: the establishment of close links between universities and industry and the availability of venture capital.

First, academic scientists and universities readily responded to the opportunities the new technology presented. By the middle 1980s, 46 percent of biotechnology firms were supporting university R&D.[62] By one estimate, nearly every molecular biologist had a corporation supporting his laboratory.[63] Unlike in Japan, where the key academic researchers were severely constrained in their relations with industry, researchers in American universities had already established a dense network of linkages with industry. Land grant universities and medical schools were especially well connected to the private sector, as were major engineering schools such as MIT, Georgia Tech, and California Institute of Technology.[64] The most common form of linkage with the private sector was, and still is, contract research. In this type of agreement, a company commits to funding a narrowly defined project for a short period of time in return for rights to any products or patents generated by that research. After 1980, long-term, multi-million-dollar contracts became increasingly common, many of which involved entire academic research teams and granted the company exclusive rights to all discoveries arising from that research. Other forms of corporate sponsorship include funding of grants and fellowships, participation in industrial affiliates, such as MIT's Industrial Liaison Program, and funding of consortia and research centers, such as the University of Michigan's Center for Molecular Genetics.[65]

During the 1970s, a number of factors compelled universities and industries to move closer to each other. First, for companies, the expenses associated with facilities and staffing created high transaction costs; given the uncertainty surrounding the new science, it was simply cheaper to contract out a minimal level of basic research. In addition, large corporations interested in biotechnology were locked into older technological trajectories in which large investments had already been made; testing the waters through academic tie-ups thus appeared to be a more efficient response than plunging headlong into a new and untested technology. On the academic side, the advent of the Reagan Administration triggered fears of large cuts in science budgets, thus increasing the appeal of corporate sponsorship. In addition, concern that America's technological supremacy was in jeopardy led to a flurry of legislation aimed at easing anti-trust restrictions and promoting technology transfer. Among the most crucial were the Patent and Trademark Amendments Act of 1980 and Stevenson–Wydler Technology Innovation Act of 1980, which permitted companies to negotiate exclusive licenses to patents resulting from federally funded academic research.[66] Over the course of the decade, additional legislation would further ease transaction costs associated with technology transfer, with important consequences for biotechnology.

The evolution of university–industry interaction, however, was not without glitches. As commercial interest increased, scientists and universities suddenly found themselves with a monopoly on a critical asset in high demand – knowledge. As James Watson recalls, "The 1980s would see changes in the relationship of science and commerce that were unimaginable a decade before. Biology was now a big-money game, and with the money came a whole new mindset, and new complications."[67] Many scientists cashed in quickly; others resisted subordinating science to corporate control. At the heart of the conflict was the fundamental contradiction between science, whose practitioners seek the widest possible dissemination of knowledge, and applied technology, whose practitioners strive to keep knowledge private. Opponents argued that corporate sponsorship would distort research agendas, squeezing out basic research in favor of profitable projects. A related issue, conflict of interest, also became fodder for critics, especially when scientists whose work was largely funded by federal grants began starting their own companies.

Despite criticisms of this emerging "university–industrial complex," to use Martin Kenney's terminology, it must be remembered that industry had exerted even more influence over academic research agendas before World War II. As late as the mid 1950s, industry funded 11 percent of university research, more than twice the level of the mid 1980s.[68] In addition, the American chemical industry profoundly influenced, and was influenced by, academic chemistry.[69] Thus, biotechnology did not mark a discontinuity in relations between industry and academia; it merely confirmed patterns of interaction between university and industry that had long been part of the American NIS.

The second factor critical to the industry's emergence was the availability of venture capital and other creative financing mechanisms. Most DBCs got their initial start-up funds from venture capital sources. Unlike bankers, venture capitalists do not lend money; rather they take an ownership stake in the company in hopes that it will become self-sustaining. By doing so, they "thus play the dual role of financial capitalist and technological catalyst, providing the financial resources, management advice, and contacts needed to turn ideas into products."[70] Venture capitalists at that time generally held onto a company for five to seven years, aiming for a 500 to 1,000 percent capital gain when the company's stock was offered publicly. Among the major movers in biotechnology were Kleiner, Perkins, Caulfield & Byers, which provided start-up funding for Genentech and Hybritech, and Rothschild, which funded Amgen. Once a company showed promise, it was common in the early 1980s for managers to seek out RDLPs, which provided much of the financing for clinical development, especially at the more prominent firms. As the industry matured, public and private equity, contract research, and strategic alliances became the preferred vehicle for raising capital. Venture finance, however, remained vital as a source of early and mid-stage financing, which sustained the steady stream of new DBCs over the course of the 1980s.

Commercial take-off (1983–1990s)

Over a short five-year period, what had been to most people an abstract, even unsettling, science had become the basis for a large and growing population of new firms. Biotechnology had become such a fixture on the American industrial landscape that *Business Week* magazine could describe it in 1983 as "just another industry," in which "the push to regulate has all but vanished."[71] Yet the biotechnology revolution had only just begun.

New DBCs continued to pour forth. After reaching a peak in 1981 of 100 new companies, the number of DBC launches fell back in 1982, a year of recession, to sixty-nine. As the recovery took hold in 1983, so too did the rate of formation of new companies pick up: from eighty-six new DBCs in 1983 to ninety-seven in 1984, then a slight dip to eighty in 1985, followed by a recovery to ninety-nine in 1986, then a surge to 123 in 1987, the peak year for start-ups.[72] Venture capital investments in biotechnology tripled, from slightly less than $100 million in 1983 to just over $300 million in 1988.[73] Three-quarters of all investments flowed to a single sector, health care, reflecting the expectations that this sector would generate the greatest returns in the shortest time compared with agriculture, fine chemicals, and environmental applications.

By the mid 1980s, market selection had decisively begun acting on the budding science base. Generating the most excitement was recombinant DNA, which received 62 percent of all new investment, even though the first products were mostly still several years away. Monoclonal antibodies attracted 30 percent, a figure that rose rapidly as diagnostic products using monoclonal antibodies began to hit the market in the mid 1980s. The remaining 8 percent was distributed across fermentation and cell culture (the main areas of focus in Japan at that time). Of the cumulative total invested, 63 percent was sunk into the top ten organizations. Hybritech, which brought to market many of the first diagnostic kits based on monoclonal antibodies, attracted the largest cumulative private investment ($514 million); Genentech came in third, behind Genetic Systems, another monoclonal antibody firm. Indicative of the shake-up to come, of the top seven private companies in 1985, only two, Biogen and Amgen, remain today as fully independent entities.

Just another industry?

As cash poured into the industry, many analysts began to wonder whether the hype had gotten out of hand. By 1993, 1,272 companies were vying for a slice of investment; among these were 235 public companies.[74] Sales totaled $7 billion, most of which ($5.7 billion) was invested back in R&D. Total employment in biotechnology firms reached 97,000 and was growing at 10 to 20 percent a year.

Yet there was a problem, one that has dogged the industry to the present: despite the efforts of hundreds of firms, the flow of products onto the market remained a trickle. By 1992, a decade after recombinant human insulin became the first marketed biotechnology drug, only fourteen therapeutic drugs and vaccines, covering ten new chemical entities, had been approved for marketing by the FDA.[75] In 1994, four of the top-selling drugs sold globally were biotechnology products.[76] True, 571 monoclonal antibody-based diagnostic products had been brought to market; these devices delivered significant improvement in sensitivity and reproducibility in such areas as blood screening, drug monitoring, testing for the presence of pathogens and markers for cancer, AIDS, and other diseases. But these were, generally, low-margin products, sold mainly to hospitals, health clinics, and private testing firms. Nor were conditions any more favorable in agriculture and industrial chemistry: the first genetically modified food, the "Flavr Savr" tomato, would not reach the market until 1994; and among specialty chemicals, only recombinant versions of lipase (used in detergents, degreasers, and other industrial products), chymosin (used in making cheese), alpha amylase (used in textile manufacturing), and xylanase (used in paper making) had been brought to market. Although firms in Europe, especially Denmark-based Novo-Nordisk, achieved considerable success in applying recombinant DNA techniques to the manufacture of industrial enzymes – and Japanese firms developed a range of popular products that used them – industrial chemistry remained far down on the list of priority fields for American biotechnology firms.

The period between 1984 and 1991 was one of adjustment and uncertainty in the industry. The stock market crash in October 1987 ensured that the market for IPOs would remain shut to biotechnology firms for the next four years. Still, a lot of interesting and even breakthrough science filtered out of academic and DBC laboratories. In December 1984, Genentech's powerful cloning conveyor belt rolled out a recombinant version of tumor necrosis factor (TNF), which had the interesting property of causing tumor cells to swell up and explode in the test tube while leaving healthy cells intact. Sadly, TNF turned out to be far more toxic and unpredictable when injected into patients than it had in test tubes, which dashed the hopes of Japan's Asahi Chemical, the first company to test it in clinical trials. As science goes, however, work with TNF proved to have unforeseen benefits elsewhere; the molecule was found to be associated with the inflammation accompanying rheumatoid arthritis. Immunex, a Seattle-based DBC, discovered that TNF, used not as a drug but as a target for a drug the company's scientists had cleverly designed to bind to it, could substantially ameliorate the pain of rheumatoid arthritis. That drug, Enbrel, was approved for marketing in late 1998 and has become one of biotechnology's biggest-selling products.

Genentech went on to develop Tissue Plasminogen Activator (TPA), a clot-busting molecule that became a first-line treatment for heart attack and stroke; the FDA gave its seal of approval for marketing in late 1987. Also during this period Centocor developed the first therapeutic monoclonal antibody, ReoPro, as a treatment for reducing the risk of blood clot complications following angioplasty; it came onto the market in late 1994. Following its successful development of EPO, Amgen cloned and developed granulocyte colony stimulating factor (GSF), which boosts the immune system's production of white blood cells. Marketed first in 1991 as an adjunct to chemotherapy and bone-marrow transplants, the drug quickly took its position as the biotechnology sector's best-selling drug after EPO. Finally, scientists at Cetus cloned interleukin-2 (IL-2), one of a group of immune system modulators called lymphokines, which gave all appearances of being the next big cancer-killing drug. Cetus bet the company on IL-2, only to see the FDA ask for more data when it submitted its clinical trial results for review. Unwilling to sustain another round of trials, Cetus chose to fall into the arms of another DBC, Chiron, which in summer 1990 paid $650 million in stock for the company; Chiron went on to complete clinical trials and obtain FDA approval in 1992 for use of IL-2 in certain kidney cancers and, six years later, for metastatic melanoma. Like interferons, however, interleukins have proved too toxic and difficult to administer to permit widespread use.

Developing biotechnology drugs is fraught with risk. Getting the science right is only the beginning; without a well-conceived strategy, a competent and experienced management, and the complementary assets needed to plan and execute clinical trials, a firm cannot hope to achieve success, at least on its own. Which is why most DBCs have opted to partner with large pharmaceutical companies and with other DBCs; the other options are to integrate forward into clinical development, manufacturing, and marketing, or follow Cetus's approach and merge with or be acquired by another firm.

Public policy to the rescue

Before examining organizational evolution, however, technological change and industry response need to be situated in the broader policy context. The federal government, unlike the government in Japan, never explicitly targeted commercial development of biotechnology. Nevertheless, continued growth in funding of basic research and fine-tuning of regulatory and intellectual property protection regimes had enormous indirect influence on commercial activity. Also crucial were policies easing anti-trust restrictions on collaborative research and encouraging technology transfer from university and government laboratories to industry. Though not aimed at a single technology, these latter initiatives reflected a fundamental shift in science policy that took hold in the 1980s. The old model of funding basic research and waiting for industry to find and commercialize the results gave way to one of funding basic research, opening a channel between that research and industry, providing incentives that encourage the two sides to interact in mutually beneficial ways, and then waiting for industry to commercialize the results.

Regulatory issues have consistently topped the private sector's list of factors influencing its ability to develop new products.[77] As discussed above, the NIH guidelines represented a cautious attempt to balance public fears with growing commercial interest in the new recombinant DNA technology. Over the following decade, hundreds of thousands of genetic engineering experiments were performed without incident, leading to a gradual relaxation of the guidelines.[78] By the mid 1980s, the focus of public concern had shifted from oversight of research to promoting the industrial development of new products.[79] Biotechnology came to be viewed not as a monster in need of restraint but as a crown jewel in America's competitive arsenal.

Attempts to develop a coherent regulatory framework, however, raised a host of new difficulties. Most of the products being commercialized were already heavily regulated. The main question was thus whether products made using biotechnology would require stricter control than the same products made conventionally. Because they are contained within a patient's body, medical products presented few headaches; besides, the FDA could easily accommodate new drugs within its existing regulatory framework.[80] Developing transgenic plants and microorganisms, on the other hand, involved releasing genetically altered organisms into the environment without absolute certainty that their spread beyond the point of cultivation could be contained and with no standard procedures in place for assessing risk. Because of uncertainties over the direction federal regulations would take, and lengthy product development cycles intrinsic to experimentation with plants, commercialization of genetically modified plants proceeded at a much slower pace than it had with drugs, diagnostics, and vaccines; the first products reached the market only in the mid 1990s.

One of the main sources of regulatory uncertainty has been the fragmentation of regulatory and oversight functions across a number of federal agencies and Congressional committees. The fact that several agencies both promoted and regulated the technology added to the confusion. According to Plein, at least eleven federal agencies and sixteen Congressional committees had a stake in regulating or promoting biotechnology.[81] A report by the Government Accounting Office noted that USDA, FDA, and USDA could not even agree on a common definition of biotechnology, much less on a common strategy for regulating it.[82] Researchers in both corporate and academic sectors found that officials at different government agencies were applying different rules, laws, and philosophies to their different definitions. For example, FDA, EPA, USDA, NIH, and the Occupational Safety and Health Administration (OSHA) each claimed jurisdiction over the deliberate release of genetically altered microbes. An example of the resulting confusion was the case of Advanced Genetic Sciences, a company which had developed a spray containing a genetically altered bacterium that, when applied to plants, made them resistant to frost damage. In 1985, after obtaining NIH approval, the company tested the spray on plants growing on the roof of one of its buildings. In this case, however, EPA approval was required, and its regulations concerning deliberate release were more stringent than those of NIH. EPA subsequently fined the company, and it was forced to repeat its tests using complete physical containment of its test facilities.[83]

Uncertainty over outdoor testing prompted industry to step up pressure for federal and state governments to fashion a consistent and coherent regulatory regime.[84] In an attempt to harmonize regulations and coordinate their administration, the Office of Science and Technology Policy (OSTP) in the Executive Office of the Presidency took the initiative. In April 1984, it formed the Domestic Policy Council Working Group on Biotechnology, which it charged with the task of drafting an interagency regulatory regime that would provide consistent, science-based regulation consistent with the maintenance of US technological leadership – a difficult task indeed. The result was the "Coordinated Framework for Regulation of Biotechnology," the final version of which was released in June 1986.[85] Coordinating authority was vested in a Biotechnology Science Coordinating Committee (BSCC) composed of senior representatives from five federal agencies; its role was purely advisory.[86] Among the accomplishments of the committee was agreement on common definitions of products to be regulated, especially those considered to be biological pathogens. The committee also decided which agency would have principal responsibility for a given class of genetically modified products.[87] In general, the FDA was to have responsibility for pharmaceutical products (though it would later implement voluntary guidance for firms developing transgenic plants); the USDA was to ensure that transgenic plants did not introduce an unapproved plant pest; and the EPA was to certify plants genetically modified to produce proteins that act as insecticides. Although the USDA has eased its requirements and simplified notification procedures for the most commonly modified plants, the division of responsibilities under the Coordinated Framework has remained largely intact to the present.

On the other hand, the BSCC's days were numbered. After only five years in operation, it was disbanded on the grounds that it had become "too politicized."[88] Industry groups had expressed concern about closed-door decisions and the preponderance of high-level political appointees in working meetings. As one analyst noted, instead of tackling tough regulatory issues that "cut across agency lines," the committee "has been active behind the scenes trying to thwart EPA's rulemaking."[89] It did just that, persuading the Office of Management and Budget to block EPA's attempt to regulate genetically modified microorganisms under the Toxic Substances Control Act.[90] In response, representatives from EPA stopped attending deliberations. Meanwhile, states began enacting their own patchwork of regulations, prompting industry to intensify its lobbying for unified, national guidelines.[91] The final result was that the BSCC not only failed to bridge agencies and eliminate redundancies, it further alienated and confused an industry sorely in need of a sensible, consistent regulatory regime.

In 1990, the BSCC was replaced by the Biotechnology Research Subcommittee of OSTP's Federal Coordinating Council for Science, Engineering, and Technology (FCCSET), which was headed by the President's science advisor.[92] Though its responsibility was similar to that of the BSCC, its membership was broader, and it concerned itself more with promoting science and technology research across relevant federal agencies.

A year later, Vice President Dan Quayle's Council on Competitiveness issued recommendations that became the Bush Administration's official policy position on biotechnology and the basis for subsequent biotechnology regulation. These included the recommendation that risk assessment should focus on the product, not the process by which the product is made. This had been the long-standing position of FDA in its approach to regulating biopharmaceuticals, and was consistent with recommendations made by the National Research Council in 1989. The Competitiveness Council also urged that regulations related to health and the environment use performance standards rather than mandating rigid targets or fixed design criteria.[93] A performance standard sets the end to be achieved, then allows the regulated party to choose the best means to ensure compliance.

Oversight is conducted on the basis of "substantial equivalence," meaning that if the genetic modification of a food crop yields a product chemically and nutritionally equivalent to an approved variety, testing of the new variety for safety is not mandated, nor are firms required to label products as genetically modified.

The FDA implemented this new regulatory approach in its "Statement of Policy" published in the Federal Register in May 1992; it covers both genetically modified and non-genetically modified foods.[94] Included in this policy is a voluntary consultation mechanism, not unlike that applied to industry in the NIH guidelines for recombinant DNA in research. Though strongly opposed by some environmental and consumer advocacy groups, the regulatory approach contained in the 1992 statement has withstood legal challenge by opponents who support mandatory labeling of GM foods.[95] Industry has also responded positively: through October 2002, the FDA had completed voluntary consultations on fifty-five genetically modified foods, including all the products brought to market in the US to date.[96]

Since the first products were approved for marketing in 1993, the cultivation and consumption of genetically modified crops has expanded rapidly. At the beginning of 2003, farmers in the US were marketing genetically modified versions of eleven crops. The percentage of American crops planted with genetically modified seeds in 2002 stood at 74 percent for soy beans (introduced in 1996), 71 percent for cotton (introduced in 1998), and 32 percent for corn (also introduced in 1998).[97] Of the total global land area planted with genetically modified seed, 88 percent is in the US; the only other countries with significant shares are Argentina (29 percent), Canada (7.9 percent), and China (3.7 percent). Virtually no acreage is given to genetically modified plants in the European Union or Japan, neither of which has completely accepted the standard of substantial equivalence that underpins the US regulatory approach.

By the late 1980s, the discourse on biotechnology at the federal level had turned decisively away from restraining it through regulation and toward promoting it as an antidote to the competitive decline of American industry. Congress led the way with a barrage of legislative proposals aimed at expanding federal support of commercial biotechnology. While Congress earlier had been sympathetic to the arguments of groups opposed to biotechnology on moral and environmental grounds, tough lobbying by industry, coupled with the growing prominence of competitiveness as an issue area, galvanized support for biotechnology in both the House and Senate.[98] Echoing the new line in the House, Don Fuqua, then-chairman of the House Committee on Science and Technology, writes in 1986:

> America has been the world's leader in biotechnology research. We have the opportunity and the capability to continue this prominence and to be the world's foremost competitor for biotechnology products and

> processes in the international marketplace. We all share that same goal. However, the only way to achieve it is for all the concerned sectors and groups to communicate and cooperate with each other. Cooperation does not mean that there should be no dissenters or disagreements, but rather that all those concerned share the responsibility for reasonable resolutions. If we polarize our efforts or work at cross-purposes, we will relinquish our lead.[99]

Consistent with its new stance, Congress tried twice, in 1987 and 1988, to pass the Biotechnology Competitiveness Act. The new law would have authorized a National Center for Biotechnology Information in NIH. In addition, it would have created a Biotechnology Policy Board, composed of representatives from federal and state governments, industry, and universities, which would make recommendations to Congress and the President on government biotechnology activities.[100] On both occasions, backers used arguments that Japanese industry, with government support, was zeroing in on America's lead. Senator Patrick Leahy, a supporter of the new legislation, spoke for many lawmakers in saying, "The biotech race is a race America can't afford to lose."[101] On both occasions, however, political squabbling over which agency, NIH or DOE, would play the lead role in sponsoring commercial activity torpedoed the bills.[102]

Congress fared better in legislation broadly impacting American industry. In 1986, it passed the Federal Technology Transfer Act, which authorized national laboratories to make their research accessible to the private sector. Companies could approach federal laboratories and negotiate a Cooperative Research and Development Agreement (CRADA). The CRADA specifies, among other things, the division of rights to any patents resulting from joint research and allows firms to take out exclusive licenses on patents owned by the government. Within three years of passage, NIH had signed eighty agreements and had another eighty pending.[103] An early result of this policy was the emergence of a regional cluster of biotechnology firms surrounding the NIH campus in suburban Maryland, many of whose firms worked closely with NIH researchers. (See Chapter 3 for more details on the impact of CRADAs on biotechnology.)

Also critical to the industry's take-off in the 1980s and 1990s was the strengthening of intellectual property protection and its more aggressive enforcement by the courts. The Supreme Court's Chakrabary decision in 1980 had already established the legal precedent for recognizing plants and nonhuman animals as patentable subject matter. In 1988, the Patent and Trademark Office (PTO) granted the first patent on a nonhuman animal, the so-called "Harvard onco-mouse," genetically modified with a gene that makes the mouse susceptible to tumor growth. Then in early 1991, Craig Venter, at the time a researcher at NIH, dropped a bombshell: at the urging of officials at NIH, he applied for patents on 337 human gene sequences, igniting a firestorm of controversy. Gene patents themselves were nothing new; the PTO had been granting them since the early 1980s. The difference was that gene patents granted to that point had been limited to genes whose activity was known: the primary invention to be protected was the protein itself; patents on the gene and the cell system expressing it were pursued to add further layers of protection. In addition, before the advent of automated high-speed DNA sequencing, a researcher usually started with a known protein, then worked backward to deduce the sequence of the gene that encodes it. By the time the Human Genome Project was gearing up in the early 1990s, it had became possible to isolate and sequence genes and gene fragments before their biological function could be determined. From the perspective of the biotechnology industry, tens of millions of dollars of investment would likely be needed to translate knowledge of gene sequences into commercially useful products; without a priority date for the discovery of the gene that patent protection confers on the holder, the private sector would have no incentive to make that investment. The industry thus kept up the pressure on the PTO to treat gene sequences as patentable subject matter.

By early 1997, the PTO had received 350 applications, covering more than 500,000 gene fragments.[104] Before it could begin to respond, however, the PTO had to decide on a threshold for patentability using the standard three criteria of novelty, non-obviousness, and utility. Novelty had been dealt with before: a gene is novel if its sequence has not been made public and it is in an isolated, purified state. Non-obviousness was trickier but hinges on the PTO's long-standing position that the process by which a composition is produced should have no bearing on its patentability.[105] The problem was utility: an isolated DNA molecule has no utility apart from the protein products and biological activity its expression brings about. The question became: how much knowledge of the genes' usefulness is sufficient to conform to the legal definition of utility in patent law?[106] The answer came in the form of new patenting guidelines issued in January 2001.[107] Covering a range of technologies, the guidelines include a new dimension of utility that requires applicants to link the gene sequence to a real-world application. In other words, it is not enough to link the gene to a protein or specific biological process; that protein or process must in turn be linked to a specific application, such as use in a diagnostic kit to test for a specific disease or as a target for a new drug to treat a specific disease. The aim is to reduce the number of frivolous patent applications and encourage a focus on understanding what genes actually do, while at the same time acknowledging the value of gene patents.

In short, the federal role in biotechnology has primarily been one of balancing regulation with promotion but with a clear shift toward the latter after 1990. Promotion has taken the form of a strong commitment to funding biomedical research, breaking down of barriers to technology transfer between university and industry, and strengthening the regime of intellectual property protection. Despite efforts to unify the policy-making framework in biotechnology, coordination has not been easy; the FDA, EPA, NSF, and NIH all resisted efforts to create an overarching coordinating authority. Regulatory policy making rather has been *ad hoc* and somewhat fragmented, though it has not been as compartmentalized or prone to jurisdictional conflicts as policy making in Japan has been. In every case, both industry and the research community have had ample opportunity to project their preferences into the policy arena; they have done so, for the most part, in a disciplined manner, which has made the policy process flexible and largely responsive to their changing needs. The exception is the PTO's decision to accept applications for patents on gene sequences, which has strong support in industry but significant resistance among academic researchers worried about the possibility of a small number of firms gaining a monopoly over the handling and use of genes. Undoubtedly, the responsiveness of public policy to the evolving science and propensity to deregulate has created a supportive environment for DBCs and large firms alike. The costs too have been significant: soaring health care costs, frequent and costly patent litigation, and the exclusion at times of the general public and parties with opposing views from deliberations about regulatory policy. Unless the policy-making system can somehow address these concerns, the continued prosperity of American biotechnology is by no means assured.

Biotechnology firms approach maturity

In the late 1980s, most DBCs still harbored hopes of becoming full-fledged drug companies. When a product was ready for clinical testing, they sought to develop the capabilities to carry it out in house. At the same time, most large drug companies, aware of the potential impact of biotechnology on drug discovery, began dabbling in research of their own. Eventually, most found that they could stay apprised of developments in biotechnology more efficiently, and position themselves to pluck the fruit of biotechnology innovation as it ripened, by partnering with DBCs. Consequently, the defining characteristic of this period was the emergence of the strategic alliance between DBCs and drug companies as the preferred organizational vehicles for product development. Strategic alliances, to summarize the points made in Chapter 3, provide stable yet flexible governance structures that integrate the knowledge base of the DBC with the financial, clinical development, manufacturing, and marketing resources of the drug firm, cementing the core elements of a biopharmaceutical value chain. DBCs often benefit from a tie-up with a large drug firm because of the signal it sends to investors of the DBC's viability and attractiveness as a potential investment.

At first, an alliance usually meant a DBC simply selling the rights to a drug in development, or licensing a technology to a drug company in return for a modest up-front payment and royalties on future product sales. Eli

Lilly was the first drug company to move decisively into biotechnology when it bought the rights to recombinant human insulin from Genentech in 1978 and went on to develop and market the drug. As DBCs have matured and gained bargaining power, deals with large firms have become more complex, the risks and rewards more evenly shared. The advent of second-generation technologies such as genomics made big drug firms especially anxious to negotiate deals out of fear of being left behind. In the deal that launched the genomics era in 1993, drug giant SmithKline-Beecham paid $125 million to newly formed Human Genome Sciences in return for a 7 percent equity stake in the company and exclusive commercial rights to its data base of genes.[108] Not to be outdone, Bayer struck a $465 million deal with Millennium Pharmaceuticals in 1998, in which Bayer received a 14 percent equity stake and access to 225 drug targets from Millennium's data base of genomic information.[109] By the end of the decade, nearly all the major pharmaceutical firms had planted themselves at the center of large networks of strategic alliances with DBCs. One source documented 1,100 such alliances formed between 1988 and 1999; Hoffmann-La Roche alone entered into 129 such alliances during that period, followed by SmithKline-Beecham with ninety-two and American Home Products with ninety.[110]

Monsanto relied heavily on its partnerships with universities and DBCs to transform itself from a traditional maker of bulk chemicals to a diversified life sciences company. A research contract with Washington University had given the company crucial know-how in plant biotechnology in the early 1980s. Additional opportunities to learn the new technologies came when it took a $20 million equity position in Biogen and a $5.5 million stake in Collagen; in 1994, few large firms benefited as much as Monsanto from early strategic investments in biotechnology. One recipient of Monsanto's support was Mary Dell Chilton, a researcher at Washington University who had earlier characterized the process by which *Agrobacterium tumefaciens*, a common soil-dwelling microbe, infects plants, causing crown gall disease. In the process of infecting the plant, *Agrobacterium* delivers a stretch of its DNA, where it is integrated into the plant's own genome. Monsanto was one of the first to realize that *Agrobacterium* would enable genetic engineers to do in plants what they were doing in bacteria: add foreign genes that induce them to make useful proteins. In this case the new proteins might confer pest resistance, improve taste or nutrition, or make the plant resistant to herbicides. Monsanto incorporated this technology into a family of genetically modified plants, including varieties of soybean, cotton, and corn engineered to withstand application of its Roundup brand of herbicide; and varieties of corn and cotton engineered to produce their own insecticides. Monsanto now controls 90 percent of the world market for genes used to impart new traits to crop plants.[111]

The number of collaborations tends to rise when financing from other sources is tight. Except for 1991 and 2000, most DBCs have found it difficult to raise funds through public stock offerings; although private sources of capital remain important, many DBCs have had to enter into partnerships with other companies as a matter of survival. At the same time, drug makers began to suffer declining productivity in their R&D and expiration of patent protection on profitable products. The two parties thus saw their interests converge. According to data compiled by J. Hagedoorn at the Maastricht Economic Research Institute and tabulated by the National Science Foundation (Figure 4.3), strategic technology alliances in biotechnology involving at least one US-based firm rose to a peak of seventy-eight new alliances in 1987 before dropping off to thirty-two in 1990, a time of some retrenchment in biotechnology against the backdrop of a recession in the US economy. In the mid 1980s nearly half of new alliances involved a foreign partner, and of those between a third and half involved a Japanese firm. In the 1990s, European drug firms aggressively pursued alliances with DBCs, becoming partners in nearly half of all alliances by mid decade. Alliances involving Japanese partners, however, shrank sharply, both as a proportion of total alliances and in absolute terms. That trend is likely to change as a result of the resurgence of investment in biotechnology in Japan since 2000, the strength of Japanese firms in certain technologies such as tissue engineering and stem cell research, and efforts by regional governments and trade associations to promote the industry.[112]

In some cases, DBCs stumble in their effort to maintain viability. Failure to secure patent protection or coming out on the wrong end of a patent

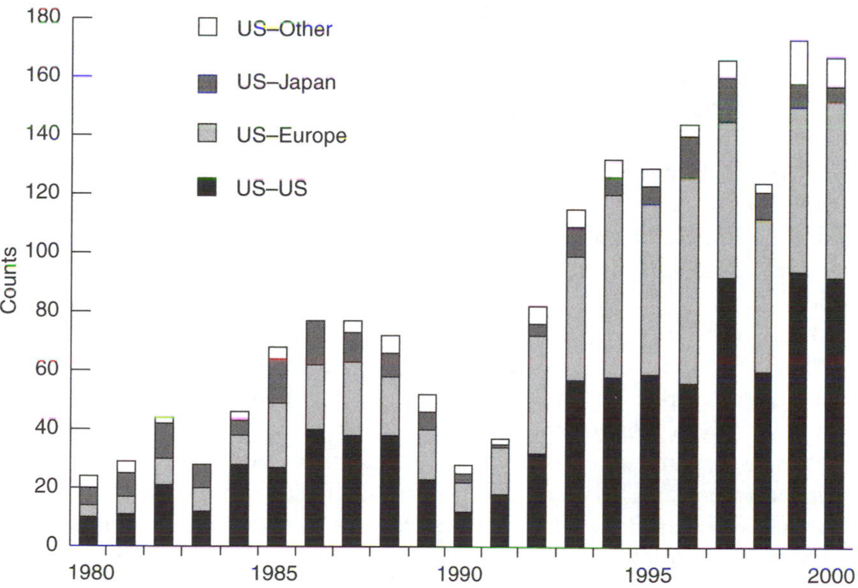

Figure 4.3 Strategic alliances in biotechnology involving at least one US firm

Source: National Science Board, *Science and Engineering Indicators, 2002*, Appendix Table 4–39.

infringement ruling, for example, can seriously erode a firm's value. Failure to win FDA approval for a drug on which the firm has heavily invested can spell disaster. Such firms are prime candidates for a merger or acquisition. Even the strongest firms have sometimes found it strategically or financially advantageous to sell a large or even a controlling stake in themselves to a large drug company. Genentech has fared especially well since Swiss giant Hoffmann-La Roche bought 60 percent of the company in 1990, then wisely chose to allow it to retain its autonomy. Already mentioned was Chiron's acquisition of Cetus; shortly thereafter, Swiss firm Ciba-Geigy, one of Chiron's long-time partners, acquired just under half of the company's stock. Another pioneering DBC, Genetics Institute, founded in 1980 by two Harvard molecular biologists, spent most of that decade in the front ranks of DBCs. Then it lost a costly patent suit with Amgen over the rights to the blockbuster drug EPO, making it a prime candidate for acquisition; American Home Products bought two-thirds of the company in 1992 and a few years later bought out the outstanding shares, turning the firm into a wholly owned subsidiary. Amgen and American Home Products also figure prominently in the recent story of Immunex. A Seattle-based company formed in 1981, Immunex has already been mentioned as the developer of the anti-inflammatory drug Enbrel, one of the most successful biotechnology products to date. To improve its ability to market its first major product Leukine in the early 1990s, the company sold 53.5 percent of itself to Lederle Laboratories, at the time a subsidiary of American Cyanamid. The following year Lederle Laboratories was acquired by American Home Products, which trimmed its ownership share of Immunex to 44 percent. Then in December 2001, in the largest biotechnology acquisition ever, Amgen purchased Immunex from AHP for $11 billion, creating what the *Financial Times* has termed a "biotechnology colossus."[113] The twists and turns in the Immunex story are indicative not only of the complexity of strategy and financing in biotechnology but also the beginning of a consolidation as biotechnology firms seek to broaden their portfolios of complementary products over which to leverage growing R&D costs. Indeed, since 1995 DBCs have been far more likely to merge with each other in their quest for synergies than to be acquired outright by a big drug maker.

The fact remains that the biotechnology sector in the US is a crowded field and thus ripe for a shake-out. Nearly 1,500 companies still throng the sector. Of those, only nineteen manage to earn a profit, a record not substantially different from a decade ago.[114] Although twenty new biopharmaceuticals received FDA approval in 2002, and fifteen existing products were approved for new indications, the mean time required for FDA approval of all new medicines has been rising, from twelve months in 2000 to 15.3 months in 2002.[115] Part of the problem stems from the after-effects of an investment bubble that between 1999 and 2001 enticed the formation of nearly 200 new companies. The announcement of the completion of the first draft of the sequence of the human genome in 2000 had an especially stimulatory effect. Investors poured $38 billion into biotechnology that year, more than the sum that had been invested in the previous five years; fifty-eight companies went public, a record.[116] Market capitalization shot up to nearly $30 billion, triple that of the previous year. By 2001, however, the markets turned south, casting a shadow over the entire sector. By 2002, the market capitalization of biotechnology firms had fallen to half its level in 2000. Only five companies managed initial public offerings, while 69 percent of public companies found their stock trading below $5 per share at some point during the year.[117] By early 2003, 22 percent of publicly traded biotechnology firms had market values less than the value of cash on hand, making them prime candidates for liquidation or acquisition.[118] At the same time, big drug companies face not only maturing product lines but intense criticism over high drug prices; health care costs in sum have risen to the point where one is forced to wonder whether thesystem can bear the costs of further innovation. Under these circumstances, more consolidation is likely as firms struggle to achieve sustainable growth.

Conclusions

Commercial biotechnology emerged in the US primarily because of the proximity of American firms to the new knowledge base and an institutional context that enabled them to harness it without undue delay. That knowledge base had accumulated in the laboratories of American universities whose researchers were funded by federal grants mostly channeled through the NIH. As a result of the NIH's institutional mission to promote research aimed at treating and curing human disease, innovation has been strongly biased toward the health care sector. Consequently, most commercial activity has been directed at developing human therapeutic and diagnostic products.

Firms responsible for early innovative efforts were generally chemical and pharmaceutical companies already endowed with large internal R&D organizations. However, because their expertise largely was in traditional organic chemistry and not molecular biology, most large firms forged links with universities to access cutting-edge breakthroughs. Once the stock of scientific know-how had reached a critical mass after Cohen and Boyer's successful demonstration of the recombinant DNA process, the driving force behind commercial development shifted to the DBC. Built around a nucleus composed of entrepreneur, key scientist, and venture capitalist, DBCs evolved organizational qualities ideally adapted to the task of massaging the stream of scientific breakthroughs into new products and services capable of meeting Americans' insatiable demand for high-quality health care.

As more and more products began moving into expensive clinical trials, however, DBCs quickly found they were burning capital at unsustainable rates. Their cause was not helped by the fickleness of capital markets, which either flooded companies with cash or shut the spigot off entirely. In addition, only a handful of DBCs had their own manufacturing and marketing operations. Facing enormous costs to push a product through the final stages of development, DBCs pursued alliance strategies with pharmaceutical giants. Flush with capital, though too slow off the mark in the early stages, large firms welcomed the opportunity to integrate backward into biotechnology R&D, especially in an area in which they had little internal expertise. The resulting institutional network has proved remarkably well suited to solving the technical and organizational problems which distinguish the biotechnology regime.

The story, however, neither ends nor begins with the firm. In accordance with the reasoning in Chapter 2, America's leadership in biotechnology turns on the network of public and private institutions whose reinforcing strengths make up the American NIS. A well-endowed system of research universities, an unrivaled national research institute of biomedical research, and a strong supporting cast in the chemical and pharmaceutical industries have contributed mightily to America's success. Equally important have been innovative regulatory and intellectual property protection policies, which responded quickly to the emergence of the new techniques and maintained open channels of communication with both academic and industrial researchers. Indeed, policies that eased regulatory burdens in health care relative to agriculture and other applications probably forestalled innovation in these latter areas. Public policies, moreover, have for decades funneled resources into biomedical R&D; only defense has taken more tax dollars. Ironically, a massive medical establishment that feeds at the trough of government, and which contributes to the high cost of medical care, is the price the nation pays for its leadership in biotechnology.

5 The emergence of commercial biotechnology in Japan

Introduction

Compared with the US, Japan's biotechnology sector has achieved modest commercial success. According to figures on the size of national biotechnology markets compiled by Japan's Patent Office, the market for biotechnology products in Japan reached 834 billion yen in 1999, only about one-sixth the size of the 5.2 trillion yen market in the US, and less than half the size of the 2.4 trillion yen market in the European Union.[1] Product sales are growing rapidly, however, topping 1.3 trillion yen in 2001, a seven-fold increase over the past twelve years; they are expected to approach 25 trillion yen by 2010.

Policy makers have very high expectations of biotechnology; they see it not only as a potent source of economic revitalization but also as a means of improving the quality of life, curing disease, and restoring the environment. To that effect, an advisory panel recently called for the doubling of the government's biotechnology-related budget over the next five years, hailing 2003 as "the first year of biotechnology human resources development."[2] Lofty targets have been set, and science resources mobilized as perhaps they have never been before in the hopes of achieving them. Does Japan's national innovation system possess the resources and capabilities required to grow the market for biotechnology products and services by a factor of twenty in less than a decade? Chapter 3 gave clear evidence of major changes in science and technology policy related to biotechnology that could very well lead to the fulfillment of expectations. Yet for long-time observers of Japanese biotechnology, the rush to mobilize the NIS for a big push in biotechnology will sound very familiar; a similar push was made in the early 1980s to close a yawning technological gap with the US. How that gap opened up and why it has remained stubbornly resistant to being closed is the main purpose of this chapter.

Biotechnology's birth and development in Japan cannot be understood apart from the institutional context in which it has taken root. As Chapter 3 made clear, neither Japan's universities nor its public research institutes provided the kind of fertile environment conducive to cutting-edge research in molecular biology and genetics comparable to that which occurred in the US and Europe. Nor has there been a single vanguard institution that, like America's NIH, could set the agenda for biomedical research. On the other hand, Japanese industry quickly imported and adapted the technology for mass producing antibiotics, added many important process and product innovations, and went on to become the leading exporter of antibiotics and antimicrobial products. The food-processing and chemical industries employed similar fermentation and cell culture technologies to develop a wide range of innovative products. Finally, Japanese researchers have made important contributions in protein engineering, biocatalysis, biosensors, and, more recently, in nano-biotechnology, structural analysis of proteins, and the identification and analysis of single-nucleotide polymorphyisms (SNPs). Japan's experience with biotechnology fits the pattern of technological catch-up – an all-out mobilization of technological resources to exploit science that had been mostly developed elsewhere, only to find that continued innovation depends on strengthening the underpinning science base. Decisions to undertake that strengthening have been made; policies to carry it out are in place. It is thus plausible to conclude that, at least in biotechnology, the country has indeed turned the corner onto a path of science-driven technological innovation.

In this chapter I distinguish three phases in the history of commercial biotechnology. In the first phase, from the 1920s until 1980, Japanese industry developed world-class expertise in fermentation and industrial microbiology. In particular food and chemical companies used this expertise to become world leaders in the production of food additives, antibiotics, and other niche products in which process innovation conferred competitive advantage. In the early 1970s, responding to breakthroughs in molecular biology and genetics emanating from the US, the government and a few large companies subtly began promoting basic research in the life sciences. Not until Genentech's initial public offering in 1980, however, did public and private sectors converge on a strategy for promoting commercialization of the new genetic technologies, marking the start of the second phase. For the next five years, firms from diverse industries, often working in conjunction with research associations sponsored by the government, launched new programs in biotechnology at a breathtaking pace. Japan's first "bio-boom," however, lost energy after the middle of the decade. In the third phase, which lasted from 1985 until the present, firms focused more on core technological and institutional strengths, using various alliance strategies to access key complementary assets. The government, meanwhile, intensified efforts to improve basic research, leaving applied research and commercialization to industry. Although Japan's science community pushed to increase the government's commitment to the Human Genome Project, the Ministry of Finance kept a tight lid on budgets. Near the end of the period, the government revised the legal framework governing university–industry relations along the lines discussed in Chapter 3. Increased opportunities for technology transfer, coupled with a surge in funds brought on by the Millennium Project, finally created conditions for the emergence of dedicated biotechnology start-ups. At the time of writing, a second "bio-boom" had just run its course. A small but steadily growing cluster of small biotechnology companies appears to have taken root, which could change the dynamics of the sector considerably in the years ahead.

The origins of Japan's bioindustry: 1920–1980

Whereas molecular biology and genetics defined technological trajectories in the US, the impetus for innovation in Japan came from industrial applications. In the US, science paved the way for commercial development; in Japan, commercial need determined relevant fields for subsequent scientific inquiry. Generally, private firms were the center of action, though they enjoyed a steady stream of highly capable new researchers from engineering and agricultural science departments of the national universities. Rather than probe scientific frontiers, firms concentrated on shoring up areas close to their own traditional technological strengths in food processing and fine chemicals. Institutional linkages were few, government promotion weak or absent entirely. Nevertheless, food and chemical companies undertook a series of innovations that established Japan as a global leader in modern industrial fermentation and bioprocess engineering. Based on their accumulated skills in conventional process technologies, these firms would later spearhead Japan's thrust into genetic engineering and cell fusion-based biotechnology in the early 1980s.

Industrial fermentation and Japan's traditional industries

Commercial biotechnology in Japan grew out of a centuries-old tradition of craft-based fermentation, brewing, and applied microbiology. Agricultural technologies practiced since ancient times provided a wealth of opportunities for tinkering with and manipulating living organisms and their byproducts. The production of sake (*nihon-shu*), an alcoholic beverage derived from fermented rice, is documented as early as AD 712 in the ancient historical chronicle *Kojiki*; its use is intimated as far back as the third century in the Chinese chronicle *Wajinden*.[3] In addition, production of traditional cuisine such as *shoyu* (soy sauce), *miso* (fermented soy bean paste, typically used as a base for soup), *tofu* (soy bean curd), and *natto* (fermented whole soy bean) gave Japan's food-processing industry early experience with microbial fermentation.[4] Many of the major producers of brewed products today trace their origins back to the Edo Era (1603–1868).[5] One of Japan's oldest extant corporations, Yamasa Shoyu, began as a producer of soy sauce in 1645; in the 1980s, it was one of scores of food-processing companies that diversified into biopharmaceuticals. Initially, contributions from theoretical science were few; technology was mostly in the form of experiential or tacit knowledge embodied in craftsmen.[6] And although other countries, especially in Europe, had also mastered craft-based fermentation by the middle of the nineteenth century, none approached the level of sophistication commonly found in Japan. In particular, Japan was the only country at that time thought to be capable of carrying out fermentation using more than one type of microorganism.[7] Indeed, there is evidence that brewers and fermentors used quite elaborate mixtures of organisms, which they could vary depending on characteristics desired in the final product. According to Karube, this early experience in applied microbiology provided a solid foundation on which Japanese firms would later build world-class expertise in antibiotics and amino acid production.[8]

During the Meiji Era (1868–1912), scientific knowledge of fermentation and other microbial processes grew rapidly; for the first time, brewers actually understood the biochemical processes responsible for fermentation. Brewing began to be industrialized. In addition to the science itself, new laboratory techniques were imported from the West, including steam sterilization and methods of screening out useful microbes from a mixture and growing them in pure cultures. Beer making came to Japan from Germany, adding a new dimension to the brewing sector; like their counterparts in the food and fine chemicals industries, beer makers would be among the first firms to make major investments in biotechnology. To help brewers understand the science of fermentation, in 1903 the Ministry of Finance established the Fermentation Laboratory, funded by a tax on liquor. There, scientists uncovered the mysteries of the workings of the *koji* mold used in the *sake* brewing process and devised ways of improving *sake*'s quality and shelf life.[9] Academic technical support was also important, especially that provided by the new schools of agriculture attached to the imperial universities, which the government had established as a means of promoting absorption of foreign technology.[10] These schools housed departments of applied microbiology (or in some cases departments of biochemistry), whose original faculty had been trained largely by German organic chemists, and whose focus was fermentation engineering. Graduates often moved directly into industries that manufactured traditional food and beverage products. Working through the *Nihon Nogei Kagakukai* (Japan Agricultural Chemistry Society), which was formed in 1927, these scientists contributed to several key product and process innovations. The most significant of these was the food flavor enhancer monosodium glutamate (MSG), which in the 1930s became one of Japan's major export products.[11] Because of the nearly complete absence of modern research capabilities in the private sector, firms relied strongly on infusions of such newly trained scientists into their organizational structures.[12]

During the Taisho Era (1912–1926) and early Showa Era (1926–1988), Japan's government, increasingly concerned about ensuring stable supplies of raw materials, increasingly looked to microbial fermentation technology as a solution to the problem of over-dependence on imports.[13] In 1925, Japan's navy commissioned research on a technique for producing butanol, an alcohol used as a fuel, through fermentation using microbes imported from the UK. In 1937, the government passed the Alcohol Monopoly Law, which empowered it to take actions needed to maintain a stable supply of liquid fuels. Finally, it succeeded in developing an alcohol fermentation process on its colony of Taiwan; the technique, which used juice squeezed from sugar cane as raw material, was quickly introduced at some thirty giant alcohol-production plants across Japan. By that time, war with the US was about to commence and the US had ended its exports of butanol and other fuels to Japan. The government responded by converting more than half the country's alcohol plants to production of butanol for use as aircraft fuel and in solvents and lubricants. Plans called for the importation of sugar cane from throughout Southeast Asia to use as raw material.

In the early postwar period, process innovations in fermentation and microbiology contributed to the revival of Japanese industry. Two early beneficiaries were the drug and food-processing industries. In 1948, the US Occupation forces introduced strains of penicillin, mass production of which had begun in the US during the war, into Japan for the first time. More than seventy companies quickly set up operations. According to one estimate, virtually the entire class of 1942 of the department of Applied Microbiology at Tokyo University became chief executive officers of these new companies.[14] Although only four of the original seventy firms survived, Japan quickly emerged as the world's foremost producer and exporter of antibiotics; by 1990, it was supplying about 60 percent of global demand.[15] One important reason for this success was the development of large, enclosed fermentation vats that employed new techniques of agitation and aeration. Although the first large-scale, aerated fermentation was carried out in the US and Europe, the improvements contributed by Japanese firms facilitated the shift to mass production.[16] Many of the processes pioneered in Japanese firms in the early postwar period remain standard practice worldwide in the production of antibiotics.[17]

Process innovations in large-scale microbial fermentation quickly diffused through the drug, food, and fine chemical industries. In the 1950s and 1960s, Japanese firms achieved breakthrough innovations in the manufacture of amino and nucleic acids for food and specialty chemical applications. Among the most important of these was Yoshiro Kinoshita's discovery in 1955 of an organism that permits efficient, single-step synthesis of glutamate, an amino acid that gives MSG its distinctive flavor. Commercialized in 1909 by Ajinomoto Corporation, MSG originally required the costly extraction of glutamic acid first from seaweed, then from Chinese soybean.[18] Capitalizing on Kinoshita's discovery, the chemical company Kyowa Hakko in 1956 conducted the world's first large-scale production of L-glutamic acid by fermentation, using a microbial metabolic control fermentation process. In 1951, Kyowa Hakko, perhaps best known today as a maker of wine and *shochu* (a distilled spirit), had imported production technology for mass-producing the antibiotic streptomycin from the US drug maker Merck. By 1960, advances in metabolic suppression techniques had made possible mass production of a variety of commercially important amino and nucleic acids, hormones, and vitamins.[19] Intense competition fueled technological change: Ajinomoto, determined not to surrender market share to Kyowa Hakko, fought back by quickly developing an even more efficient fermentation technology for making MSG and other amino acids, the "Ajinomoto Process." In addition, in a move reflecting the crucial importance of fermentation in shaping subsequent technological trajectories, Ajinomoto began using byproducts from glutamic acid production as starting materials for making a new generation of pharmaceutical products; it went on to become the world's leading producer of amino acids and related products. Kyowa Hakko too used its strengths in fermentation to become a leading pharmaceutical and biotechnology firm, which in recent years has helped start several biotechnology venture businesses.[20]

The emergence of modern biochemical process technology

By 1970 Japan was firmly established as the world leader in bioprocess technology applied to production of fine and specialty chemicals. In addition, its laboratories possessed the world's largest and most varied library of microorganisms that had been screened, mutated, and cultured for industrial use. In the late 1960s and early 1970s, another cluster of biological process innovations reinforced Japan's competitive position by vastly improving the performance and range of application of industrial bioreactors. A bioreactor is a large tank in which nutrients, cultured microbes, and enzymes interact chemically to yield a desired final product. It differs structurally from a simple fermentation vat in that it contains "immobilized" (*koteika*) enzyme or microbial cultures, usually fastened to a solid support, whose function is to catalyze, or quicken the pace of, the desired chemical reaction. Glass beads, roller bottles, and flat plates are among the materials used to support the catalyst, thereby immobilizing it within the culture medium.[21]

The breakthrough innovation came in 1969, when Tanabe Seiyaku, a mid-size drug maker, pioneered the immobilized enzyme technique for production of L-glutamic acid. Tanabe's breakthrough involved isolating the necessary enzyme and then depositing it onto a sticky solid support immersed in the reaction vessel, hence immobilizing it. Through continuous contact with the vessel's liquid contents, the immobilized enzyme hastened conversion of starting materials to desired final product. Though simple in principle, the technique had a profound impact on productivity: by consuming less enzyme and energy than conventional methods, Tanabe's technique slashed the cost of producing amino acids by 30 to 40 percent.[22]

A few years later, researchers applied the concept to microbes, whose immobilization in ceramic packing or other suspension greatly broadened the scope of applications for the bioreactor. By the mid 1970s, it had become the standard process in the production of syrups and oils, glucose and other sugars, enzymes, detergents, nutritional supplements, specialty chemicals, antibiotics, and even cosmetics.[23]

Although lacking the high drama of molecular biology research, which was about to give rise in the US to the recombinant DNA process and in Britain to the hybridoma technique of making monoclonal antibodies, innovations in fermentation and bioreactor technologies provided a base of tacit knowledge and organizational learning that would later prove useful when these same firms made their first forays into biotechnology. This is because the production of biotechnology-based drugs almost always involves cultivation of live microbial cultures, fermentation, and the recovery of final products on a grand scale; by the 1970s, Japanese companies led the world in these technologies. The bioreactor's importance for the future of biotechnology, though perhaps overstated at the time, was acknowledged by MITI when, in 1981, it incorporated the technology as one of four target processes in its Next Generation Biotechnology project.

On the other hand, there were clear limits on the extent to which process technologies could drive technological change. In the first place, before it could be applied to biotechnology, Japanese firms first had to acquire and master the new laboratory techniques for producing recombinant DNA and monoclonal antibodies, which involve a combination of product and process innovation. Because the ability to apply these techniques is strongly dependent on a solid research foundation in molecular biology and genetics, firms hoping to use these new techniques would first need to build up their research capabilities in these areas, which itself would require access to external sources of knowledge elsewhere in the innovation system. The trouble was that such sources simply did not exist, at least in a form readily accessible to domestic firms. Thus Japanese biotechnology would quickly become dependent on knowledge in-licensed from the US. Second, Japan's major developers and users of bioreactor technology by the 1970s faced maturing markets for their products, both at home and abroad; the usual diminishing returns to innovation set in as firms approached a limit on the returns that could be squeezed out of products derived from amino acids and antibiotics. Perversely, bioreactors may have even deterred subsequent innovation by driving down prices: glutamic acid in 1980 was selling at its 1950 price, despite the more than six-fold increase in consumer prices during that time span. Many companies after the twin oil shocks moved production overseas. On the eve of the genetic engineering revolution, the fear was that productivity gains from recombinant DNA technology might destroy rather than rejuvenate Japan's chemicals industry.[24]

Also weakening Japan's position after 1970 was the surprising ambivalence of Japanese companies toward the new genetic technologies, even as they were beginning to take off in the US. The only major firm to undertake a substantial commitment to research in the life sciences was Mitsubishi Kasei, which in 1971 established one of Japan's first private laboratories dedicated solely to research in the life sciences. Its mission was not only to support basic research in the life sciences but in doing so establish a model of cooperation between academic researchers and industry. The extent of Japan's nonparticipation was subtly criticized in an early MITI study, which noted that of the forty key research breakthroughs in molecular biology stretching from 1665 to 1981, Japanese researchers were credited with only four.[25] When the achievements of Genentech and other American start-ups finally galvanized Japanese companies into action in the early 1980s, they were so far behind as to render catch up a nearly impossible task, even with a head start in process technology. Nevertheless, not a few analysts of Japan's competitive potential in biotechnology in the early 1980s, including the US Office of Technology Assessment, interpreted Japan's strengths in bioprocess technology as a powerful asset that would enable Japanese firms to rise quickly to dominance in commercial biotechnology. Those strengths were real, indeed.[26] Evidence of their potential came when Japanese firms that had licensed new product technology from the US in the 1980s quickly commercialized the results, sometimes before the product reached the market in the US. Yet in hindsight, they could not compensate for weaknesses elsewhere in the NIS, especially the lack of institutional channels for technology transfer from university to industry and an academic research culture that simply ruled out the close interaction between academic researchers and industry that led to the growth of DBCs in the US.

Rumblings in the laboratory

Japan's scientific institutions were not well prepared for the arrival of genetic engineering technology. As explained in Chapter 4, the precursors to biotechnology in the US – a globally competitive pharmaceutical industry and a well-funded research base in molecular biology – evolved along separate trajectories until the 1970s, when the prospect that recombinant DNA would revolutionize the drug industry became clear. The two trajectories converged in the creation of the DBC. Drawing them together were the high returns that investors, scientists, and entrepreneurs expected the market to deliver; academic scientists willing and able to participate in starting up a company, relatively abundant venture capital, and government policies that were biased strongly in the direction of support for the industry served as enabling conditions. Strikingly, almost none of these conditions applied to Japan. This does not mean, of course, that commercial biotechnology was dead in the water. Rather its beginnings and early take-off were almost completely dependent on, and in reaction to, technological and policy developments in the US.

An analyst jumping forward into the 1970s from the late Meiji Era might have been surprised by the extent to which the country's biological and biomedical research base had fallen behind that of the West. By the turn of the century, Japan had forged the institutions of modern science almost from scratch, and a growing number of its scientists were making important scientific contributions, especially in biomedical research. As James Bartholomew argues, the period before World War I was a golden age for medicine: of the 1,360 doctorates awarded in Japan between 1888 (the first year of conferrals) and 1920, almost half (656) were in medicine.[27] The strong public commitment to medical research and public health provided fertile ground for some of the world's most impressive scientific achievements of the period. While working in the laboratory of the German bacteriologist Robert Koch in the late 1880s, Shibasaburo Kitasato isolated the infectious agent that causes tetanus and developed serum therapy as a means of priming the immune system to resist it. He later discovered the bacterial agent that causes bubonic plague and went on to found two research institutes in Tokyo devoted to bacteriology and public health (the Institute of Infectious Diseases, established in 1892 as a nonprofit institute but absorbed in 1914 by the Ministry of Education into Tokyo University, and the Kitasato Institute, established in 1914). Kanehiro Takagi demonstrated that the cause of beriberi is a nutritional deficiency, not a pathogen. Kiyoshi Shiga, Kitasato's second hire from Tokyo University at his Institute of Infectious Diseases, isolated the bacterium that causes dysentery. Finally, Mendelian genetics was introduced into Japan in 1905 by Kenjiro Fujii, who returned from a three-year stint in Europe to resume his post on Tokyo University's faculty of science.[28] Bartholomew points out that at least two scientists during this period, Kitasato and Katsusaburo Yamagawa, were denied Nobel Prizes due them: Kitasato for the discovery of natural immunity, Yamagawa for discovering a technique for inducing tumor growth in mice.[29] Had those prizes been awarded, biomedical research in Japan might well have followed a very different path.

Alas, Japanese scientists played only a minor role in the history of molecular biology leading up to the development of the recombinant DNA process. Several scientists did work actively to introduce molecular biology into the biological sciences around the time that Watson and Crick determined the structure of DNA. In 1949, Fujio Egami, Itaru Watanabe, and Atsuhiro Shibatani organized the first symposium in Japan on nucleic acids. Egami later served as the founding president of the Mitsubishi Kasei Institute of Life Sciences. Hamao Umezawa discovered several powerful new antibiotics, including kanamycin. Shibatani wrote a series of articles in 1960 exhorting the biology community to shift away from the traditional "enumerative" biology, which involves mainly classifying and maintaining lists of organisms, to "fundamental" biology centered on the study of molecular processes.[30] The most significant contribution in research by far was Susumu Tonegawa's elucidation of the role of genes in generating antibody diversity, a stunning scientific feat that earned him a Nobel Prize in 1987, the first awarded to a Japanese national in medicine. Most of the research, however, was done at the Basel Institute for Immunology in Switzerland and at the Massachusetts Institute of Technology, and Professor Tonegawa himself has criticized the research environment in Japan for not supporting the kind of free-spirited research that led to his discovery.[31] The upshot is that the academic research environment in postwar Japan simply did not provide an institutional setting conducive to the free-wheeling interdisciplinary approaches to molecular biology comparable to what was then being undertaken in the US and Europe. Nor were government agencies or other funding sources taking the lead in defining new research agendas; Japan had nothing comparable to the Rockefeller Foundation, which in the US conceived research programs and funded projects consistent with its socioeconomic values.[32]

Divisions within the government in postwar science and technology policy have made research and commercial development even more uncertain. In terms of public policy, the Ministry of International Trade and Industry (MITI) maintained exclusive jurisdiction over matters pertaining to industrial science and technology. The Ministry of Education (Monbusho), though reorganized under the US Occupation, quickly re-centralized administration of university research under its tight jurisdiction. Scientists themselves were polarized ideologically between the "*minka*" group, which resisted the industrial orientation of science and dependence on imports of foreign technology, and the "technocratic group," which went along with the status quo – a schism whose influence still reverberates through the academy.[33] The creation of the Science and Technology Agency (*Kagaku gijutsucho*) in the mid 1950s was aimed at unifying science policy within a single administrative unit; yet the practical effect was to add yet another competitor for relatively scarce science funding.[34] The resulting institutional structure produced a schizophrenic policy environment in which research in basic sciences within the universities became almost completely disconnected from applied research and development in industry, while different ministries wandered off in different directions in support of research tied to their own respective interests – a problem that still evokes much hand-wringing in Japan's science policy community. Although steps have been taken to increase joint research between universities and industries, there simply has been no counterpart in Japan to the tight institutional nexus between biotechnology firms, universities, and the National Institutes of Health (NIH) that has been at the center of American biotechnology.

Not until the early 1970s did references to molecular biology begin to appear widely in science policy discourse. The turning point came in 1971, when the Council for Science and Technology (CST), which officially advises the Prime Minister and Cabinet on science policy, issued the fifth in a series of broad policy statements on science and technology. It noted

Japan's lagging investment in R&D as a proportion of national income, which, at less than 2 percent, was roughly half that of the US and one-third that of West Germany. Most significantly, the report called for application of the principles of molecular biology in five areas: treating cancer, improving animal and plant breeds, developing information processing devices, engineering of microorganisms, and environmental preservation.[35] A few years later, the Council's newly formed Committee on the Life Sciences (*raifusaiensu bukai*) issued an interim report that linked elucidation of life phenomena on the molecular level to applications in preventive medicine, treatment of the elderly, cancer therapy, animal agriculture, and development of new food resources.[36] Although, curiously, the interim report failed to acknowledge the recombinant DNA process which had been demonstrated in the US a year earlier, it galvanized the scientific community to the potential importance of this new and expanding field of inquiry.

Initially, only the Science and Technology Agency moved aggressively on the CST's recommendations. In 1974, it established the Center for Promotion of the Life Sciences in its leading laboratory, the Institute of Chemical and Physical Research (Riken). The new center initiated projects grouped under five themes: control of aging, engineered enzymes and bioreactors, the biology of thinking, artificial organs, and physiologically active substances.[37] Three years later, it was elevated into a full-fledged institute within Riken. Elsewhere, mission-oriented research related to life sciences slowly increased in prominence, especially in the national laboratories of the Ministry of Health and Welfare and in research institutes of public universities associated with Monbusho's anti-cancer research program.[38]

Astonishingly, not until the CST's "Sixth Recommendation," in May 1977, did science policy officially respond to the first experiments on recombinant DNA that had been taking place in the US since the early 1970s. While the policy statement echoed old themes, it for the first time called for a policy promoting research in recombinant DNA and proposed guidelines for its safe conduct.[39] This set in motion a chain of events by which both CST and Monbusho drew up separate guidelines for regulating research using genetically modified organisms. A year earlier, in 1976, the Recombinant DNA Advisory Committee of the American NIH had issued the world's first comprehensive guidelines. Using the NIH's guidelines as a blueprint, the Science Council of the Ministry of Education (*gakujutsu shingikai*) issued its policy in March 1979 – but only after more than two years of intense lobbying by Japanese scientists. The guidelines covered only research conducted in universities or affiliated institutes, or with grant funds obtained from Monbusho. Five months later, the CST, in response to a Cabinet request, issued its own set of guidelines covering research in government institutes not associated with Monbusho.[40] These were somewhat less restrictive than those of Monbusho, an indication of industry's participation in drawing them up.[41]

The government's delay in setting up a regulatory framework and responding to developments in the US has cost Japan dearly. In the first place, the reaction began a full four years after Cohen and Boyer had first spliced foreign DNA into a bacterial host cell. During that interval, public and private research in the US had boomed, giving American researchers a virtually insurmountable lead. To make things worse, few Japanese firms showed any interest at all in applications of the new techniques, squandering any advantages attributable to their strengths in bioprocessing.

Finally, by the time Japan's regulatory framework coalesced, America's NIH had already eased or eliminated 90 percent of the restrictions in its original draft.[42] This left Japanese researchers encumbered with regulations with which American researchers did not have to contend. Although these were eased in 1982, and again in 1983 under intense pressure from industry, many companies by that time had already invested in costly safety facilities that suddenly became obsolete.[43] Without the flexibility to respond nimbly as knowledge accumulated – NIH had revised its guidelines five times by 1982, compared to the Japanese government's single revision – Japanese firms limped into the commercialization stage at a severe disadvantage relative to firms in the US.

Biotechnology fever hits Japan (1980–1985)

Barriers to commercializing new biotechnology

Industry's leadership in bioprocess technology, coupled with the government's failure to move expeditiously on new scientific advances, left Japan's biotechnology effort in an awkwardly ambiguous position. On the one hand, Japan had garnered 60 percent of the 2,400 biotechnology-related patents awarded worldwide between 1977 and 1981, though the vast majority covered innovations related to bioreactors and other "old" biotechnologies.[44] Beginning in 1980, moreover, the new regulatory framework unleashed a flurry of activity in the nation's university, public, and private research laboratories: the number of registered experiments involving recombinant DNA rose from 284 in 1980 to more than 3,500 in 1986.[45] On the other hand, Japan remained far behind the US and Europe in terms of resources committed to research related to the life sciences, even correcting for differences in GNP. Though estimates varied, one source suggested that Japan had fallen as far as ten years behind the US.[46] In 1980, total funds committed to biotechnology research in public research institutes amounted to only 13 percent of those in the US and one-third of those in West Germany; funding for biomedical research, of which biotechnology was a component, amounted to a mere one-thirtieth of the level in the US. The private sector, too, lagged far behind: funding of biotechnology R&D in Japan's five leading firms amounted to only 14 percent of that being spent in the five leading western companies, which also had more than 17 times the number of researchers (Tables 5.1(a) and 5.1(b).[47]

The effects of relatively low levels of research appear in Japan's patent data for the period, which show a high level of foreign ownership of key patents related to recombinant DNA. In 1978, foreigners received two of six recombinant DNA patents, six of nine in 1979, and ten of eleven in 1980, after which the proportion awarded to Japanese parties gradually began to take off; overall from 1973 to 1981 foreigners filed for more than three-quarters of all patents in fields related to the life sciences.[48] Only after 1983 do Japanese applications even begin to outnumber those of foreigners. Such foreign penetration of Japanese patenting is striking considering that the proportion of foreign ownership of all patents awarded in Japan during this period ranged from 13 to 15 percent.[49]

Japanese firms planning entry into biotechnology thus found themselves in a position quite different from that of firms in the US. Large chemical, food, and pharmaceutical companies, though strong in downstream process technologies and distribution networks, had little access to the relevant stocks of scientific knowledge; there were literally no researchers working in genetic engineering in private industry. Nor was there a pot of venture capital awaiting potential investors not already affiliated with an established company. Not that such funds would have mattered; for Japanese universities, which had only just received permission to conduct experiments using recombinant DNA, had few molecular biologists whose research

Table 5.1(a) Comparison of conditions in government laboratories at the beginning of the 1980s

Country	*Expenditure on life sciences (billions of yen)*	*Of which was biotechnology-related (billions of yen)*
Japan	25.1 (1980)	1.6 (1980)
United States	771 (1979)	12 (1979)
United Kingdom	–	2.5 (1980)
West Germany	–	5.3 (1980)

Table 5.1(b) Conditions in five leading private firms at the beginning of the 1980s

Country	*R&D Expenditures*		*Number of Researchers*	
	Total	*Life science*	*Total*	*Life science*
Japan	53.2	9.9	6,600	845
US/Europe	370	124	42,200	14,900

Source: "Baiotekunorojii," *Kogyo gijutsu* [Industrial Technology], November 1981, vol. 22, p. 28.

offered meaningful commercial prospects. In addition, restrictions on formal faculty contacts with industry and taboos on professors leaving university posts blocked the university–industry channel, which was at the heart of America's success. Such faculties in the US even drew ridicule in the Japanese media, which referred to them as *gakusha shonin* (scholar-merchants), whose sell-out to business threatened the free flow of scientific information and corrupted the mission of the basic research enterprise.[50]

The US had demonstrated that commercial success hinged on an institutional marriage of excellent basic research, risk capital, and entrepreneurial management. This had been accomplished through creation of a specialized institution – the dedicated biotechnology firm, which pulled together the complementary assets needed to fashion a biotechnology value chain. Organizationally tailored to the fluid markets in human, financial, and knowledge resources of the American NIS, DBC-style enterprises were ill suited to conditions in Japan. Yet Japanese firms faced the same technical challenges. The problem, therefore, was to craft an institutional response that could overcome the technical hurdles, while capitalizing on the distinct market conditions and resources available in the Japanese national system. Because high uncertainty and risk deterred most firms from entering the market – a classic case of market failure – the role of formulating a response fell to the government. Before that could happen, however, a consensus on the importance of mounting a commercial thrust had to obtain.

The public policy response

In 1980, biotechnology burst into the national limelight. That year, the Japanese term for biotechnology (*baiotekunorojii*), along with references to a distinct biotechnology industry (*baioindasutorii*), began to appear in government and private sector reports alike. Newspapers ran glossy spreads on the "genetic revolution" under way in the life sciences, noting in particular the degree to which Japan had fallen behind. Biotechnology, all but ignored during the 1970s, suddenly was hailed as a "base technology" (*kiban gijutsu*) that would underpin the future industrial economy. As one journalist put it, Japan was about to "catch the biotech wave" rolling in from the US.

The surge of interest in biotechnology grew out of a sense of panic that a new technological revolution was beginning without Japan's participation. Several developments raised this concern to the level of national policy. First was the growing chorus of criticism from the scientific community concerning the severity of restrictions on research using recombinant DNA and general ambivalence with which the government appeared to be responding to new breakthroughs in the US.[51] The Japan Society for Bioscience, Biotechnology, and Agrochemistry and the Chemical Society of Japan led the lobbying effort, arguing that unless the government took action, the nation would be rendered irrelevant as a meaningful contributor to the global scientific effort.[52]

Second, commercial take-off in the US, especially the record-shattering initial public offering of Genentech in the fall, 1980, and the subsequent rapid-fire emergence of American DBCs, caught experts in Japan by surprise.[53] For the Japanese, Genentech embodied the ethos of American capitalism; indeed, Genentech's CEO and co-founder Robert Swanson became a media sensation when he visited Japan late in 1980, prompting one observer to comment: "Whether biotechnology has the promise of semiconductors remains to be seen; nevertheless, Genentech will be the world's next Sony."[54] Reinforcing these fears was a flurry of patent activity by DBCs in Japan; as noted above, in no other industry were Japanese companies ceding the lion's share of intellectual property on their own turf to foreigners. In addition, the granting of an important patent in the US covering part of the original Cohen–Boyer recombinant DNA process, coupled with the US Supreme Court's landmark decision to uphold the right to patent a genetically altered organism, added to the fear that Japan might be entirely shut out of the new genetic technologies. Warning of dire consequences should that happen, Keidanren, Japan's prestigious peak industry association, brought its influence to bear on urging a decisive policy response.[55] A MITI official summed up the emerging consensus: "We're as far behind the US in biotechnology as we are in rocket technology ... For a country with no natural resources, technology is the only means of survival. Consequently, government and industry must work together to develop biotechnology."[56]

Finally, though seemingly unrelated to biotechnology, there was deepening concern over how to deal with Japan's struggling chemical industry. Since the mid 1970s, MITI and the industry had tried various attempts at reducing capacity to no avail. The twin oil shocks of the 1970s had abruptly halted two decades of stable growth. The tripling of prices of petroleum-based feedstock from 1972 to 1975, and again from 1978 to 1980, sent firms reeling; thereafter, ruinous competition and surging imports of chemical intermediates from the US, amid declining demand in the domestic market, wreaked further havoc, especially among the "Big 12" oil companies. Growing concern over pollution and a number of high-profile accidents at large processing plants, moreover, had cast a pall over the industry.[57] As the new decade began, MITI and industry were groping toward measures that would encourage firms both to reduce capacity and shift resources away from petroleum-based commodity chemicals to fine and specialty chemical products.

For MITI, this convergence of policy demands provided an extraordinary opportunity: why not fuse structural adjustment and high technology policies by persuading chemical companies to lead Japanese commercial entry into the new biotechnology in return for adjustment assistance?[58] Consequently, MITI secured funding for its Next Generation Industries Base Technology (*Jisedai*) project, which targeted biotechnology, electronic devices, and new functional materials as three core technologies which would "adjust" Japan's industrial structure (*sangyo kozo chosei*) for competition in the upcoming decade. MITI took the lead in the program by organizing the Research Association in Biotechnology (RAB), which brought together eleven of Japan's top chemical companies, along with two pharmaceutical and one food company, to work jointly on projects related to commercial applications in genetic engineering, mass cell culture, and large-scale bioreactors. MITI's first foray into biotechnology, the program mobilized industry's interest, thus helping to launch Japan's commercial biotechnology boom.[59] That MITI managed the project from its newly established Bioindustry Office in the Basic Industries Bureau, which oversees the chemical and heavy industries, gave clear indication of its aim to link high technology promotion with structural adjustment.[60]

Commercial take-off and the consequences of government policy

Judging from the acceleration in rate of market entry into biotechnology after 1980, MITI's initiation of a biotechnology policy certainly could qualify as a success. It is quite possible, however, that firms would have become active regardless of MITI's action. Indeed, my interviews with industry participants in the initial RAB projects suggest that MITI's policy helped, though only at the margins: firms viewed the seriousness with which MITI approached biotechnology as validation of the technology's potential but also as an indication that onerous regulations would soon be loosened. By 1985, at the peak of the "bio-boom," an average of thirty firms were entering the biotechnology market each year, six times the rate of the late 1970s. Between the late 1970s and 1985, more than 200 companies started major biotechnology development programs.[61] Not only did companies rush into the market, other government agencies quickly began promoting biotechnology policies for their client firms, broadening the extent of participation into agriculture and pharmaceuticals. The next few years ushered in what one analyst called the "explosive rise to power" (*bokkoki*) of government leadership (*seifushudogata*) over the fledgling industry.[62]

The speed with which MITI had implemented its program and the prestige surrounding the promotion of a national strategic technology were lessons not lost on other ministries. In 1983, the Central Pharmaceutical Affairs Bureau of the Ministry of Health and Welfare (MHW), concerned about stagnating profits in the pharmaceutical industry, convened a biotechnology study group. The group's final report, issued in the fall of 1984, called for, among other things, improvement of basic research and the establishment of a "Biotechnology Research Exchange Center." In April 1985, on the recommendation of the Pharmaceutical Industry Policy Forum, the Japan Association for Advanced Research of Pharmaceuticals was formed and charged with the task of applying advanced technologies such as genetic engineering to human health care and catalyzing cooperation among drug firms, universities, and public research institutes.[63] Fast on its heels, the

Ministry of Agriculture, Forestry, and Fisheries (MAFF) set up its Biotechnology Division and a government–industry consultative committee, the Cooperation Group for Promoting R&D in Biotechnology. Unlike MHW or MITI, MAFF has no single organization that promotes commercialization of biotechnology across the spectrum of industries falling under its jurisdiction. Instead, it established a number of small research associations (RAs) to promote cooperative research in the many sub-fields under its jurisdiction. These include the areas of enzyme function, bioreactors, agrochemical, and genetic analysis of agricultural organisms. Two aspects of MAFF's activities would have an important bearing on later commercial trends. First, more than other ministries, it has had to deal intensively with public concerns about the release of genetically altered organisms in the environment. Secondly, by virtue of the organization of MAFF's research into a large network of regional research institutes, it has become an important, if debatably effective, channel for technology transfer into rural areas.[64]

The results of government policies were mixed. On the one hand, a wide variety and number of firms entered the industry, many of which did not participate in formal Research Associations; all were large, established companies. Representing the synthetic fibers industry were Toyobo, Kuraray, Toray, Teijin, and Asahi Kasei; from pharmaceutical came Yamanouchi, Dai-ichi, Takeda, Sankyo, Dai Nippon, Chugai, Meiji Seika, Yoshitomi, Green Cross, Fujisawa, and Shionogi; food and beverage companies included Suntory, Takara Shuzo, Toyo Jozo, Ajinomoto, Yamasa Shoyu, and Snow Brand; and from the chemical industry came Mitsui Toatsu, Mitsui Seika, Mitsubishi Kasei, Mitsubishi Yuka, Sumitomo Kagaku, Showa Denko, and Kyowa Hakko.[65] Competition, therefore, was intense: no less than six companies vied to commercialize the cancer-killing drug interferon alpha; TPA, Genentech's blockbuster anti-clotting agent, drew seven Japanese competitors, including firms from the textile, dairy, chemical, and food industries.[66]

On the other hand, not all firms regarded the government's role in a positive light; some even resisted its prodding. When MITI convened its first research association in biotechnology, for example, Kyowa Hakko, widely recognized as a leader in genetic engineering at the time, declined to participate in that portion of the project for fear of losing control of proprietary technology. For the same reason, Tanabe, a mid-size pharmaceutical firm, refused to participate in the bioreactor program.[67] One anonymous participant in the project conceded that the association was merely symbolic (*tatemae*); the majority of participants in reality (*honne*) wanted the project to be discontinued.[68] Others have mentioned that firms rarely send their best researchers to joint laboratories. While I documented no such pessimism, it did appear that criticisms were stronger from firms that saw themselves at the cutting edge in a particular area. Firms whose competitive position was weak, especially the chemical industry, tend to speak more positively about their relationship with MITI.[69]

Second, MITI's crash program ultimately failed to deliver on the explicit goal of restoring the chemical industry to health. Although profits of chemical makers staged a comeback after the 1982 recession, they plummeted again after 1985. In addition, after 1981, Japan's trade balance in chemicals swung into deficit for the first time since the mid 1960s. Since that time, American and German chemical firms have far outpaced Japanese rivals in diversifying into more lucrative fine and specialty chemicals.[70]

Nor did the pharmaceutical industry, many of whose firms had their main activities in food or chemicals, receive the expected boost from new recombinant DNA-based drugs. It was certainly not for want of trying: in 1982, according to a survey of biotechnology companies conducted by Keidanren, 82 percent of firms active in biotechnology were pursuing applications in pharmaceuticals.[71] Interferon and antibiotics were the most popular targets, neither of which was to prove to be a profitable endeavor. For reasons discussed earlier, Japan's major drug firms had built dominant positions in world markets for antibiotics, partly because of their experience making them: because far more antibiotics are consumed per capita in Japan than elsewhere, Japanese pharmaceutical makers naturally specialized in their manufacture. Antibiotics, however, had become a commodities business. Worse, the reimbursement system by which the government administers the national health care system not only kept existing drug prices low, it forced them lower almost every year, even as reimbursement rates for medical treatment were rising.[72] Indeed, nothing more clearly underlines the dramatic difference between health care delivery systems in Japan and the US than the trend in drug prices: in the US prices in 1986 were 251 percent of 1975 levels; in Japan, by contrast, drug prices by 1986 had *fallen* to 54 percent of their 1975 level![73] Inability to raise margins severely crimped spending on R&D, which in the mid 1980s averaged only 8 percent of sales, or about half the amount spent by major American firms.[74] The only way for firms to increase profits and hence R&D was to pump out a continual stream of new, innovative drugs – which they did, at least some of them. This made biotechnology especially attractive and accounts for the numerous early entrants from the pharmaceutical industry. For Japanese drug firms, joint R&D to build pre-commercial capabilities was not a choice; it was a matter of survival.

Although markets were slow to develop, firms soon began turning out a varied assortment of innovative products uniquely adapted to domestic demand.[75] Cosmetics drew early attention: Kanebo's "Bio-lipstick," derived from a fungus whose rearranged genes produce a rich red pigment, took the market by storm during the "bio-boom" of the mid 1980s. MITI's National Laboratory for Chemical Technology devised a way of cheaply mass-producing lanolinic acid using mass cell culture; Shiseido, which licensed the technology from MITI, used it to produce a popular line of cosmetics (Shiseido "seltz" and "revital").[76] Ajinomoto developed a biocellulose product that it sold to Sony for use in audio speakers. Plant agriculture also attracted interest: using cell fusion technology, Mitsui Toatsu developed a high-yield hybrid strain of rice. Mitsui Petrochemical and Suntory introduced colorful virus-free flowers, based on large-scale tissue culture; they are used in miniature flower arrangements, a lucrative market in Japan. Continuing in the rich tradition of innovation in bioprocess technology, Nitto Chemical, in conjunction with a Kyoto University researcher, in the mid 1980s developed an immobilized enzyme bioreactor to mass produce acryl amide, a key raw material in the production of industrial polymers. Finally, Japan's biggest-selling biotechnology product through most of the 1990s was a laundry detergent containing a genetically engineered protease enzyme made by a European firm. Although they lack the glamor and profit potential of "blockbuster" drugs being developed in the US, these products nonetheless illustrate the novel ways in which biotechnology was adapted to the domestic market and to the capabilities of producers.

From bio-boom to bio-reality: alliance strategies and the shift to basic research (1985–present)

The early 1980s had been a heady time for Japanese biotechnology, as it had been in the US a few years earlier. Brimming with confidence, firms rushed into the industry: from a dozen or so new entrants each year in the late 1970s, the numbers rose above thirty in the early and mid 1980s.

By the second half of the decade, however, the picture had become more complicated. On the private level, firms stepped up pursuit of alliance strategies, entering into partnerships with foreign firms more frequently and on more equal terms than before. On the public level, the government shifted attention from promoting commercialization to shoring up weaknesses in basic research, though little in the way of new budget allocations was made on the commercial side. In contrast, regional governments, hoping to tap local sources of competitive advantage, began targeting biotechnology as a means of revitalizing local economies. With the collapse of asset prices in the early 1990s, commercialization went into a full retreat, even though product sales were rising sharply. Most strikingly, companies pulled back significantly from their pursuit of international alliances. The inability to mount a genome project worthy of the country's size and scientific status became a source of embarrassment, which prompted a rethinking of the government's entire approach to biotechnology. The Diet's passage of the Science and Technology Basic Plan and subsequent pumping up of budgets for science, coupled with seemingly endless economic stagnation, brought a second wind to the country's life science policies: biotechnology policy came to be linked in part to economic revitalization. Thus a new window of opportunity opened for Japanese biotechnology in the late 1990s.

Changes in industry

By the end of the 1980s, the private sector had entered a period of rapid flux. Most notably, companies that diversified into biotechnology in the early 1980s became more aggressive at expanding their boundaries to take advantage of complementary assets both within the domestic innovation system and abroad. At the same time, the flood of new entrants into biotechnology that characterized the "bio-boom" years slowed to a trickle. Though partly the result of the strengthening yen, it also reflected sobering realization of the long lead times between research and return on a new product.[77] Still, the market retained its dynamism; sales of new products derived from recombinant DNA more than doubled from 1988 to 1989, and again from 1989 to 1990.[78] By 1992, product sales had reached five times the level of 1987 and appeared to be increasing at an almost exponential rate.[79]

Two trends distinguished the evolution of commercial biotechnology trajectories in Japan during this period. First was the application to biotechnology of a new approach to cultivating new fields of technological inquiry: "technology fusion" (*gijutsu yugo*).[80] This occurs when different types of technology, often originating in different industries, are combined into a hybrid technology to yield novel products. Commonly cited as examples are robotics (fusion of mechanical engineering and electronics) and liquid crystal displays (electronic, crystal, and optical technologies). Fusion involves a process Kodama calls "demand articulation," which takes place when users transmit wants and needs to producers; networks of relationships among companies in *keiretsu* and between contractors and subcontractors drive the process.

The "fusion" concept was not new. In biotechnology, fusion began in 1974 when a triangular pattern of demand emerged among food, drugs, and industrial chemicals makers. Food and drugs had been connected for decades through common use of fermentation technology; it was the opening of a channel to chemicals that turned old bioprocessing into new biotechnology. The process has been accelerated through the growth in number of cross-industry research associations that share information in the hope of achieving cross-fertilization (*igyoshu koryu*). According to a survey by Kodama, the ten research associations related to biotechnology and founded between 1964 and 1988 involved on average companies from 3.3 different industries. Most likely to be represented were firms from the food, chemical, and textile industries.[81]

Fusion took on a striking variety of forms. One example is the field of biosensors, which fuses semiconductor, molecular biology, and, occasionally, optical technology. A biosensor is a biochemical transducer that sends out an electrical signal when it comes into contact with a biologically active substance. Developed serendipitously when Isao Karube and his team of researchers at Tokyo University tried and failed to build an organic battery powered by glucose, biosensors now command a market of 35 billion yen, fifteen times the level of a decade ago.[82] Applications include monitoring of wastewater and detection of biological hazards in environments unsuitable for conventional instrumentation. More recently, tiny enzyme sensors have been developed to measure concentrations of organic acids and sugars in the human body. Among products that have been commercialized in this category are various physiological sensors installed in toilets popular among Japanese consumers. Another example was the "wristwatch fatigue sensor" in which a tiny sensor mounted on a wristwatch would provide continuous measurement of the concentration of lactic acid in body sweat.[83]

Another example of technology fusion is in the area of "nutriceuticals," a hybrid of food and pharmaceutical technologies. Building on accumulated expertise in fine chemicals and food-processing, companies such as Hayashibara, Suntory, Meiji Seika, and Taiyo Kagaku, began experimenting with nutriceuticals in the early 1990s, using genetic engineering to boost nutritional value, while lowering caloric content.[84] Targeted products include wheat bran and corn fiber, dextrin, and erythritol, a low-calorie sweetener used in various chocolates and sweets in Japan. Another new market was "physiologically functional foods," whose introduction had just then received approval from the Ministry of Health and Welfare. These included Morinaga Dairy's low-phosphate milk intended for patients with chronic kidney disorders and a bioengineered rice designed by Shiseido, a large cosmetics firm; the rice was said to employ a special enzyme that deactivates an allergen responsible for severe skin lesions on thousands of Japanese afflicted with rice allergy.[85] That Shiseido's primary field is cosmetics exemplifies the extent to which firms use biotechnology to create hybrid technological trajectories. Such a phenomenon, to my knowledge, has not yet been seen in the US.

The second trend to emerge in this period was the rapid growth in number of strategic alliances between Japanese and foreign firms, followed by an equally rapid retreat. Like large American firms, large firms in Japan have pursued strategic alliances as a means of accessing new products and technologies, especially from the US. And several American DBCs sought Japanese partners both as a source of capital and as means of penetrating markets in Japan and East Asia. Between 1981 and 1986, Biogen entered into nine agreements with Japanese firms, including Fujisawa, Meiji Seika, Shionogi, and Yamanouchi. Genentech linked seven deals with Japanese companies during this period.[86] Although a wide variety of linkages has been employed, the predominant strategy reflects prevailing technological and institutional capabilities and needs at a given point in time. In the early 1980s, licensing agreements proliferated as Japanese companies rushed to acquire new products and technology from American companies and, in some cases, universities.[87] Later in the decade, marketing agreements and joint product development supplanted licensing as the most popular strategy.

Perhaps the most successful and enduring of all Japanese–US corporate biotechnology partnerships was the one Amgen struck with Kirin, a large Japanese brewer. A relative late-starter in the biotechnology field, Kirin tied its fate to a joint-venture corporation it set up with Amgen to jointly develop erythropoietin (EPO) in 1984. Amgen, which had cloned EPO, supplied the science and production know-how; Kirin contributed its roller-bottle fermentation technology and a fistful of capital. The result was biotechnology's first blockbuster drug, turning both companies into the premier biotechnology firms in their respective countries. More recently, the companies pooled their expertise to develop G-CSF, a colony-stimulating factor used in cancer treatment as an adjunct to chemotherapy; it now trails only EPO in sales of biotechnology-based drugs.[88]

By 1991, Japanese companies had negotiated at least 282 alliances with American biotechnology companies and twenty-seven tie-ups with large American companies active in biotechnology.[89] Interestingly, an examination of 231 of the former found eleven cases of technology transfer from Japan to the US and only eight cases of two-way technology flow. Perhaps for these reasons, American firms tend to prefer partnering with each other or with European firms: according to a survey done in 1992, in only 13 percent of worldwide alliances involving an American DBC was the DBC paired with a Japanese partner.[90] An exception has been in the field of genomics; Japanese pharmaceutical firms have moved aggressively in the past decade to form multilateral partnerships in which they share genome data and related information. Dai-ichi, Yamanouchi, Kyowa Hakko, and Eisai have formed one team; a third group composed of Fujisawa, Shionogi, Mitsubishi Tokyo Seiyaku, Dai-ichi, Tanabe, Yamanouchi, Chugai, and Mitsui enters into tie-ups with venture businesses.[91] Over the past decade, however, Japanese partnerships have come to be a far smaller proportion of total alliances than they were in the 1980s. According to the Maastricht Economic Research Institute data reported by the National Science Foundation, the peak years for strategic alliances involving at least one Japanese firm were 1985 through 1987; roughly half of those involved an American partner (Figure 5.1). Two points should be noted. First, Japanese firms during the more recent upswing in the cycle show less tendency to partner with each other than they did in the mid 1980s. Second, Japanese firms in recent years have shown a greater tendency to partner with European firms than they did in the earlier period.

Japanese firms also sought to compensate for weaknesses in infrastructure for basic research by tapping into the intellectual resources of American universities and research institutes. Shiseido made waves in 1989 when it pledged $85 million to Massachusetts General Hospital and Harvard University to support basic research in dermatology.[92] At the same time, Kirin set up a non-profit research center, the La Jolla Institute for Allergy and Immunology, in close proximity to the University of California, San Diego. And Hitachi Chemical built a 20 million dollar research center in the

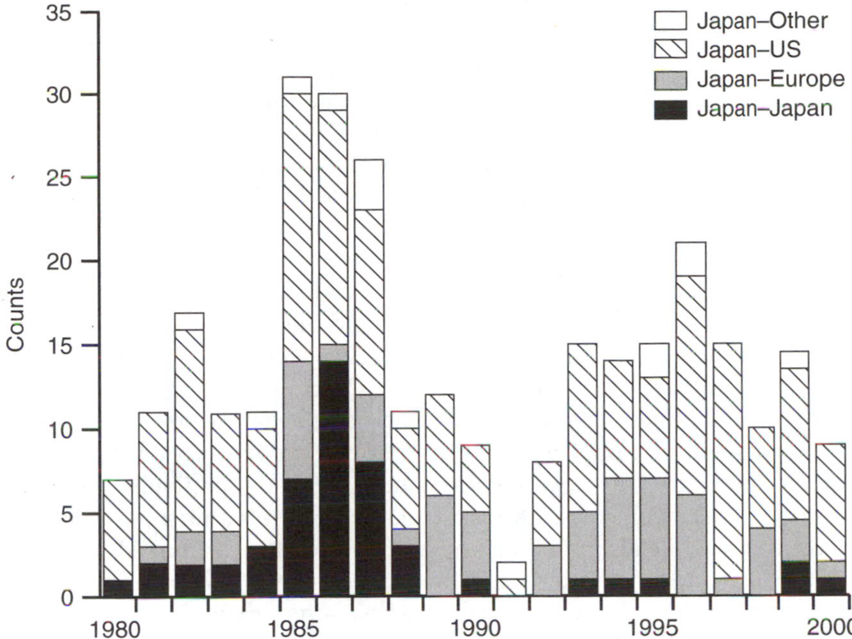

Figure 5.1 Strategic alliances in biotechnology involving at least one Japanese firm

Source: National Science Board, *Science and Engineering Indicators, 2002*, Appendix Table 4–39.

same building as the biochemistry department at the University of California, Irvine.[93] Together with expanded corporate tie-ups, these investments drew widespread criticism that American biotechnology was heading down the same road as the electronics industry a generation earlier. Such fears proved unfounded. Japan's investment in American basic research appears to have generated few returns.[94] Furthermore, according to one study, European firms represented more of a cause for concern than did Japanese firms, as the latter had only about a tenth the number of collaborations with American firms as the former had.[95]

Changes in public policies

In the late 1980s, the emphasis of government policies evinced a discernible shift. A general awareness that the country had gained little ground on the US, the emergence of new "quality of life" issues, and a subtle change in the private sector's perception of its relationship with government had altered societal expectations of government policies. By 1985, funding of the biotechnology portion of MITI's Next Generation Project had peaked and soon began dropping steadily, largely because of the dearth of commercial success.[96] Funding for superconductivity and new materials, which had come to bask in the glow once enjoyed by biotechnology, crowded out the latter in the competition for funds. Changing priorities were reflected in MITI's new comprehensive "vision" for the industry. Issued within three years of Keidanren report, and apparently incorporating many of its recommendations, it called for consolidating biotechnology infrastructure, revitalizing regional industry, integrating biotechnology with downstream "user" industries, and increasing participation in international projects.[97] In short, the report was a recognition that government policies were out of step with the requirements of the technological regime.

The nature of the technological regime and the new policy environment challenged the government to develop novel concepts and mechanisms for stimulating the creation and diffusion of generic knowledge. In addition, MITI began looking to biotechnology to provide solutions to environmental problems such as global warming and extracting resources from marine aquatic systems.[98] These were entirely new demands that called for novel approaches that would assist firms and organizations within a bureaucracy's constituency while also fulfilling important societal needs. For MITI, as the 1990s wore on, its programs and funding requests had increasingly to be justified in terms of broad social benefits rather than simply achieving narrow industrial policy goals.

The Japan Key Technology Center (JKTC) was a completely new type of research consortium that appears to overcome many of the problems associated with conventional research associations. In particular, two problems needed to be resolved: funds had to be found outside traditional budgetary channels, and participating firms needed authority to initiate projects and negotiate terms of participation and division of patent rights. It was precisely these problems that led by this time to widespread dissatisfaction with the RA concept in general. The Key Technology Center was established jointly by MITI and the Ministry of Posts and Telecommunications in 1985, using funds released from the partial privatization of NTT.[99] Under its capital investment program, two or more companies could form a joint-stock company for the purpose of conducting research that neither firm would be inclined to undertake individually. JKTC funded up to 70 percent of the capital of the project for up to seven years. Several companies related to biotechnology have been established under JKTC, the first of which was the Protein Engineering Research Institute (PERI). PERI was established in 1985 as a ten-year program to study the folding properties of proteins. Supported by a core of five companies, it established its permanent headquarters near Osaka University; researchers drawn from both academia and the corporate sponsors worked together in a collaborative setting. JKTC and its corporate sponsors provided 17 billion yen in funding over the ten-year life of the center.[100] PERI was succeeded in 1995 by the Biomolecular Engineering Research Institute (BERI), whose mission extends beyond proteins to encompass the full range of biological molecules; it has since then become a magnet for researchers worldwide in the important new field of protein engineering.[101] Its corporate partners include eighteen of Japan's most distinguished drug and food companies, including one European company.

PERI had been widely acclaimed as a new model of basic research that brought together researchers from university and corporate laboratories in a well-appointed research setting. Its researchers managed to publish nine papers in the British journal *Nature* over a ten-year period, an impressive achievement by any standard.[102] Coleman, however, reports some division between corporate and academic researchers in their manner of recruitment and degree status – corporate researchers tend to hold the MS, while academic researchers hold the PhD. PERI also suffered from a problem endemic to academic institutions in Japan: recruitment by personal connections rather than through competitive interviews.[103] The WTEC Panel Report also expresses concern over the emphasis on patents and licensing income as measures of economic and commercial impact.[104] Alas, the JKTC, PERI's parent, had its fate sealed in the current round of administrative reform, being one of eighteen public entities targeted for elimination by Prime Minister Koizumi in 2001.[105] On 12 May 2003, the JKTC was officially disbanded, with a reported cumulative loss of more than 276 trillion yen, or more than 96 percent of the total amount invested. Of the 4,417 patents the center had acquired, only 1,753 had been sold, "with most of them selling only at low prices."[106]

For all its faults, the JKTC proved a popular model for other ministries to follow. Not long after its establishment, both the Ministry of Health and Welfare and Ministry of Agriculture, Forestry, and Fisheries set up similar organizations. MHW's Adverse Drug Sufferings Relief and Promotion Fund spawned joint-stock companies in the fields of biosensors, drug-delivery systems, and human diagnostics. MAFF's Bio-Oriented Technology Research Advancement Institution (BRAIN), founded in 1986, funds research centers in plant and animal breeding, aquaculture, and environmental resources.

Public policies impacting on biotechnology also changed during this period. By the mid 1980s, interest groups that had pressed government into action five years earlier were once again calling for something to be done about the country's failure to catch up. This time the demand was for greater spending on basic research to put the Japanese innovation system on a more equal footing with those of the United States and Europe. Among the more strident voices was that of Keidanren, which had issued a special report on biotechnology in February 1985.[107] Echoing criticisms made elsewhere, the report singled out deteriorating conditions in university and national laboratories, and it urged that these institutions fulfill their role in promoting basic R&D, cultivating human resources, and strengthening the diffusion of information. Most importantly, it stressed that there were clear limits to what industry alone could achieve. The government could contribute most effectively, it suggested, through provision of tax and financial incentives, a unified regulatory structure, improved mechanisms of personnel exchange, and more effective regional policies. Interestingly, MITI's new vision for biotechnology, released in 1988, echoed many of these recommendations.

To some extent, the thrust of science and technology policy had already begun to change. Since the early 1980s, the Science and Technology Agency had been leading the charge toward greater levels of spending on basic research and a higher profile for science in the national budget. The efforts bore fruit in the life sciences, which experienced double-digit increases in government R&D funding in four of eight years since 1986. Expenditures by nine ministries on biotechnology reached 170 billion yen in 1994. Among the most active areas was genome research, in which human, dog, and rice genome projects drew 5 billion yen, up 24 percent over the figure for 1993. But here, Japan's government faced criticism not only from within Japan but also from without. At an international conference on international cooperation on the Human Genome Project in June 1989, James Watson, head of the genome project in the US, confronted the Japanese delegate, warning him that Japan risked being shut out of the project if it could not come up with an amount of funding befitting the nation's economic clout.[108] Alert to Watson's influence, scientists in Japan used the incident as *gaiatsu* (pressure applied from outside the country) to try to wrest more funding from the Ministry of Finance. Not only were the Education and Health Ministries lobbying hard for genome funding in 1990 and 1991, MITI also saw the project as an opportunity for electronics and machinery companies under its jurisdiction. Neither the country's finances, nor the disagreement among the project's supporters over the rationale for Japan's participation in the project, favored generous amounts of funding at that time. The result was emblematic of the politics behind Japan's science policy. As Cook-Deegan called it:

> Policies in the United States and Japan were, in many respects, drifting in opposite directions. In the United States, a relatively small number of administrators in science agencies successfully launched the genome project. In Japan, the ministries vied for dominance without the same pressure for cooperation faced by the DOE and NIH in the United States. The resulting effort was more atomized.[109]

Not until the end of the decade with the implementation of the Millennium Project would the government have in place a strategy for cross-ministry coordination in the planning of biotechnology policies (see Chapter 3).

Conclusions

Technological development is by nature a path-dependent process. The dynamic pattern of innovation and commercial development of Japanese biotechnology cannot be understood apart from its historical and institutional roots. The findings here are thus in agreement with conclusions reached by Landau and Rosenberg in their study of the chemical industry and Samuels in his study of Japan's defense industry.[110]

As argued above, by the time the techniques of genetic engineering and cell fusion became widely available, the only companies capable of responding were locked into a set of technological trajectories oriented around industrial fermentation and bioreactor technology. Drug firms, burdened by a centrally administered pricing system and heavily dependent on imported foreign technology, were unable to set the pace. The immobility of researchers across sectors, lack of venture capital, and proscriptions on research using genetically engineered organisms ruled out the creation of new forms of enterprise like the American DBC. Firms thus faced a narrow range of options in attempting to catch up with the US. The important point, however, is that all these factors derive from the particular historical experiences of institutions that comprise a national system of innovation.

Once the transformative power of the new techniques became clear, the government, under relentless pressure from researchers and firms, eased regulations; bureaucrats cobbled together programs to spur market entry and rally firms to catch up with sprinting American DBCs. Through the middle 1980s, firms from diverse industries, often participating in or following the leads of research associations sponsored by the government, fused the new techniques into existing product lines, then bombarded markets with a variety of new products. Again, the possibilities open to innovators were largely set by national institutional factors – in this case, the industrial policy-making process, regulatory regimes in drug pricing and research, and national developmental goals stressing importation and indiginization of foreign technology.

The dynamic pattern of innovation and commercial development of Japanese biotechnology reflects the interaction of national conditions and specific demands of the technological regime. Unlike the US, Japan had little experience in basic research related to molecular biology, human genetics, and biomedicine. Weaknesses in the academic research system and general emphasis on applied research elsewhere in the national system meant that firms had little in the way of a relevant knowledge base in the surrounding institutional environment. Strict controls on formal interaction of academic researchers with industry, along with a general tendency for researchers to remain in the same institution for the duration of their careers, aggravated the problem by effectively freezing knowledge resources at their point of origin. Even if Japan had the equivalent of America's NIH or Fred Hutchinson Cancer Research Center, the absence of a true venture capital market and enormous barriers to entry of new firms would have precluded emergence of American-style DBCs. In addition, competitive weaknesses in the pharmaceutical and chemical industries reduced the potential for productive knowledge spillover that might have neutralized deficiencies in basic research elsewhere in the system. Finally, the government's delay in permitting experiments using recombinant DNA, and subsequent slowness in relaxing the regulatory regime, further deterred innovative activity.

The delay in easing regulations produced a classic case of market failure. While scores of American firms were being formed, most Japanese companies watched from the sidelines. Only after MITI targeted the industry and organized the first research association did market entry begin in earnest. Although cause and effect cannot be established with certainty, that private resources began pouring into the industry after MITI's initiation of biotechnology policy is certainly suggestive of the *hata buri*, or flag-waving, role so often associated with the historical development of other high technology industries. As subsequent events bear out, however, government policies alone could do little to erase an American lead that was decades in the making.

What government policy did do, however, was to catalyze a process of path-dependent learning through which firms gradually capitalized on their own rich stocks of technological and institutional resources, in addition to those available in their immediate external environments. This explains the pattern of innovation that unfolded after the middle 1980s. By licensing innovative products developed in the US, while at the same time using the new techniques to make novel consumer and industrial products, Japanese firms enjoyed the best of both worlds. No characteristic is more distinctive in this approach than "technology fusion." Through fusion, firms have "tamed" genetic technologies by linking them to technologies in which they enjoyed competitive advantage: today, such talks of fusion center on nanotechnology and biotechnology. This process might be likened to the technique of genetic engineering itself: firms have spliced the "gene" associated with genetic engineering knowledge into their own institutional "genome," yielding a hybrid with superior innovative capabilities.

6 Conclusions

Summary

Patterns of technological innovation within a country depend on the distribution and accessibility of capabilities across the national system of innovation. A new technological trajectory opens up when demand conditions align with institutional capabilities and organizational resources available within the innovation system. The direction of the trajectory of innovation depends on the pattern of scientific and institutional capabilities, factor endowments, market structure, and the nature of demand. Firms are most likely to exhibit movement along a trajectory when the pull of demand reinforces the push of institutional capabilities and scientific resources searching for opportunities to bring new technologies to the market. The distance moved depends on the extent to which the endowment of institutions, knowledge, and other resources within the national innovation system (NIS) can solve the problems and mitigate the uncertainties corresponding to the technological regime. For biotechnology, these problems and uncertainties center on the breadth of the technology's application across the economy and strong dependence on basic research, as well as the challenges it poses for existing regulatory institutions.

In the US, commercialization of biotechnology began in the mid 1970s, soon after the basic techniques of recombinant DNA and cell fusion had emerged from the laboratory. A new industry of small, specialized companies sprang up to translate these novel laboratory techniques into new products and processes. The pace of innovation was fast, the technological trajectory skewed heavily toward pharmaceuticals. Driving it was a combination of supply and demand conditions unique to the US innovation system. These included on the supply side an abundance of basic knowledge that was the cumulative result of decades of generous public funding of academic research in molecular biology and medicine. Intellectual property protection and technology transfer regimes channeled this knowledge into the market, where highly mobile scientists and entrepreneurs, supported by a large venture capital industry, shouldered the burdens of founding and growing companies around it. Flexible regulatory institutions and market structure conducive to the formation of diverse forms of inter-firm alliances kept risk at manageable levels and reduced transaction costs associated with moving products from laboratory to market. On the demand side, consumer spending on health care products rocketed in the 1980s and 1990s. At the same time, public policy eschewed price controls on drugs and other health care products. Consequently, high rents were available to firms applying biotechnology to the development of new drug and diagnostic products, inducing market entry but concentrating commercial development in the pharmaceutical sector.

In Japan, commercialization of biotechnology not only began later than in the US but took on a substantially different character. Large chemical and food companies led the way; few dedicated biotechnology companies appeared until the latter half of the 1990s, when the venture capital market matured and regulations restricting the entrepreneurial activities of academic scientists were eased. The pace of innovation was moderate, though broadly based, the technological trajectory less skewed toward pharmaceutical applications. Driving it was a combination of supply and demand conditions quite unlike those of the US. On the supply side, comparatively modest levels of public funding and an academic culture that discouraged risk-taking conspired to limit the potential of the domestic science base to power innovation in biotechnology, though care should be taken not to exaggerate this weakness. More damaging has been the absence of a technology transfer regime to bring market forces to bear on the knowledge stocks that have lain dormant in universities and research institutes. As a result, firms have been heavily dependent on their own internal R&D or on knowledge obtained from abroad, often through alliances with American and European firms. Although industrial policies encouraged established firms to enter the field, no fewer than five ministries have claimed jurisdiction over biotechnology, leading to a patchwork of programs with little coordination among them. On the demand side, a rapidly aging population and high per capita consumption of drugs ensured a large and growing domestic market for pharmaceuticals. However, government regulation of drug prices kept a lid on profits, limiting the appeal of pharmaceuticals as an early target for commercial development. As a result, the technological trajectory in Japan was less skewed toward pharmaceuticals than it was in the US.

Explaining the pattern of innovation requires more than understanding the institutional structure of the national system. More important is the degree to which those institutions solve the distinctive problems embedded in the particular technology. In other words, the study suggests the possibility of specifying *a priori* a set of institutional arrangements that lead to successful innovation along a given technological trajectory. To permit such determination, I proposed the "technological regime" as the conceptual variable that distinguishes one technological system from another. The assumption behind this concept is that technologies have certain inevitabilities whose manifestations are independent of micro- or macro-level factors. To put it another way, technologies have paradigmatic qualities associated with the types of problems that have to be solved, routines that need to be mastered, nooks and crannies into which light has to be shined. In this way, new knowledge – or new ways of looking at old knowledge – heralds new technology, which in turn offers a set of potential "natural" trajectories for commercial development. Which trajectories are pursued and the extent to which they generate real economic returns depend on the set of institutions orchestrating the innovative response.

I argued that the tacitness of knowledge underpinning the technology and its pervasiveness of application fix the properties of the technological regime. Stylizing the variable as such draws attention to the type of learning employed in mastering the technology and the potential penetration of the technology across existing industries. Along these two dimensions, biotechnology is characterized first by low tacitness of learning, which results from the fact that innovation flows largely out of breakthroughs from basic scientific research. Second, biotechnology is pervasive in the sense that the techniques of genetic engineering and cell fusion have potential application in a broad range of existing industries. This maximizes the chances that firms will experience real economic returns by pursuing options along any given technological trajectory. Finally, the combination of high pervasiveness and low tacitness of learning produces high uncertainty, raising barriers to entry to unusually high levels.

In short, the properties of the technological regime suggest that for firms to "get it right" in terms of innovating requires bringing to bear appropriate capabilities and resources that reside within the national system. Happily for biotechnology, the broad range of potential natural trajectories gives innovating firms lots of possibilities for hedging their bets. This explains why Japanese and American firms have successfully exploited biotechnology in widely differing ways. On the other hand, low tacitness of learning gives the edge in the innovation race to firms that have their own sophisticated research organizations and which have easy access to research sources elsewhere in the national system. On this point, Japan lags the US, which is evident from the fact that the US clearly leads in cutting-edge applications of biotechnology in the pharmaceutical and agricultural sectors. Finally, for firms to get it right requires an abundance of resources for dealing with high uncertainty. Here, fluid capital markets and diverse sources of private capital give the United States the edge. Yet Japanese firms compensate through accessing inter-firm networks and other means of partial integration unavailable to firms in the US.

Biotechnology in the US and Japan

Proximity to the world's premier biomedical research institutions gave American firms a crucial head start in opening new technological trajectories. However, Japan's ability to deploy fusion strategies in fields largely ignored in the US, while employing the usual catch-up mechanisms in fields targeted by American firms, has kept it in the race. These differences, as noted above, stem from variation across the national systems of innovation. Tables 6.1 and 6.2 summarize the major sources of variation discussed in Chapters 3–5.

In the United States, large firms moved quickly to capitalize on the new technology. Chemical companies tested the waters, searching out biochemical pathways around conventional petroleum feedstock for producing bulk chemicals. Pharmaceutical companies were next, seizing on the new techniques as a means of producing the next generation of drug products. The cautious and defensive nature of large firms' strategies, coupled with accumulating stocks of knowledge in search of application, left an opening for new entrants, thus opening the way for the DBC. Taking advantage of the mobility of academic scientists and a permissive legal climate surrounding

Table 6.1 Comparison of US and Japanese national innovation systems in biotechnology

	United States	*Japan*
Firms/industry structure	Forward-integrating DBC's; backward-integrating large firms	Forward- and backward-integrating medium and large firms
Related and supporting industries	Chemical and pharmaceutical industry strongly competitive domestically and globally	Chemical and pharmaceutical industry moderately competitive in domestic market; weak globally
Public research institutes	NIH as vanguard agency in life sciences; intramural and extramural R&D	No vanguard institute in life sciences; little or no extramural R&D
University research system	Very strong in health and life sciences; high levels of public funding; NIH dominant funder; low barriers to technology transfer and labor mobility	Spotty record of basic research in health sciences; funded through centralized education ministry; high barriers to technology transfer and labor mobility
Public policy – promotional	Strong in science, weak in technology; preference for mission-oriented research through extramural grant programs and financial incentives	Strong in technology, weak in science; preference for tax incentives, sponsored cooperative research, non-financial incentives
Public policy – regulatory	No mandated regulation of drug prices; global leader in easing regulations on recombinant drugs, tough elsewhere	Drug prices regulated; follows US on safety and product regulations but with lag, tough outside drugs

Table 6.2 Comparison of national innovation systems in the US and Japan with respect to the regime characteristics of biotechnology

	High pervasiveness	*High intensity of basic research*	*High uncertainty*
United States	– Innovation concentrated in health care sector; low opportunity conditions elsewhere	++ World-class public and academic R&D; DBCs; strong support industry in drugs and chemicals	+ Pluses are vigorous and diverse markets in private capital, flexible regulatory regime in health care; minuses are volatile and capricious capital markets, regulatory problems outside drugs
Japan	+ Fusion strategies employed in food, chemicals, fibers, electronics, and other industries	– Weak public and academic basic R&D; weak support industry in drugs and chemicals	– Pluses are inter-firm linkages lowering transaction costs; minuses are rigid, stifling regulatory system, drug price controls

industry–university relations, DBCs quickly filled the commercial void. They mediated between the push of academic science and pull of commercial opportunity from lucrative markets for new anti-cancer, anti-AIDS, and other therapeutic drugs.

As way-stations between basic research and the delivery and marketing of new products, DBCs brought virtually all biotechnology's first generation of products from concept to reality. Making and marketing them, however, required complementary assets in manufacturing, management and financing of clinical trials, and marketing, which most DBCs did not have. To access them, DBCs looked first to their large counterparts in the pharmaceutical industry, and more recently even to other DBCs. Large drug firms, conversely, sought out the resources of DBCs as a means of integrating backwards into R&D. The resulting marriage in the form of strategic alliances has become the engine driving the final stage of the innovation process – delivery of new products to the market.

Japan took a different tack. Barred from doing research that used recombinant organisms, Japanese researchers watched developments in the US largely as spectators. Spurred on by the pace of technological change in the US, researchers and industry leaders pressed the government to ease regulations. When it appeared that the US government would lock up the new techniques behind a wall of patents, in conjunction with the explosion of DBCs, the Japanese government acted. Through sponsoring research associations, MITI galvanized the private sector, stimulating market entry.

In contrast with the US, most entrants were large established companies. Many firms had a long history of working with microorganisms, having achieved global acclaim in the fields of fermentation and bioreactors.

Once firms had ramped up activities in biotechnology, government policies faded into the background. The government continued to support formation of research associations in areas targeted for their high social returns. The engine of innovation, nonetheless, shifted to the private sector, where it has remained. There have been two elements to the private sector's response. First, in cutting-edge applications where Japan's basic research has traditionally been weak, firms have sought to contract for the necessary knowledge from American firms. Second, in areas close to firms' existing markets and core expertise, firms have incorporated biotechnology as a means to accelerate product innovation, forging alliances with other firms when necessary. This so-called fusion approach, so named because it combines unrelated technologies in ways that yield new hybrid products, has to some degree been reinforced by the government, whose research associations often bring together firms from widely different industries. Because most early entrants into biotechnology hailed from sectors other than pharmaceuticals, the portfolio of new products looks strikingly different from that of the US.

In both countries, institutions supporting technological change have evolved in a path-dependent process from widely different points of origin. In the US, concentration of resources in basic science happened not by chance but as a result of key decisions made at the end of the Second World War concerning the centrality of science in the nation's economic development and national security. Those decisions vaulted the university to the forefront as the institution of choice for performing federally funded R&D, established human health care as the highest priority for basic research, and cemented the role of the research grant, allocated on the basis of peer review, as the primary vehicle for awarding federal funds. This new vision for science made possible the subsequent explosive expansion of the biomedical research enterprise, which in turn gave rise to the science of biotechnology.

In Japan, too, concentration of resources in technological development and commercialization reflects decisions made in the past concerning appropriate strategies of development in light of developmental goals and needs. For Japan, since the Meiji Era the focus of policy has been to catch up with the West economically and technologically. To do so required large investments in manufacturing, practical education, and research relevant to commercialization; there was little room for pie-in-the-sky, curiosity-driven R&D. Consequently, technological development has been primarily industry-led; government, mainly through its sponsorship of cooperative research, has played a largely supporting role.

In short, the American strategy somewhat parallels what Florida and Kenney more than a decade ago called the "breakthrough" approach to innovation.[1] This involves mobilizing a distinctive set of institutions – venture capital, high labor mobility, creative genius, high caliber research universities, and clusters of core knowledge and complementary assets in regions such as Silicon Valley. They go on to argue, however, that in the rush to turn out breakthroughs, the "follow-through" gets ignored; American firms invent but fail at translating invention into new products and hence bottom line. On this point, they were wrong. The technology transfer system put in place in the early 1980s has provided both legal protection for intellectual property and incentives for universities to license their inventions to industry. The DBC, moreover, has evolved into an institution specializing in following through on breakthroughs generated elsewhere in the system. Once its work is completed, the strategic alliance becomes the next stage in carrying the follow-through to its logical end point.

Japan, by contrast, most closely resembles what Fumio Kodama terms the "technology fusion" approach. This approach "blends incremental technical improvements from several previously separate fields of technology to create products that revolutionize markets."[2] It happens when market forces drive R&D rather than the other way around, firms capitalize on knowledge that is mostly outside the industry, and companies from many industries share cooperative R&D ties. In biotechnology, the fusion approach has permitted Japan to bring the weight of its strongest industries to bear on mastering the new technological regime. Although it has not compensated for the absence of basic research, it has proved a viable alternative to America's breakthrough approach in fields outside the biomedical sector.

Concluding thoughts

When I first began this research in the early 1990s, I was immediately struck by the differences in policy processes between Japan and the US as they related to biotechnology. My reading in graduate school prepared me for an encounter in Japan with a centralized, coherent policy framework; what I found instead was quite the opposite. In fact, it was the US that came across as the stronger, more centralized state, at least in this issue area. Well before the advent of commercial biotechnology, the US exerted the political leadership that elevated promotion of biomedical research – peer reviewed, science-driven research – as a cornerstone of national policy. In this sense, support for biotechnology came about by accident: it was the unintended consequence of America's postwar science policy. More recently, however, that policy has become more overtly commercial, especially in its promotion of technology transfer and licensing of patents on terms favorable to the private sector. When industrial policy can be cloaked as science policy, as has been the case in aerospace, energy, and defense, as well as in health sciences, the government's influence on technological trajectories will be strong in sectors where technological innovation is strongly science driven.

Likewise, for Japan the evidence calls for rethinking the government's role as a driving force of technological change. A collection of bickering ministries competing for funds and the prestige of winning the next big biotechnology project presents an image not too different from that of the US, or at least the conventional view of the US. If anything, government policies probably worsened Japan's competitive position through the middle 1980s; at the very least, strict regulatory policies delayed the onset of genetic engineering research in Japan until well after the US had established its lead. Nor did biotechnology policies even achieve the limited goal of restoring the health of Japan's ailing chemical industry. Policies framed in the grand context of technological catch-up simply did not work. On the other hand, policies having more narrowly defined goals, especially those centering on the use of research associations, exerted an important cumulative effect, namely that of encouraging market entry and catalyzing the private sector's independent pursuit of fusion strategies. More like the typical portrayal of the US government, however, Japanese government policies have been primarily reactive, *ad hoc*, and responsive to pressures from politically active groups.

In the future, progress in biotechnology will likely involve issues that played only a peripheral role in this story. The prospect of human cloning, the spread of genetically modified foods, questions over the moral standing of human embryos and genes, and widespread use of genetic testing pose troubling questions that will have to be debated in the public square. Few efforts were made to permit a wide-ranging discussion on the wisdom and safety of recombinant DNA; the few who chose to oppose it or advocated caution usually found themselves alone on the losing end of the debate. The controversy over genetically modified foods has been more intense, and differences in national responses more pronounced than was the case with recombinant DNA. Interestingly, though opposition to genetically modified food in Japan has been strong, far fewer concerns have been voiced about the use of left-over human IVF embryos as sources of stem cells. The opposite has been the case in the US. From a purely business point of view, a firm developing stem-cell-based therapies will likely find the going easier in Japan than in the US; conversely, a firm doing research on plants genetically modified to produce a drug will likely find a more supportive environment in the US. The point is that as the implications of the technology encroach more upon closely held moral and ethical principles, these principles, or at least their distribution across society, will need to be given more weight in our models of how nations respond to biotechnology.

A second problem peculiar to biotechnology is its effect on health care costs through its influence on drug pricing. In both countries health care costs have been increasing far faster than the rate of inflation. In 2001 Herceptin, Genentech's innovative monoclonal antibody-based drug for treating a type of metastatic breast cancer, went on the market in Japan for 80,879 yen ($670) per 150 milligrams. That would yield for the average patient receiving standard treatment a monthly cost of 200,000 yen ($1,700) per month. In ten years, sales of the drug could reach 7.73 billion yen each year. Rituxan, a monoclonal antibody approved for treating non-Hodgkins lymphoma, could see even higher annual sales, perhaps as high as 4 billion yen. Who will pay for these costly new drugs? Of course, the price of health care must be balanced against the added economic value that comes from treating or curing a disease. According to one scholarly study, curing cancer would add $47 trillion to the US GDP; reducing the death rate by 20 percent would add around $10 trillion.[3] But the point is that novelty generation and value creation in biotechnology is not necessarily an unalloyed good. When one considers, moreover, that significant amounts of tax dollars fund research that ultimately gives rise to new drugs, consumers end up paying twice for many drugs. The increase in costs raises an interesting question: could too much innovation in biotechnology actually be bad for social welfare?

Notes

1 Introduction

1 US Congress, Office of Technology Assessment, *Commercial Biotechnology: An International Assessment*, Washington, DC: Government Printing Office, 1984.

2 National Research Council, *US–Japan Technology Linkages in Biotechnology*, Washington, DC: National Academy Press, 1992, p. 51.

3 Kenichi Arai, *Tokyo genomu bei keikaku* [Tokyo Genome Bay Project], Tokyo: Kodansha, 2002, p. 36.

4 BT senryaku kaigi kiso iinkai [Drafting Committee of the Cabinet Council on Biotechnology Strategy], "Baiotekurunoroji-senryaku taiko (soan)" [Outline of a Strategy for Biotechnology (Draft)], 26 November 2002, p. 6.

5 Keizai sangyosho [Ministry of Economics, Trade, and Industry], *Waga kuni no baio sangyo o meguru jokyo ni tsuite* [Conditions in our Country's Bioindustry], 23 May 2002, p. 1.

6 Kosei rodosho [Ministry of Health, Labor, and Welfare], "'Seimei no seiki' o sasaeru iyakuhin sangyo no kokusai kyosoryoku kyoka ni mukete: iyakuhin sangyo bijion no gaiyo" [Strengthening the Competitiveness of the Pharmaceutical Industry to Support the "Century of Life": Outline of the Pharmaceutical Industry Vision], 30 August 2002, p. 3.

7 The number 334 comes from a recent survey of biotechnology venture firms conducted by the Japan Bioindustry Association. See Baioindasutori-kyokai, "Baiobencha-ni kansuru tokei" [Statistics Related to Biotechnology Venture Businesses], 11 June 2003, online, available HTTP: <http://www.jba.or.jp/bv/pr030611.pdf> (accessed 19 June 2003). Consultants Ernst & Young reckon that in 2001 there were 1,115 private biotechnology firms in the US and 1,775 in Europe.

8 These figures come from the Prime Minister's Cabinet Council on Biotechnology Strategy. See note 4.

9 The scientific community was especially stung by President Clinton's omission of Japan in a speech he made in June 2001 announcing the impending completion of the Human Genome Project. Although the speech omitted Japan, it acknowledged the contributions of the UK, Germany, France, and China to the project's completion. "Research Requires National Strategy," *Nikkei Weekly*, 19 March 2001.

10 R. Triendl, "Large-Scale Projects See Increased Spending in Japan's Budget," *Nature Biotechnology*, March 2003, p. 218.

11 "Alleged Biotech Espionage Rocks Japan," *The Lancet*, 20 June 2001, vol. 357, p. 2111.

12 "Idenshi supai jiken de shintenkai" [New Developments in Gene Spy Case], *Nikkei Baiobijinesu*, January 2003, p. 23; "Espionage Charges Threaten to Undermine Research Relations," *Nature*, 17 May 2001, pp. 225–6.

13 "Scientists Jailed for Alleged Theft from Harvard Laboratory," *Nature*, 27 June 2002, p. 886.

14 "'Tokkyo arasoi' no kanetsu ga haikei ni" [Overheating of Patent Wars in the Background], *Nihon Keizai Shimbun*, 19 July 2002.

15 "Shinyaku supai, bei piripiri" [America Stung by New Drug Spy], *Yomiuri Shimbun*, 21 June 2002; "Chiteki zaisan hogo: Nihon okureru hoseibi" [Protecting Intellectual Property: Japan Lags in Revising Law], *Yomiuri Shimbun*, 21 June 2002.

16 "Mapping the Human Genome: Patent Setbacks Hamper Japan in Life Sciences," *Daily Yomiuri*, 7 August 2000, p. 1.

17 R.J. Samuels, *Rich Nation, Strong Army: National Security and the Technological Transformation of Japan*, Ithaca, NY: Cornell University Press, 1994.

18 "Keizai sangyosho, Seibutsu kagaku sangyoka, Baiotekunoroji-senryaku taiko no torimatome ni tsuite" [Regarding the Outline on Biotechnology Strategy], April 2003, p. 8, online, available HTTP: <http://www.meti.go.jp/policy/bio/BT%taikou/BT%Presentation-04.pdf> (accessed 26 April 2003).

19 "The Power of Knowledge," *Financial Times*, 16 April 2003, Survey, p. 2.

20 "Starting to Grow a Culture of Consolidation: The Biotechnology Industry," *Financial Times*, 9 April 2003, Survey, p. 4.

21 "Biotechs Hold their own in Shifting Industry," *Nature Biotechnology*, November 2002, p. 1066.

22 "States, Insurers Find Prescriptions for High Drug Costs," *Wall Street Journal*, 11 September 2002, p. A1; "Where the Money Is," *The Economist*, 26 April 2003, p. 53.

23 Ernst & Young, "Global Biotechnology at a Glance," online, available HTTP: <http://www.ey.com/global/download.nsf/International/Biotechnology_at_a_Glance/$file/Biotechataglance_2002.pdf> (accessed 16 May 2003).

24 Representative works are M. Anchordoguy, *Computers Inc.*, Cambridge, MA: Council on East Asian Studies, 1989; S. Casper, "Institutional Adaptiveness, Technology Policy, and the Diffusion of New Business Models: The Case of German Biotechnology," *Organization Studies*, 2000, vol. 21, 887–914; H. Ergas, "Does Technology Policy Matter?" in B. Guile and H. Brooks (eds) *Technology and Global Industry: Companies and Nations in the World Economy*, Washington, DC: National Academy Press, 1987; P.A. Hall and D. Soskice (eds) *Varieties of Capitalism: The Institutional Foundations of Comparative Advantage*, New York: Oxford University Press, 2001; J.R. Hollingsworth, W.S. Schmitter, and W. Streeck (eds) *Governing Capitalist Economies*, New York: Oxford University Press, 1994.

25 B. Achilladelis and N. Antonakis, "The Dynamics of Technological Innovation: The Case of the Pharmaceutical Industry," *Research Policy*, 2001, vol. 30, 535–88; M. Kenney, *Biotechnology: The University–Industrial Complex*, New Haven, CN: Yale University Press, 1986; L.H. Lynn, N.M. Reddy, and J.D. Aram, "Linking Technology and Institutions: The Innovation Community Framework," *Research Policy*, 1996, vol. 25, 91–106; M.D. McKelvey, *Evolutionary Innovations: The Business of Biotechnology*, New York: Oxford University Press, 1996; W. Powell, "Learning from Collaboration: Knowledge and Networks in the Biotechnology and Pharmaceutical Industries," *California Management Review*, 1998, vol. 40, 228–40; and D. Teece (ed.) *The Competitive Challenge*, Cambridge, MA: Ballinger, 1987.

26 H. Gottweis, *Governing Molecules: The Discursive Politics of Genetic Engineering in Europe and the United States*, Cambridge, MA: MIT Press,

1998; S. Wright, *Molecular Politics: Developing American and British Regulatory Policy for Genetic Engineering, 1972–1982*, Chicago: University of Chicago Press, 1994.

27 S. Coleman, *Japanese Science: From the Inside*, London: Routledge, 1999; P. Rabinow, *Making PCR: A Story of Biotechnology*, Reprint Edition, Chicago: University of Chicago Press, 1997.

28 S. Bartholomew, "National Systems of Biotechnology Innovation: Complex Interdependence in the Global System," *Journal of International Business Studies*, 1997, vol. 28, 241–66; R.R. Nelson (ed.) *National Innovation Systems: A Comparative Analysis*, New York: Oxford University Press, 1993; M. Porter, *The Competitive Advantage of Nations*, New York: Free Press, 1990; R. Samuels, *Rich Nation, Strong Army.*

29 C. Edquist "Systems of Innovation Approaches – Their Emergence and Character-istics," in C. Edquist (ed.) *Systems of Innovation: Technologies, Institutions, and Organizations*, London: Pinter, 1997; C. Freeman, "The 'National System of Innovation' in Historical Perspective," *Cambridge Journal of Economics*, 1995, vol. 19, 5–24; R.R. Nelson (ed.) *National Innovation Systems*.

30 B. Steil, D.G. Victor, and R.R. Nelson, "Introduction and Overview," in B. Steil, D.G. Victor, and R.R. Nelson (eds) *Technological Innovation and Economic Performance*, Princeton: Princeton University Press, 2002.

31 For a rare comparative analysis of Japan's globally competitive and uncompetitive industries, see M.E. Porter, H. Takeuchi, and M. Sakakibara, *Can Japan Compete?* Cambridge, MA: Perseus Publishing, 2000; and H. Itami, *Nihon sangyo mitsu no nami* [Japanese Industry: Three Waves], Tokyo: NTT Shuppansha, 1998.

32 E. Mansfield, "Industrial R&D in Japan and the United States," *American Economic Review*, 1988, vol. 78, 223–8.

33 R. Rosenbloom and M. Cusumano, "Technological Pioneering and Competitive Advantage: The Birth of the VCR Industry," *California Management Review*, 1987, vol. 4, 51–75.

34 Anchordoguy, *Computers, Inc.*; and C. Johnson, *MITI and the Japanese Miracle: The Growth of Industrial Policy, 1925–1975*, Stanford, CA: Stanford University Press, 1982. The point is not that these earlier studies were flawed; they remain seminal works on Japanese high technology policy and general industrial policy, respectively. Rather they portray the actions and effectiveness of the bureaucracy in different sectors and at different times in history. The field of Japanese political economy still awaits scholarship that convincingly explains how the bureaucracy can appear unified, competent, and coherent in its actions under one set of circumstances but divided, confused, and incoherent under other circumstances.

35 D.I. Okimoto, *Between MITI and the Market: Japanese Industrial Policy for High Technology*, Stanford, CA: Stanford University Press, 1989, p. 226.

36 S. Callon, *Divided Sun: MITI and the Breakdown of Japanese High-Tech Industrial Policy, 1975–1993*, Stanford, CA: Stanford University Press, 1995, p. 186.

37 L. Thurow, *Head to Head: The Coming Economic Battle Among Japan, Europe, and America*, New York: Morrow, 1992; J. Zysman, *Governments, Markets, and Growth: Financial Systems and the Politics of Industrial Change*, Ithaca, NY: Cornell University Press, 1983.

38 S. Coleman, *Japanese Science*.

39 S. Wright, *Molecular Politics*.

40 D.S. Greenberg, *Science, Money, and Politics: Political Triumph and Ethical Erosion*, Chicago: University of Chicago Press, 2001.

41 "Biotechnology: A Collection of Technologies," Biotechnology Industry Organization, online, available HTTP:<http://www.bio.org/er/technology_collection.asp> (accessed 27 June 2003).

42 Also important was the research that led to an understanding of protein synthesis, the role of proteins in disease, and the role of enzymes as regulators of biochemical processes. Biochemists performed much of this research, though their role has often been overshadowed by that of molecular biologists. Especially crucial here were the contributions of Linus Pauling, much of whose research was funded by the Rockefeller Foundation. See M. Morange, *A History of Molecular Biology* (Cambridge, MA: Harvard University Press, 1998), ch. 12.

43 Data presented in this paragraph come from the website of the Biotechnology Industry Association and are current as of June 2003, online, available HTTP: <http://www.bio.org/er/statistics.asp> (last accessed 28 June 2003).

44 "Baio kanren shijo wa 1 cho 3000 oku en toppa" [Biotechnology and Related Markets Break through 1.3 billion Yen], *Nikkei Baiobijinesu*, March 2002, 50–4.

45 "2005 nen made wa 10% seicho tsuzuku" [10 Percent Growth to Continue through 2005], *Nikkei Baiobijinesu*, June 2002, 46–51.

2 Firms, technological regimes, and national innovation systems

1 The state, of course, may participate in the process, or even direct it, especially in industries closely connected to national security, such as telecommunications, aircraft, and defense, but also in sectors broadly related to national welfare, such as health care and transportation.

2 P.A. Geroski, "Vertical Relations between Firms and Industrial Policy," *The Economic Journal*, 1992, vol. 102 (January), 138–47; and D. Teece, "Strategies for Capturing the Financial Benefits of Technological Innovation," in N. Rosenberg *et al.* (eds) *Technology and the Wealth of Nations*, Stanford: Stanford University Press, 1992.

3 This conception of path dependence derives from North, who applied it to institutional change, and Arthur, who applied it to technological change. B.W. Arthur, "Self-Reinforcing Mechanisms in Economics," in K. Arrow and D. Pines (eds) *The Economy as an Evolving Complex System*, Reading, MA: Addison-Wesley, 1988; D. North, *Institutions, Institutional Change, and Economic Performance*, Cambridge: Cambridge University Press, 1990. For another classic expression of the often profound impacts of path dependence and lock-in, see P.A. David, "Clio and the Economics of QWERTY," *American Economic Review*, 1985, vol. 76, 332–7.

4 W.J. Baumol, *The Free-Market Innovation Machine*, Princeton: Princeton University Press, 2001, ch. 1; V.W. Ruttan, *Technology, Growth, and Development*, New York: Oxford University Press, 2001, ch. 2.

5 Paul Romer was among the first economists explicitly to model the influence of knowledge accumulation as an endogenous source of economic growth. See the discussion in Baumol, *Free-Market Innovation Machine*, pp. 263–7; and Ruttan, *Technology, Growth, and Development*, pp. 25–9.

6 I. Nonaka, N. Konno, and R. Toyama, "Emergence of 'Ba'," in I. Nonaka and T. Nishiguchi (eds) *Knowledge Emergence: Social, Technical, and Evolutionary Dimensions of Knowledge Creation*, New York: Oxford University Press, 2001.

7 This is in part because different mixtures of knowledge types typically correspond to different organizational forms, four of which are identified by Lam. See A. Lam, "Tacit Knowledge, Organizational Learning and Societal Institutions: An Integrated Framework," *Organization Studies*, 2000, vol. 21, 487–513.

8 Ibid. See also A.K. Klevorick *et al.*, "On the Sources and Significances of Interindustry Differences in Technological Opportunities," *Research Policy*, 1995, vol. 24, 185–205.

9 R. Nelson and S. Winter, "In Search of a Useful Theory of Innovation," *Research Policy*, 1977, vol. 6, 36–76.

10 Ibid.

11 G. Dosi, "The Nature of the Innovative Process," in Dosi *et al.* (eds) *Technical Change and Economic Theory*, London: Pinter, 1988, p. 224.

12 Nelson and Winter explain technological regimes with reference to the emergence of large, piston-powered commercial aircraft in the 1930s. On microelectronics as a "new techno-economic paradigm," see C. Perez, "Microelectronics, Long Waves and World Structural Change: New Perspectives for Developing Countries," *World Development*, 1985, vol. 13, 441–63. Freeman, in a more nuanced interpretation, looks at change within an existing paradigm in C. Freeman, "Technical Innovation in the World Chemical Industry and Changes of Techno-Economic Paradigm," in C. Freeman and L. Soete (eds) *New Explorations in the Economics of Technical Change*, London: Pinter, 1990.

13 Dosi, "The Nature of the Innovative Process," p. 229.

14 Freeman, "Technical Innovation in the World Chemical Industry and Changes of Techno-Economic Paradigm," pp. 74–5.

15 H. Kitschelt, "Industrial Governance Structures, Innovation Strategies and the Case of Japan," *International Organization*, 1991, vol. 45, 453–93.

16 R. Nelson, "What is Commercial and What is Public about Technology, and What Should Be?" in N. Rosenberg *et al.* (eds) *Technology and the Wealth of Nations*, Stanford: Stanford University Press, 1992. Nelson's scheme is based on extensive empirical work on cross-sectoral variance in degrees of appropriability and effectiveness of patents in protecting innovations. See R. Levin *et al.*, "Appropriating the Returns to Industrial R&D," *Brookings Papers on Economic Activity*, 1987, vol. 3.

17 Pavitt's writings on this question have evolved over the years. For an early conceptualization, see K. Pavitt, "Sectoral Patterns of Technical Change," *Research Policy*, 1984, vol. 13, 343–73. I follow here his later groupings found in idem, "What We Know about the Strategic Management of Technology," *California Management Review*, 1990, vol. 32 (Spring), 17–26.

18 Kitschelt, "Industrial Governance Structures." A major drawback in Kitschelt's theory is imprecise use of the term "governance." In transaction cost theory, from which he draws many of his insights, "governance" is a microanalytic concept describing the extent to which a firm coordinates market transactions. There is nothing political, or even sectoral, in its meaning.

19 This is another source of confusion arising from Kitschelt's use of terms. Sectors do not adopt governance structures; firms do. This becomes clear when one recalls that "governance" refers to the way in which market transactions are organized. Whether that is done through arm's-length exchange, vertical integration, strategic alliance, or any other form of organization depends on the preferences of individual firms.

20 L.H. Lynn, N.M. Reddy, and J.D. Aram, "Linking Technology and Institutions: The Innovation Community Framework," *Research Policy*, 1996, vol. 25, 91–106.

21 S. Winter, "Knowledge and Competence as Strategic Assets," in D. Teece (ed.) *The Competitive Challenge*, Cambridge, MA: Ballinger Press, 1987, pp. 159–84.

22 W. Powell, "Learning from Collaboration: Knowledge and Networks in the Biotechnology and Pharmaceutical Industries," *California Management Review*, 1998, vol. 40 (Spring), 228–40; N. Greis, M. Dibner, and S. Alden, "External

Partnering as a Response to Innovation Barriers and Global Competition in Biotechnology," *Research Policy*, 1995, vol. 24, 608–40.

23 N. Rosenberg, *Perspectives on Technology*, Cambridge: Cambridge University Press, 1976, p. 170.

24 Examples of works employing this approach include H. Ergas, "Does Technology Policy Matter?" in B. Guile and H. Brooks (eds) *Technology and Global Industry*, Washington, DC: National Academy Press, 1987; N. Reingold, "The Peculiarities of the Americans or Are There National Styles in the Sciences?" *Science in Context*, 1991, vol. 4, 347–66; D. Mowery, "The US National Innovation System: Origins and Prospects for Change," *Research Policy*, 1992, vol. 21, 125–44; C. Edquist, "Systems of Innovation Approaches – Their Emergence and Characteristics," in C. Edquist (ed.) *Systems of Innovation: Technologies, Institutions and Organizations*, London: Pinter, 1997; and R. Whitley, "The Institutional Structuring of Innovation Strategies: Business Systems, Firm Types and Patterns of Technical Change in Different Market Economies," *Organization Studies*, 2000, vol. 21, 855–86.

25 C. Freeman, *Technology Policy and Economic Performance: Lessons from Japan*, New York: Frances Pinter, 1987, p. 1.

26 Ibid., and C. Freeman, "Japan: A New National System of Innovation?" in Dosi *et al.* (eds) *Technical Change and Economic Theory.*

27 Lynn, "Linking Technology and Institutions," p. 102.

28 B.A. Lundvall, "Innovation as an Interactive Process: From User–Producer Interaction to the National System of Innovation," in Dosi *et al.* (eds) *Technical Change and Economic Theory.* Though Porter does not use the expression "national innovation system", his theory implicitly accepts its premises. See M. Porter, *The Competitive Advantage of Nations*, New York: Free Press, 1990. The most ambitious effort to apply the concept not only to advanced industrial countries but Third World nations as well is R. Nelson (ed.) *National Innovation Systems: A Comparative Analysis*, New York: Oxford University Press, 1993.

29 My use of the term "related or supporting industries" follows that of Porter, who incorporates it as one of four key attributes of the national environment that shapes competitive success. See Porter, *Competitive Advantage of Nations*, pp. 100–7.

3 Biotechnology and national innovation systems in the US and Japan

1 Office of Technology Assessment, *New Developments in Biotechnology: US Investment in Biotechnology – Special Report*, OTA-BA-360, Washington, DC: Government Printing Office, July 1988. An earlier OTA report in 1981 referred to these companies as "new biotechnology firms" (NBFs), as have other sources. See, for example, S. Krimsky, *Biotechnics and Society: The Rise of Industrial Genetics*, New York: Praeger, 1991.

2 M. Kenney, *Biotechnology: The University–Industrial Complex*, New Haven: Yale University Press, 1986, ch. 7; Arthur Kornberg, *The Golden Helix: Inside Biotech Ventures*, Sausalito, CA: University Science Books, 1995, pp. 28–9.

3 Biotechnology Industry Organization, *BIO Editors' and Reporters' Guide to Biotechnology 2002–2003*, online, available HTTP: <http://www.bio.org> (accessed 9 July 2002).

4 Not surprisingly, the drug industry insists on the higher figure, while its critics counter with the lower. See "Too High? Debate Continues over Drug Development Costs," *Chemical & Engineering News*, 28 January 2002, pp. 27–33.

5 Ernst & Young, *Convergence: The Biotechnology Industry Report*, Ernst & Young, 2000, p. 31.

6 Slightly less than a third of the companies in its data set are based outside the US. "Public Biotechnology 2001 – The Numbers," *Nature Biotechnology*, June 2002, pp. 551–5.
7 Standard & Poor's, *Biotechnology Industry Survey*, 21 November 2002, pp. 7–8.
8 L.G. Zucker, M.R. Darby, and M.B. Brewer, "Intellectual Human Capital and the Birth of US Biotechnology Enterprises," *American Economic Review*, March 1998, vol. 88, 290–306.
9 J. Cortright and H. Mayer, "Signs of Life: The Growth of Biotechnology Clusters in the U.S.," Brookings Institution, June 2002, online, available HTTP: <http://www.brook.edu/dybdocroot/es/urban/publications/biotech.html> (accessed 9 August 2002).
10 C. Robbins-Roth, *From Alchemy to IPO: The Business of Biotechnology*, Cambridge, MA: Perseus Publishing, 2000, p. 166.
11 "How the Elephants Dance," *Recombinant Capital*, 2 January 1997, online, available HTTP: <http://www.recap.com> (accessed 7 January 1997).
12 G.S. Burrill, "Life Sciences: State of the Industry," June 2002, Burrill & Company, online, available HTTP: <http://www.burillandco.com> (accessed 4 July 2002).
13 "Drug Deal-Making Dynamics Change," *Chemical & Engineering News*, 28 January 2002, pp. 37–44.
14 W.W. Powell, "Learning from Collaboration: Knowledge and Networks in the Biotechnology and Pharmaceutical Industries," *California Management Review*, Spring 1998, pp. 228–40.
15 S. Nicholson, P.M. Danzon, and J. McCullough, "Biotech–Pharmaceutical Alliances as a Signal of Asset and Firm Quality," NBER Working Paper 9007, National Bureau of Economic Research, 2002.
16 "Tracking Trends in U.S. Biotechnology," *Bio/Technology*, December 1991, p. 1334.
17 Ernst & Young, *Biotech '95: Reform, Restructure, Renewal*, 1994; Standard & Poor's, *Biotechnology Industry Survey*, 16 May 2002.
18 M. McKelvey, *Evolutionary Innovations*, New York, Oxford University Press, 1996, p. 261.
19 Kenney, *Biotechnology: The University–Industrial Complex*, pp. 194–5; "Chemical Engineering Focuses Increasingly on the Biological," *Chemical & Engineering News*, 11 January 1993, pp. 26–36
20 Kenney, *Biotechnology: The University–Industrial Complex*, pp. 203–11.
21 Ernst & Young, *Biotech 2001: Focus on Fundamentals*, 2001.
22 Ernst & Young, *Convergence*.
23 National Science Board, *Science & Engineering Indicators – 2002*, Volume 2, Appendix Table 6–1.
24 Ibid., Text Table 4–19 and Appendix Table 4–32; Ernst & Young LLP, Center for Industry Change, *The Global Pharmaceutical Marketplace*, Table 5, online, available HTTP: <http://www.ey.com/global> (accessed 6 August 2002).
25 National Science Board, *Science & Engineering Indicators – 2002*, Volume 2, Appendix Table 6–1.
26 "Pharma Overview," *Chemical & Engineering News*, 2 December 2002, pp. 39–49; *Yakuji Handobukku* [Pharmaceuticals Handbook], 2002, Tokyo: Jiho, 2002, p. 153.
27 Organization for Economic Cooperation and Development, *Health at a Glance*, Paris: OECD, 2001, pp. 41, 47, and 93.
28 Organization for Economic Cooperation and Development, *Main Science and Technology Indicators*, Volume 2001/2, Paris: OECD, 2001, p. 36, Table 38.
29 Tsushosangyosho, Baioindasutoriishitsu, *Baioindasutorii bijion* [Vision for the Bioindustry], Tokyo: Tsushosangyo chosakai, 1988, p. 103.
30 Tsushosangyosho, kisosangyokyoku, seibutsu kagaku sangyoka, *Baioteku Benran, 1991* [Biotechnology Handbook, 1991], pp. 66–8.

31 JETRO, Market Information, "Biotechnology-Related Products," Japanese Market Report 2000, online, available HTTP: <http://www.jetro.go.jp/ec/e/market/jmr/047/1.html> (accessed 26 June 2002).

32 Monbukagakusho, kenkyu shinkokyoku, raifusaiensuka, *et al.*, "Heisei 13 nendo baiosangyo sozo kiso chosa hokokusho" [Report on the Basic Survey of Bioindustry Creation], March 2002, available HTTP: <http://www.meti.go.jp/policy/bio/BioIndustry-Statistics/ 13FYBiotoukei.pdf> (accessed 16 November 2002). The survey classifies products produced by these firms into six categories based on the technology used to make the product. These are as follows: (1) conventional fermentation and cell culture techniques; (2) cell fusion, tissue culture, animal cloning, and other advanced cell manipulation techniques; (3) recombinant DNA; (4) bioreactors and other techniques based on fixed-bed cell culture; (5) waste treatment and environmental remediation techniques that use conventional biology; and (6) sensors and analytical hardware and software that uses biological knowledge. "Traditional biotechnology products" are defined as articles manufactured using technologies from categories 1 and 5, "new biotechnology products" as ones made using technologies from categories 2, 3, 4, and 6.

33 Ibid.

34 These figures are reported in Nihon baiosangyojin kaigi, Baiosangyo gijutsu senryaku iinkai, "Baiosangyo gijutsu senryaku" (Bioindustry Technology Strategy), 24 November 1999, p. 18.

35 The food category refers not to genetically modified seeds sold to farmers, which come under agriculture, but to foods for final consumption. Expectations were, and still are, high for so-called "functional foods" that use techniques from biotechnology to improve nutritional content, eliminate allergens, and tailor the nutritional content to individual needs.

36 The difficulty of forecasting has great relevance in the current technology policy debate in Japan about the future of the biotechnology industry. Policy discussion is premised on the assumption, based on a MITI study done in 2000, that the biotechnology market will swell to 25 trillion yen in 2010. The market in 2001 was only 1.3 trillion yen, and it has been growing at an annual rate of about 10 percent. Extrapolating that growth rate into the future yields a market size in 2010 of only 3.4 trillion yen. The government's forecast assumes a sharp increase in the rate of new product introductions, especially after 2005. The trade journal *Nikkei Baiobijinesu* recently polled its readers about the future of commercial biotechnology. Asked to forecast the size of the market in 2015, roughly 47 percent of the 394 respondents felt that it would be less than 10 trillion yen; only 10 percent believed that it would exceed 30 trillion yen, which would be in line with official growth projections. As for the fields most likely to be growing the fastest in 2015, some 80 percent of respondents chose therapeutic drugs, and a little over half chose diagnostics. Following in popularity were research outsourcing services and environmental products. See "2005 nen made wa 10% seicho tsuzuku" [Ten percent Growth will Continue until 2005], *Nikkei Baiobijinesu*, June 2002, pp. 46–51.

37 Gerlach refers to this process as "*keiretsuization*." See M. Gerlach, *Alliance Capitalism*, Berkeley: University of California Press, 1992, ch. VI.

38 These and the following figures on production and trade of pharmaceutical products are for the year 1998 and are calculated from data presented in National Science Board, *Science and Engineering Indicators – 2002*, Volume 2, Appendix Table 6–1.

39 Kosei Rodosho, "'Seimei no seiki' o sasaeru iyakuhin sangyo no kokusai kyosoryoku kyoka ni mukete: Iyakuhin sangyo bijion no gaiyo" [Strengthening the International Competitiveness of the Pharmaceutical Industry to Support the

Century of Life: Outline of the Vision for the Pharmaceutical Industry], 30 August 2001, p. 5.

40 IMS HEALTH, "US Innovation will Drive Domination," 27 March 2001, online, available HTTP: <http://www.ims-global.com//insight/news_story/0103/news_story_010327.html> (accessed 4 May 2003).

41 Takashi Endo, *Iyakuhin gyokai* [Pharmaceutical Business], Tokyo: Paru Shuppan, 2002, pp. 68–78.

42 *Yakuji Handobukku* [Pharmaceuticals Handbook], 2002, p. 83.

43 OECD, *Health at a Glance*, pp. 47 and 93. Among large industrialized countries, France, Italy, and Spain, in that order, devote a larger share of health care spending to drugs (21.9, 20.7, and 17.5 percent, respectively).

44 Kosei Rodosho, "'Seimei no seiki' o sasaeru iyakuhin sangyo no kokusai kyosoryoku kyoka ni mukete," p. 6.

45 *Yakuji Handobukku* [Pharmaceuticals Handbook], 2002, pp. 139 and 158.

46 Ibid., p. 159.

47 C. Oberlander, "R&D in Japan's Pharmaceutical Industry," in M. Hemmert and C. Oberlander (eds) *Technology and Innovation in Japan*, London and New York: Routledge, 1998, p. 180.

48 On the problems brought about by the intertwining of health and welfare with industrial promotion policies, see M. Reich, "Why the Japanese Don't Export More Pharmaceuticals: Health Policy as Industrial Policy," *California Management Review*, Winter 1990, 124–50.

49 R. Henderson, L. Orsenigo, and G. Pisano, "The Pharmaceutical Industry and the Revolution in Biotechnology," in D. Mowery and R. Nelson (eds) *Sources of Industrial Leadership*, New York: Cambridge University Press, 1999, p. 282.

50 National Science Board, *Science and Engineering Indicators – 2002*, Volume 2, Appendix Tables 4–5 and 4–29. The figure cited for total research is for the year 2000; the figure for research in the life sciences is for the year 1998.

51 Ibid., Appendix Table 4–27.

52 National Science Board, *Science and Engineering Indicators – 2002*, Volume 1, pp. 4–12.

53 "The NIH Budget in the 'Postdoubling' Era," *Science*, 24 May 2002, pp. 1401–2.

54 Data obtained from the NIH website.

55 "NIH Report Knocks Tax on Blockbusters," *Science*, 31 August 2001, p. 1575.

56 J. Paugh and J.C. Lafrance, "Meeting the Challenge: US Industry Faces the Twenty-first Century – The US Biotechnology Industry," US Department of Commerce, Office of Technology Policy, July 1997, pp. 68–70.

57 This section draws on D. Guston, "Technology Transfer and CRADAs at the NIH," in L. Branscomb and J. Keller (eds) *Investing in Innovation*, Cambridge: MIT Press, 1999, pp. 221–49; and R. Kneller, "Technology Transfer: A Review for Biomedical Researchers," *Clinical Cancer Research*, 2001, vol. 7, April, pp. 761–74.

58 The material transfer CRADA was authorized for use by NIH beginning fiscal year 1996 to promote the transfer into NIH of proprietary research materials such as reagents, cell lines, and chemical compounds held by external organizations. In this type of CRADA, the two parties negotiate terms under which the external organization retains rights to inventions resulting from the NIH's use of the supplied materials.

59 Guston, "Technology Transfer and CRADAs at the NIH," pp. 232–3, supplemented with more recent data from the NIH web site.

60 National Science Board, *Science and Engineering Indicators – 2002*, Volume 2, Appendix Table 4–35.

61 The following is drawn from the account of Taxol's development given by Ruttan in V.W. Ruttan, *Technology, Growth, and Development*, New York: Oxford University Press, 2001, pp. 579–80.

62 General Accounting Office, "Technology Transfer: NIH–Private Sector Partnership in the Development of Taxol," Report to the Honorable Ron Wyden, US Senate, GAO-03-829, June 2003, pp. 3–4.

63 Office of the Secretary, US Department of Commerce, "Summary Report on Federal Laboratory Technology Transfer," September 2002.

64 Government Accounting Office, "Technology Transfer: Number and Characteristics of Inventions Licensed by Six Federal Agencies," GAO/RCED-99-173, June 1999.

65 Guston, "Technology Transfer and CRADAs at NIH," pp. 228–9.

66 R&D related to health rose from representing 27.5 percent of federal nondefense R&D obligations in 1982 to 45.6 percent in 2001.

67 R. Evenson, "Agriculture," in R. Nelson (ed.) *Government and Technical Progress*, New York: Pergamon, 1982.

68 Office of the Secretary, US Department of Commerce, "Summary Report on Federal Laboratory Technology Transfer."

69 For a review of this history, see N. Rosenberg and R. Nelson, "American Universities and Technical Advance in Industry," *Research Policy*, 1994, vol. 23, 323–48.

70 The Morrill Act of 1862, Sec. 2, online, available HTTP: <http://usinfo.state.gov/usa/infousa/facts/democrac/27.html> (accessed 13 March 2003).

71 R. Landau and N. Rosenberg, "Successful Commercialization in the Chemical Process Industry," in N. Rosenberg *et al.* (eds) *Technology and the Wealth of Nations*, Stanford: Stanford University Press, 1992, pp. 85–93.

72 R. Nelson, "The Rise and Fall of American Technological Leadership: The Postwar Era in Historical Perspective," *Journal of Economic Literature*, December 1992, vol. XXX, p. 1951.

73 National Science Board, *Science and Engineering Indicators – 2002*, Volume 2, Appendix Tables 5–2 and 5–10.

74 Ibid., Volume 2, Appendix Table 5–9.

75 Ibid., Volume 2, Appendix Table 4–29.

76 M. Kenney, *Biotechnology: The University–Industrial Complex*.

77 D. Blumenthal, N. Causino, E. Campbell, and K.S. Louis, "Relationships between Academic Institutions and Industry in the Life Sciences," *The New England Journal of Medicine*, 8 February 1996, vol. 334, 368–73.

78 F. Narin, K.S. Hamilton, and D. Olivastro, "The Increasing Linkage between U.S. Technology and Public Science," *Research Policy*, 1997, vol. 26, 317–30; G.S. McMillan, F. Narin, and D.L. Deeds, "An Analysis of the Critical Role of Public Science in Innovation: The Case of Biotechnology," *Research Policy*, 2000, vol. 29, 1–8.

79 National Science Board, *Science and Engineering Indicators – 2002*, Volume 1, pp. 5–52.

80 Ibid., Volume 2, Appendix Table 5–54.

81 D.C. Mowery, R.R. Nelson, B.N. Sampat, and A.A. Ziedonis, "The Growth of Patenting and Licensing by U.S. Universities: An Assessment of the Effects of the Bayh–Dole Act of 1980," *Research Policy*, 2001, vol. 30, 99–119.

82 National Science Board, *Science and Engineering Indicators – 2002*, Volume 2, Appendix Table 5–56.

83 Association of University Technology Managers, *AUTM Licensing Survey: FY2000*, online, available HTTP: <http://www.autm.net> (accessed 22 September 2002), p. 1.

84 The STTR Program requires the five federal agencies with more than $1 billion in extramural R&D to set aside 0.15 percent of their R&D budgets for STTR grants to small businesses. The purpose is to facilitate partnerships between small businesses and federally funded nonprofit organizations that involve technology transfer to the small business. A small program, its budget was $65 million in 1999 with about a third of the total coming from HHS.

85 "University Licenses: How Big a Piece of the Pie?" *Signals Magazine*, online, available HTTP: <http://recap.com/signals.nsf> (accessed 4 July 1997).

86 L.G. Zucker and M.R. Darby, "Star Scientists and Institutional Transformation: Patterns of Invention and Innovation in the Formation of the Biotechnology Industry," *Proceedings of the National Academy of Sciences of the United States of America*, 12 November 1996, vol. 93, 12709–16.

87 J. Cortright and H. Mayer, "Signs of Life: The Growth of Biotechnology Clusters in the U.S.," Brookings Institution, June 2002, online, available HTTP: <http://www.brook.edu/dybdocroot/es/urban/publications/biotech.html> (accessed 9 August 2002).

88 Monbu kagakusho, *Heisei 14 nenhan kagaku gijutsu hakusho* [Science and Technology White Paper, 2002 Edition], Appendix Table 14, online, available HTTP: <http://wwwwp.mext.go.jp/kag2002/index-58.html> (accessed 20 August 2002).

89 Ibid.

90 T. Morris-Suzuki, *The Technological Transformation of Japan*, Cambridge: Cambridge University Press, 1994, p. 99.

91 Mitsubishi Sogo Kenkyusho, *Genomu bijinesu* [Genome Business], Tokyo: Mitsubishi Sogo Kenkyusho, 2001, pp. 22–7.

92 Ibid., p. 58.

93 Built at a cost of 120 billion yen, the Spring-8 facility was jointly developed by Riken and the Japan Atomic Energy Research Institute, both of which have the status of special corporations under MEXT. Development commenced in 1991, and operation began in 1997.

94 For details on Riken's genomics and proteomics initiatives, I have relied on K. Arai, *Tokyo Genomu Bei Keikaku* [Tokyo Genome Bay Plan], Tokyo: Kodansha, 2002, ch. 2; A. Saegusa, "Japan's Genome Program Goes Ahead, with Protein Analysis," *Nature*, 19 March 1998, p. 219; and personal visits to Riken's Yokohama Research Center in July 2002 and the Spring-8 accelerator in October 1998.

95 D. Cyranoski, "Japan Speeds up Mission to Unravel Genetic Diseases," *Nature*, 26 April 2001, p. 1013.

96 Kogyo gijutsuin and chushokigyocho, *Heisei 9 nendo Kosetsu shiken kenkyu kikan genkyo* [Conditions in Public Experiment Research Institutes in 1997], p. 13.

97 The procedure used was somatic cell nuclear transfer using cells derived from the oviducts of an adult cow. Researchers in Japan have been experimenting with this technique as a means of improving the breeding of cattle that yield high-quality beef. See "Cloning Hopes Rise as Successes are Duplicated," *Nikkei Weekly*, 3 August 1998, p. 1.

98 "Kachiku kuro-n kenkyu no jokyo ni tsuite" [Conditions of Livestock Cloning Research], online, available HTTP: <http://www.s.affrc.go.jp/docs/press/2002/1115genjou.html> (accessed 16 March 2003).

99 Monbukagakusho, *Heisei 14 nenhan kagaku gijutsu hakusho*, Appendices 3.4 and 3.14.

100 Different accounting standards make problematic a direct comparison of R&D expenditures and personnel in the academic sector. In particular, Japan, along

with Canada and several European countries, include as academic R&D expenditures "general university funds," which the government generally distributes to universities as block grants that can be used for functions other than research; the US has no such budget category. On the other hand, the US government reports as academic research expenditures only the obligations of federal agencies that have a specific research objective. Consequently, the figures for Japan probably significantly overstate the amount spent on academic R&D, while those for the US understate it. See National Science Board, *Science and Engineering Indicators – 2002*, Volume 1, pp. 4–51, note 60.

101 For the US, see Association of University Technology Managers, *AUTM Licensing Survey: FY 2000*, Survey Summary, p. 22; for Japan, see Monbukagakusho, "Daigaku-hatsu Bencha-no Jokyo" [Conditions of University Spin-offs], online, available HTTP: <http://www.mext.go.jp/a_menu/shinkou/sangaku/sangakub/sangakub6.html> (accessed 25 March 2003).

102 Anges MG, started by Osaka University Associate Professor Ryuichi Morishita to develop a gene therapy technique using hepatic growth factor (HGF) to clear blocked arteries, went public in September 2002. Transgenic Inc. followed in December. Founded by Tsuyoshi Ide, an entrepreneur and former director of Shikibo Lifetech, Transgenic aims to commercialize antibodies and transgenic mice being developed by faculty in the School of Medicine at Kumamoto University. See "Kokai aitsugu bio kigyo kigyo mu-do sara ni takamaru" [Succession of Biotech Firms Going Public Further Lifts Start-Up Mood], *Nikkei Biobijinesu*, January 2003, pp. 58–60.

103 Japan Patent Office, "Baiotekunoroji-kiban gijutsu ni kansuru gijutsu doko chosa" [Survey of Technological Trends Related to Biotechnology Base Technologies], 31 May 2001, online, available HTTP: <http://www.jpo.go.jp/techno/pdf/bio.pdf> (accessed 11 December 2002). The six core technologies are recombinant DNA techniques, gene analysis, embryo engineering, protein engineering, carbohydrate engineering, and bioinformatics.

104 OECD, *Main Science and Technology Indicators*, p. 39, Table 43.

105 Y. Miyata, *Amerika no sangaku renkei* [University–Industry Relations in the US], Tokyo: Toyo Keizai Shinposha, 2002, p. 211.

106 National Science Board, *Science and Engineering Indicators – 2002*, Volume 2, Appendix Table 5–43.

107 Takashi Tachibana, *21 seiki: chi no chosen* [The Knowledge Challenge of the Twenty-first Century], Tokyo: Bungei Shunju, 2000, p. 128.

108 National Science Board, *Science and Engineering Indicators – 2002*, Volume 2, Appendix Table 5–52.

109 On the importance of history in shaping the technology transfer system in Japan, see S. Collins and H. Wakoh, "Universities and Technology Transfer in Japan," *Journal of Technology Transfer*, vol. 25, 2000, 213–22.

110 Miyata, *Amerika no Sangaku Renkei*, p. 208.

111 S. Yamamoto, "The Role of the Japanese Higher Education System in Relation to Industry," in A. Goto and H. Odagiri (eds) *Innovation in Japan*, New York: Clarendon Press, 1997, pp. 295–301.

112 Consisting usually of a full professor, an associate professor, and two assistants, a *koza* (or *ikyoku* in medical schools) is the basic research unit within the Japanese university. The amount each *koza* receives is determined by a formula and is based on the field, number of graduate students, type of research, and other circumstances.

113 B. Barker, "Internationalizing Japanese Science," in *Technology and Innovation* in Japan, p. 76.

114 S. Coleman, *Japanese Science from the Inside*, London: Routledge, 1999, pp. 10–12.

115 "At Tokyo University, a Parting Shot," *Nature*, 9 April 1993, p. 155.
116 Kagaku gijtsucho, *Kagaku gijutsu kihon keikaku (kaisetsu)* [Explanation of the Science and Technology Basic Plan], Tokyo: Ministry of Finance, 1997, p. 12.
117 Ibid., pp. 22–7.
118 Partly in response to complaints from the private sector that the first Basic Plan did too little to address economic competitiveness, the second five-year plan, released in 2001, calls on universities to play an even greater role in improving the short-term competitiveness of industry. See Miyata, *Amerika no sangaku renkei*, pp. 209–10.
119 Keizai Sangyosho, "Shonin TLO ni okeru tokkyo iten no joyko (heisei 14 nen 9 gatsu no ruikei)" [Conditions of Patent Transfers in Approved TLOs, Cumulative through September 2002].
120 "Daigaku TLO no tadashii tsukaikata" [The Correct Use of University TLOs], *Nikkei Baiobijinesu*, November 2001, p. 55.
121 Miyata, *Amerika no sangaku renkei*, p. 213.
122 R. Kneller, "Intellectual Property Rights and University–Industry Technology Transfer in Japan," in Branscomb and Kodama (eds) *Industrializing Knowledge*, p. 315.
123 Y. Nakamura and H. Odagiri, "Nihon no baio-tekunorojii bunya no kenkyu kaihatsu no genjo to 3tsu no kadai" [Three Problems and the Current Conditions of Research and Development in the Field of Biotechnology], *RIETI Discussion Paper Series 02-J-003*, February 2002, Table 7, online, available HTTP: <http://www.rieti.go.jp/publications> (accessed 9 February 2003).
124 The postwar paradigm grew out of the recommendations of Vannevar Bush, director of the President's Office of Scientific Research and Development at the close of World War II. Bush stressed the need for government support of basic research with special emphasis on military and medical applications. He called for government to play an active role in providing funds while allowing scientists themselves to determine their allocation. See V. Bush, *Science: The Endless Frontier*, Washington, DC: Government Printing Office, 1945, pp. 14–15.
125 D. Mowery, "U.S. National System of Innovation," in R. Nelson (ed.) *National Innovation Systems: A Comparative Analysis*, New York: Oxford University Press, 1992, pp. 39–52; A. Teich and J. Pace, *Science and Technology in the U.S.A.*, London: Longman, 1986, pp. 25–7.
126 Office of Science and Technology Policy, *Biotechnology for the 21st Century*, p. 17; National Science Board, *Science Indicators – 1991*.
127 "Senate Panel Adds 16% to Complete Doubling," *Science*, 26 July 2002, p. 493.
128 D.S. Greenberg, *Science, Money, and Politics*, Chicago: University of Chicago Press, 2001, p. 426.
129 National Science Board, *Science and Engineering Indicators – 2002*, Volume 1, pp. 4–12.
130 Greenberg, *Science, Money, and Politics*, ch. 27.
131 "Biotech Investment Catches Congressional Eye," *Bio/Technology*, September 1988, pp. 1001–2.
132 I am grateful to Ms. Jeane Van Lear, a former Director of Membership Services for the Association of Biotechnology Companies (now the Biotechnology Industry Organization), for providing information contained in this section.
133 Telephone interview with Mr. James Derderian, legislative assistant for Representative Thomas Bliley, July, 1992.
134 "The Capitol Hill Gang," *Bio/Technology*, April 1991, p. 316.

135 "Biotechnology Lobbyists Find Growing Clout on Capitol Hill," *Seattle Times*, 3 June 2002.
136 "America's Other Drug Problem: A Briefing Book on the Rx Drug Debate," Prepared by Public Citizen's Congress Watch, p. 67, online, available HTTP: <http://www.citizen.org/rxfacts> (accessed 3 May 2003).
137 "Drug Companies are Spending Record Amounts on Lobbying and Campaign Contributions," *Wall Street Journal*, 7 July 2000, p. A14.
138 "America's Other Drug Problem," p. 67.
139 "A Big Drug, a Big Lobbying Push," *Los Angeles Times*, 9 November 1999, p. B8.
140 Lisa Raines, "Protecting Biotechnology's Pioneers," *Issues in Science and Technology*, Winter 1991/92, pp. 33–9.
141 Reid Adler, "Genome Research: Fulfilling the Public's Expectations for Knowledge and Commercialization," *Science*, 14 August 1992, 908–14; "PTO Opens Floodgates on Animal Patents," *Bio/Technology*, March 1993, p. 270.
142 "NIH Seeks Patent Protection for Human Genes," *The Washington Post*, 13 February 1992, p. A16; "DNA Patent Dispute Rages On," *Bio/Technology*, July 1992, p. 740.
143 Monbukagakusho, *Heisei 14 nenhan kagaku gijutsu hakusho*, ch. 3.
144 Sogo kagaku gijutsu kaigi [CSTP], "Sogo kagaku gijutsu kaigi ga jisshi suru kyosoteki kenkyu shikin seido no hyoka ni tsuite (an)" [Proposal Regarding Evaluation of the Competitive Research Funding System Administered by the CSTP], 28 January 2003.
145 Kakugi kettei [Cabinet Decision], "Kagaku gijutsu kihon keikaku ni tsuite" [Regarding the Science and Technology Basic Plan], 30 March 2001, online, available HTTP: <http://www.mext.go.jp/a_menu/kagaku/kihon/honbun.html> (accessed 5 April 2003).
146 Nihon baiosangyojin kaigi, Baiosangyo gijutsu senryaku iinkai, "Baiosangyo gijutsu senryaku," p. v, Appendix Table 12.
147 Ibid., pp. v–vi, Appendix Tables 13 and 14.
148 Naikaku sori daijin kettei [Resolution of the Prime Minister], "Mireniamu purojekuto (atarashii sennenki purojekuto) ni tsuite)" [The Millennium Project (Project for the New Millennium)], 19 December 1999, p. 1.
149 Interview, Mr. Masayuki Sakaguchi, Life Sciences Section, Basic Industries Bureau, Ministry of International Trade and Industry, November 1991.
150 Cited in Nakamura and Odagiri, "Nihon no baio-tekunorojii bunya no kenkyu kaihatsu no genjo to 3tsu no kadai," p. 19.
151 Interviews with MITI and MHW officials, November 1991.
152 For criticism along these lines of MITI's Next Generation Base Technology Program, see Baio 21 Guruupu, *Baiobijinesu no yume to genjitsu* [Dreams and Reality of Bio-business], Tokyo: IPEC, 1988, pp. 30–8.
153 Nakamura and Odagiri, "Nihon no baio-tekunorojii bunya no kenkyu kaihatsu no genjo to 3tsu no kadai," pp. 19–20.
154 Y. Tanaka and R. Hirasawa, "Features of Policy Making Processes in Japan's Council for Science and Technology," *Research Policy*, 1996, vol. 25, 999–1011.
155 Kagaku gijutsu cho, Monbusho, Koseisho, Norinshisansho, Tsushosangyosho; "Baiotekunorojii sangyo no sozo ni muketa kihon senryaku," 13 July 1999.
156 Nakamura and Odagiri, "Nihon no baio-tekunorojii bunya no kenkyu kaihatsu no genjo to 3tsu no kadai," pp. 22–3.
157 "Futte waita 640 oku en 'Mireniamu yosan' no yukigata" [64 Billion Yen from the Clouds: The Millennium Budget], *Shukan Daiyamondo*, 25 November 2000, p. 30.

158 Interviews with members of the Science and Technology Committee of the House of Representatives, Fall, 1991.

159 C. Johnson, "MITI, MPT, and the Telecom Wars," in C. Johnson *et al.* (eds) *Politics and Productivity*, Cambridge: Ballinger, 1989.

160 J. Lewis, "Collision of Interests: The Role of the Ruling Party in Science and Technology Policy," *Japan Forum*, 1994, vol. 6, 62–72.

161 Interview with Yohei Kono, former Director General, Science and Technology Agency, and member of the Science and Technology Committee of the LDP's Policy Affairs Research Council, November 1991.

162 Y.S. Lee, K. Kitazawa, and S. Nakayama, "A Radical Restructuring of Japan's Postwar Science and Technology Policy and Institutions: The Politics and Rationality of the New Century," NSF Report Memorandum #00-08, 15 May 2000, online, available HTTP: <http://www.nsftokyo.org/rm00-08.html> (accessed 3 June 2003).

163 Interviews, Saburo Okabe, member of the House of Councillors and Chair of the LDP's Science and Technology Subcommittee of the Policy Affairs Research Council (PARC); Eita Yashiro, member of the House of Councillors and former Parliamentary Vice-Minister, Science and Technology Agency; Jin Murai, member of the House of Representatives and member of the LDP's Commerce Subcommittee of the PARC; Yukio Hatoyama, then-member of the House of Representatives and member, House Science and Technology Committee, November–December 1991.

164 This is the gist of the argument Lee, Kitazawa, and Nakayama make in "A Radical Restructuring of Japan's Postwar S&T Policy and Institutions" cited in note 162.

4 The emergence of commercial biotechnology in the US

1 This paragraph draws on B. Achilladelis, "Innovation in the Pharmaceutical Industry," in R. Landau, B. Achilladelis, and A. Scriabine (eds) *Pharmaceutical Innovation*, Philadelphia: Chemical Heritage Press, 1999, ch. 1.

2 W. Kingston, "Antibiotics, Invention and Innovation," *Research Policy*, 2000, vol. 29, 679–710.

3 J. Drews, *In Quest of Tomorrow's Medicines*, New York: Springer-Verlag, 1999, p. 83.

4 Ibid., p. 85.

5 That such things as genes existed, and were responsible for the transmission of traits from one generation to the next, was first postulated by the German physiologist August Weismann in 1892 as a means of explaining the patterns of inheritance the Austrian monk Gregor Mendel had observed in pea plants a generation earlier. To Weismann, the bearers of inheritance had to be particles – one for each trait – carried on the chromosomes of all organisms. In 1909, Wilhelm Johannsen was probably the first to refer to these physical particles of inheritance as "genes."

6 M. Morange, *A History of Molecular Biology*, Cambridge, MA: Harvard University Press, 1998, chs 7–8.

7 Ibid., p. 80.

8 H. Gottweis, *Governing Molecules: The Discursive Politics of Genetic Engineering in Europe and the United States*, Cambridge, MA: MIT Press, 1998, p. 74.

9 Drews, *In Quest of Tomorrow's Medicines*, p. 84.

10 D.C. Mowery and N. Rosenberg, *Technology and the Pursuit of Economic Growth*, New York: Cambridge University Press, 1989, p. 93.

11 National Science Board, *Science and Engineering Indicators – 2002*, Volume 1, pp. 4–12.

12 A.J. Morin, *Science Policy and Politics*, Englewood Cliffs, NJ: Prentice-Hall, 1993, p. 52
13 M. Kenney, *Biotechnology: The University–Industrial Complex*, New Haven: Yale University Press, 1986, pp. 14–15.
14 S. Wright, *Molecular Politics*, Chicago: University of Chicago Press, 1994, p. 24.
15 Ibid., p. 69.
16 R. Teitleman, *Gene Dreams: Wall Street, Academia, and the Rise of Biotechnology*, New York: Basic Books, 1989, p. 17.
17 Office of Technology Assessment, *Commercial Biotechnology: An International Analysis*, OTA-BA-218, Washington, DC: Government Printing Office, January 1984, p. 414.
18 S. Olson, *Biotechnology: An Industry Comes of Age*, Washington, DC: National Academy Press, 1986, pp. 98–9.
19 Office of Technology Assessment, *Commercial Biotechnology*, p. 73.
20 This section follows historical accounts given in the following: H.F. Judson, "A History of the Science and Technology Behind Gene Mapping and Sequencing," in D.J. Kevles and L. Hood (eds) *The Code of Codes*, Cambridge: Harvard University Press, 1992; J. Watson, *The DNA Story*, San Francisco: Freeman Press, 1981; and Morange, *A History of Molecular Biology*, ch. 16.
21 Watson's and Crick's work was supported by Britain's Medical Research Council. That they received no funding at the time from the Rockefeller Foundation is sometimes cited as evidence that the latter's influence on molecular biology has been exaggerated. On the other hand, by this time governments in the US and Europe had ramped up spending on basic scientific research, diversifying the potential sources of research grants compared to the conditions of a decade earlier. See Morange, *A History of Molecular Biology*, ch. 8.
22 J. Watson, *DNA: The Secret of Life*, New York: Alfred A. Knopf, 2003, p. 85.
23 Wright, *Molecular Politics*, p. 68.
24 Morange, *A History of Molecular Biology*, p. 188.
25 Wright, *Molecular Politics*, p. 78.
26 H.F. Judson, "A History of the Science and Technology Behind Gene Mapping and Sequencing," pp. 65–78.
27 Cited in S. Krimsky, *Biotechnics and Society: The Rise of Industrial Genetics*, New York: Praeger, 1991, p. 197.
28 Ernst & Young, *Biotech '93: Accelerating Commercialization*, San Francisco: Ernst & Young, 1992, p. 10.
29 C. Robbins-Roth, *From Alchemy to IPO: The Business of Biotechnology*, Cambridge, MA: Perseus Publishing, 1999, pp. 13–14.
30 L.C. Plein, "Biotechnology: Issue Development and Evolution," in D.J. Webber (ed.) *Biotechnology: Assessing Social Impacts and Policy Implications*, New York: Greenwood Press, 1990, pp. 148–55.
31 L. Busch, W.L. Lacy, J. Burkhardt, and L. Lacy, *Plants, Power, and Profit: Social, Economic, and Ethical Consequences of the New Biotechnologies*, Oxford: Basil Blackwell, 1991, ch. 7.
32 Watson, *DNA*, pp. 96–7; Morange, *A History of Molecular Biology*, pp. 188–9.
33 Gottweis, *Governing Molecules*, p. 87.
34 Morange, *A History of Molecular Biology*, pp. 190–1.
35 In 1975–6, RAC meeting minutes list eighteen members, only two of whom (an ethicist and political scientist) were nonscientists. Chairing the committee was the NIH's Deputy Director for Science. See Wright, *Molecular Politics*, p. 166.
36 Gottweis, *Governing Molecules*, p. 97.
37 Watson, *DNA*, p. 98.
38 Krimsky, *Biotechnics and Society*, p. 100.

39 J. Perpich, "Genetic Engineering and Related Biotechnologies: Scientific Progress and Public Policy," in J. Perpich (ed.) *Biotechnology in Society*, New York: Pergamon, 1986, pp. 90–2; Krimsky, *Biotechnics and Society*, pp. 101–2.
40 "Can Gene-Splicers Make Good Neighbors?" *Business Week*, 10 August 1981, p. 32.
41 Wright, *Molecular Politics*, p. 158.
42 Morange, *A History of Molecular Biology*, p. 200 and ch. 17.
43 Ibid., p. 201; and Robbins-Roth, *From Alchemy to IPO*, p. 16.
44 Wright, *Molecular Politics*, p. 278.
45 Office of Technology Assessment, *Commercial Biotechnology*, Appendix; Krimsky, *Biotechnics and Society*, pp. 102–4.
46 S. Wright and D.A. Wallace, "Varieties of Secrets and Secret Varieties: The Case of Biotechnology," *Politics and the Life Sciences*, 2000, vol. 19, 45–57.
47 Office of Technology Assessment, *Biotechnology in a Global Economy*, Washington, DC: Government Printing Office, 1991, p. 175.
48 "Gene Splicing Sheds its Mad-Scientist Image," *Business Week*, 16 May 1983, p. 36.
49 Office of Technology Assessment, *Commercial Biotechnology*, p. 274.
50 Office of Technology Assessment, *New Developments in Biotechnology: US Investment in Biotechnology – Special Report*, OTA-BA-360, Washington, DC: Government Printing Office, July 1988, p. 84.
51 Kenney, *Biotechnology*, p. 166.
52 P. Daly, *The Biotechnology Business: A Strategic Analysis*, London: Pinter, 1985, pp. 81–2; Krimsky, *Biotechnics and Society*, p. 30.
53 The account here follows that in Kenney, *Biotechnology*, p. 137; Teitelman, *Gene Dreams*, pp. 24–5; and "Engineering the Therapies of Tomorrow," *New Scientist*, 24 April 1993, pp. 26–7. A more recent retelling of the story by a former Genentech employee is C. Robbins-Roth, *From Alchemy to IPO*.
54 Ernst & Young, *Biotech '93*.
55 Kenney, *Biotechnology*, pp. 96–7.
56 Nowinski had earlier declined offers from another venture capitalist, Robert Johnson, to anchor his new start-up, Genex. Teitelman chronicles the meetings, phone calls, and promises that led to the founding of Genetic Systems. See Teitelman, *Gene Dreams*, ch. 4.
57 "A Wonder Drug in the Making," *Business Week*, 19 November 1979, p. 71.
58 Scores of early investors, who had been rewarded for their contributions with penny stock, became instant paper millionaires. Teitelman makes the point that penny investors who unloaded stock at the peak on that first day would have earned 890 times their original stake! Teitelman, *Gene Dreams*, pp. 22–3.
59 G. Steven Burrill, *Biotech '89: Commercialization*, New York: Mary Ann Liebert, 1998, p. 37.
60 Robbins-Roth, *From Alchemy to IPO*, ch. 3.
61 "Biotechnology Struts into the Hen House," *Business Week*, 11 April 1983, p. 36.
62 Busch *et al.*, *Plants, Power, and Profit*, p. 15.
63 Kenney, *Biotechnology*, p. 39.
64 According to one source, the private sector provided 13 percent of all funds for biotechnology research in experiment stations affiliated with land grant universities. The same source notes that the national average for all university research was 3–4 percent. Busch *et al.*, *Plants, Power, and Profit*, p. 195.
65 Kenney, *Biotechnology*, ch. 3.
66 Busch *et al.*, *Plants, Power, and Profit*, pp. 14–15.
67 Watson, *DNA*, p. 118.

68 D. Mowery, "The U.S. National Innovation System," in R. Nelson (ed.) *National Systems of Innovation: A Comparative Analysis*, New York: Oxford University Press, 1992, pp. 53–4.
69 R. Landau and N. Rosenberg, "Successful Commercialization in the Chemical Process Industries," in N. Rosenberg, R. Landau, and D. Mowery (eds) *Technology and the Wealth of Nations*, Stanford: Stanford University Press, 1992, pp. 73–117.
70 R. Florida and M. Kenney, *The Breakthrough Illusion*, New York: Basic Books, 1990, p. 57.
71 "Gene Splicing Sheds its Mad-Scientist Image," p. 36.
72 Ernst & Young, *Biotech '93*, fold-out.
73 Ernst & Young, *Biotech '92: Promise to Reality*, p. 23.
74 Data cited in this paragraph come from Ernst & Young as reported by the Biotechnology Industry Organization, *Editors' and Reporters' Guide to Biotechnology, 2002–2003*, online, available HTTP: <http://www.bio.org> (accessed 5 March 2003).
75 Federal Coordinating Council for Science, Engineering, and Technology (FCCSET), Committee on Life Sciences and Health, *Biotechnology for the Twenty-first Century*, Washington, DC: Government Printing Office, February 1992, p. 88.
76 "An Industry Crowded with Players Faces an Ugly Reckoning," *Business Week*, 26 September 1994, p. 84.
77 Ernst & Young survey results reported in Office of Technology Assessment, *Biotechnology in a Global Economy*, p. 100; personal interviews with managers of biotechnology firms.
78 "The Gene is Out of the Bottle," *The Economist*, 30 April 1988, p. S15.
79 "A Federal Strategy for International Industrial Competitiveness," *Bio/Technology*, June 1986, pp. 522–5; Perpich, "Biotechnology, International Competition, and Regulatory Strategies," p. 204.
80 On the FDA's role in the early commercialization phase, see H. Miller, "FDA and Biotechnology: Update 1989," *Bio/Technology*, December 1988, pp. 1385–92.
81 Plein, "Issue Development and Evolution," p. 162.
82 Government Accounting Office, *Biotechnology: Analysis of Federally Funded Research*, August 1986.
83 This example comes from P. Huber, "Biotechnology and the Regulatory Hydra," *Technology Review*, November/December 1987, pp. 57–65.
84 "Larger Public Sector Role Sought on Biotech," *Science*, 6 April 1986, pp. 15–16.
85 For details on the process by which the working group arrived at the final report, see Krimsky, *Biotechnics and Society*, pp. 192–7.
86 Comprising the BSCC were the Commissioner of the FDA, the NIH Director, two assistant secretaries each from USDA and EPA, and an assistant director of NSF. A considerably stronger coordinating body had been initially proposed, only to face strong opposition from industry and the regulatory agencies.
87 Krimsky, *Biotechnics and Society*, pp. 197–8; "The Regulatory 'Coordinated Framework' for Biotechnology," *Bio/Technology*, December 1986, pp. 1071–3; "OSTP Shores up the Regulatory Framework," *Bio/Technology*, August 1986, p. 690.
88 "Open Approach to Federal Coordination Urged," *Bio/Technology*, January 1990, p. 13; "More Changes in U.S. Regulatory," *Bio/Technology*, November 1990, p. 996.
89 "BSCC Addresses Scope of Oversight," *Bio/Technology*, March 1990, p. 187.
90 OTA, *Biotechnology in a Global Economy*, p. 176.

91 "Biotech Companies Lobby for Federal Regulation," *Science*, 4 April 1990, pp. 546–7.

92 OTA, *Biotechnology in a Global Economy*, pp. 176–7.

93 The President's Council on Competitiveness, *Report on National Biotechnology Policy*, February 1991.

94 Views within the FDA, however, were by no means unanimous. Internal agency memoranda made public in 1999 give clear evidence of misgivings among some officials about treating GM and non-GM foods as equivalent. An FDA microbiologist reportedly wrote that the 1992 policy statement was not supported by available data and that the document "read very pro-industry, especially in the area of unintended effects." See "Documents Show Officials Disagreed on Altered Food," *New York Times*, 1 December 1999, p. A18.

95 "Judge Upholds F.D.A. Policy on Genetically Modified Foods," *New York Times*, 4 October 2000, p. C18.

96 US Food and Drug Administration, Center for Food Safety and Applied Nutrition, Office of Food Additive Safety, "List of Completed Consultations on Bioengineered Foods," online, available HTTP: <http://vm.cfsan.fda.gov/~lrd/biocon.html> (accessed 19 June 2003).

97 BIO, *Editors' and Reporters' Guide to Biotechnology*, pp. 66–73.

98 "Biotech Investment Catches Congressional Eye," *Bio/Technology*, September 1988, pp. 1001–2; Tom Harkin, "Biotechnology in Agriculture and America's Competitiveness," *Policy Studies Journal*, 1988, vol. 17, 68–72.

99 US Congress, House, *American Science and Science Policy Issues*, Chairman's Report to the Committee on Science and Technology, House of Representatives, 99th Cong, 2nd sess, Serial AA, December 1986, pp. 71–2.

100 US Congress, Senate, *Biotechnology Competitiveness Act of 1987*, Report to Accompany S. 1966, 100th Cong, 2nd sess, May 25, 1988; and US Congress, House, *Biotechnology Competitiveness Act of 1988*, 100th Cong, 2nd sess, October 1988; and US Congress, House, *The Biotechnology Science Coordination and Competitiveness Act of 1988*, 100th Cong, 2nd sess, September 1988.

101 "Cautious Lawmakers Fret over Biotech Issues," *Congressional Quarterly*, 27 August 1988, p. 2428.

102 Only a year before, in 1987, DOE and NIH had locked horns over which agency would head the Human Genome Project. DOE conceived the project in 1986; initially hesitant, NIH later expressed interest. Debate in the Senate featured powerful patrons – John Dingell for NIH and Pete Domenici for DOE – who each thought their side was best qualified to lead the endeavor. Compromise was reached in the initial budgetary authorization bill. DOE would later concede leadership to NIH. The definitive treatment of the politics behind the genesis of the Human Genome Project is R. Cook-Deegan, *The Gene Wars: Science, Politics, and the Human Genome*, New York: W.W. Norton, 1994, especially ch. 12.

103 "NIH Invention Development Program Advances," *Bio/Technology*, September 1989, p. 1366.

104 "Intellectual Property: Companies Rush to Patent DNA," *Science*, 7 February 1997, pp. 780–1.

105 W. Kaplan, "Biotech Patenting 101," Council for Responsible Genetics, online, available HTTP: <http://www.gene-watch.org/programs/patents/patenting101.html> (accessed 19 June 2003).

106 "Patent Office may Raise the Bar on Gene Claims," *Science*, 18 February 2000, pp. 1196–7.

107 "U.S. Issues Stiffer Regulations on Frivolous Patenting of Genes," *New York Times*, 6 January 2001, p. C3.

108 K. Davies, *Cracking the Genome*, New York: The Free Press, 2001, p. 66.
109 "Ten Deals that Changed Biotechnology," *Signals Magazine*, 17 November 1998, online, available HTTP: <http://www.recap.com/signalsmag.nsf> (accessed 1 March 1999).
110 "How the Elephants Dance Part 3," *Signals Magazine*, 4 November 1999, online, available HTTP: <http://www.recap.com/signalsmag.nsf> (accessed 22 November 1999).
111 "Monsanto Struggles even as it Dominates," *New York Times*, 31 May 2003, p. C1.
112 These thoughts are based on my discussions with the Hyogo Business and Cultural Center in Seattle, Washington, which has been heavily promoting the life science industry in the Kobe region. Only time will tell if these efforts bear fruit.
113 "Amgen's High Risk Strategy," *Financial Times*, 17 December 2001, p. 19.
114 "Biogen Puts its Formula to Test," *Financial Times*, 1 April 2003, p. 18.
115 "Approval Times for New Drugs Increase Slightly," *Wall Street Journal*, 16 January 2003, p. D4.
116 "Overview of Biotechnology in the United States," *Genetic Engineering News*, December 2001, p. 9.
117 G.S. Burrill, "Biotech 2003: Revaluation and Restructuring," March 2003, online, available HTTP: <http://www.burrillandco.com> (accessed 1 May 2003).
118 "Biotech Mergers: Cash Talks Louder than Technology," *New York Times*, 5 March 2003.

5 The emergence of commercial biotechnology in Japan

1 Tokkyocho, Gijutsu chosaka, "Baiotekunoroji-kiban gijutsu ni kansuru gijutsu doko chosa" [Survey of Trends Concerning the Biotechnology Technology Base], 11 December 2002, Table 6, online, available HTTP: <http://www.jpo.go.jp/shiryou/toushin/chousa/pdf/bio.pdf> (last accessed 23 June 2003). The figure used here for the US is considerably larger than one normally finds in American sources such as Ernst & Young's annual reports. This is because Japanese sources usually define biotechnology more broadly to include a wider range of products, making direct comparison difficult.
2 "A Bridge from Science to Life," *Japan Times*, 25 December 2002.
3 M. Hongo, *Nihon no baiteku choryu: shindai kara gendai o koete* [Trends in Japan's Biotechnology: From the Age of the Gods to Modern Times], Tokyo: HBJ Shuppankyoku, 1988, pp. 4–6.
4 Hongo writes that the first recorded use of the word *miso* was in the year 901, the word *shoyu* in 1598. The actual brewing of *shoyu* and *miso* using a microbial process is first documented in 1535 and 1645, respectively. Ibid., pp. 26–7.
5 M. Tanimoto, "Juzogyo" [Brewing], in S. Nishikawa, K. Odaka, and O. Saito (eds) *Nihon keizai no 200 nen* [200 Years of Japan's Economy], Tokyo: Nihon Hyoronsha, 1996, p. 255
6 The modern science of microbiology emerged only after the path-breaking experiments of the French scientist Louis Pasteur in the mid nineteenth century.
7 Hongo, *Nihon no baiteku choryu*, p. 51.
8 I. Karube, *Baio no hanashi: nogyo kara erekutoronikusu made nyu baiogijutsu ga hiraku kanosei* [The Biotechnology Story: The Potential of New Biotechnology from Agriculture to Electronics], Tokyo: Nihon Jitsugyo Shuppansha, 1991, pp. 20–1.
9 T. Morris-Suzuki, *The Technological Transformation of Japan*, New York: Cambridge University Press, 1994, pp. 102–3.

10 The Commission on the History of Science and Technology Policy (ed.) *Historical Review of Japanese Science and Technology Policy*, Tokyo: National Institute of Science and Technology Policy, 1991, pp. 20–1, 25.
11 M. Brock, *Biotechnology in Japan*, London: Routledge, 1989, p. 30.
12 Hongo, *Nihon no baiteku choryu*, pp. 102–3.
13 Ibid., ch. 5.
14 H. Lewis, "Biotechnology in Japan," *Scientific Bulletin*, April–June 1985, Department of the Navy, Office of Naval Research Far East, p. 13.
15 H. Katayama, "Biotech Unbound," *Business Tokyo*, September 1991, p. 23.
16 Hongo, *Nihon no baiteku choryu*, pp. 105–6; Karube, *Baio no hanashi*, p. 14.
17 Roughly fifty antibiotic compounds, including penicillins, tetracyclines, and streptomycins, are produced in commercial amounts, mostly by submerged-culture methods introduced and refined in Japan. They are used not only to treat human disease and infection, but as growth-enhancing additives in animal stock feeds. See J. Bailey and D. Ollis, *Biochemical Engineering Fundamentals*, New York: McGraw-Hill, 1981, pp. 605–7.
18 Though inefficient, extraction of glutamate from plant protein left amino acid residues which were sold as fertilizer and as flavor-enhancing additives for use in soy-sauce manufacturing. In the 1940s, companies in the US began producing MSG using the glutamate-extraction process; however, the absence of markets for by-products made it impossible for companies to defray high production costs.
19 For details, see Kogyogijutsuin somubu gijutsu chosakai, hen, *Baioindasutorii: sono kanosei o saguru* [Probing the Potential of Bioindustry] (Tokyo: Tsushosangyochosakai, 1982), pp. 16–17.
20 Nikkan kogyo shimbunsha, hen, *Nihon no kenkyujo yoran* [Survey of Japanese Research Laboratories] (Tokyo: Nikkan shobo, 1991), pp. 6–7, 56–7; T. Ohta and K. Ishii, *Baiobijinesu no shikumi* [Organization of Biotechnology Business], Tokyo: Toyo Keizai Shimposha, 2002, pp. 108 and 118.
21 K. Yoshitaro, "Kogyo bunya ni okeru baio no oyo: biaoriakutaa o chushin toshite" [Biotechnology Applications in Manufacturing: Focus on Bioreactors], *Purometiusu*, March–April 1987, pp. 40–3.
22 Hongo, *Nihon no baiteku choryu*, pp. 144–5. Tanabe's process involved mounting in the reactor vessel a resin on which a precise quantity of enzyme needed to control the reaction (in this case amino acylase) had been affixed. In older methods, large quantities of costly enzyme had to be added continuously to the process.
23 Karube, *Baio no hanashi*, pp. 108–9.
24 "Baiotekunorojii no shogeki: aminosan shijo ijo ari" [Biotechnology Shock: Disorder in Amino Acid Markets], *Nikkei Sangyo Shimbun*, 16 July 1981.
25 Kogyogijutsuin somubu gijutsu chosakai, *Baioindasutorii*, pp. 25–30.
26 On this point, see Japanese Technology Evaluation Center (JTEC), *Bioprocess Engineering in Japan*, Springfield, VA: National Technical Information Service, 1992.
27 J.R. Bartholomew, *The Formation of Science in Japan*, New Haven: Yale University Press, 1989, pp. 51–2. Bartholomew argues that medicine predominates because of the high standing of medical academies during the preceding Edo Era and the relative lack of constraints on social and geographic mobility and professional practice.
28 Ibid., pp. 76, 79, 167–8, 227.
29 Ibid., p. 5.
30 S. Sugiyama, *Nihon no kindai kagakushi* [Recent History of Science in Japan], Tokyo: Asakura Shoten, 1994, pp. 94–5, 107.
31 "Japan Asks Why Scientists Go West to Thrive," *New York Times*, 8 November 1987, p. 9.

32 Coleman makes the same point with respect to private foundations: "Private Foundations play a far smaller public service role in Japan than in the United States, with far less societal influence." He goes on to cite evidence showing that in the early 1990s, at most only 15 percent of the estimated 21,000 to 25,000 nonprofit foundations made grants. S. Coleman, *Japanese Science From the Inside*, New York: Routledge, 1999, p. 120.

33 Interview with Hiroyuki Nambu, Professor of Economics, Gakushuin University, July 1995. Nambu, who has studied the history of the pharmaceutical industry in Japan, contends that the arm's-length relationship between academic researchers and drug firms has hobbled commercial development, especially in the area of clinical trials.

34 Prior to being merged with the Ministry of Education (Monbusho) in January 2001, the STA had two roles: it administered six national laboratories and seven special public corporations, and it formulated and administered science policy along lines proposed by the Prime Minister's Council for Science and Technology (CST). Although it has been said that the STA "coordinated" interministerial science policies, that in fact is too strong a term. STA officials themselves used the phrase *kokuzentai toshite seigosei o tamotsu*, which might be translated as "keeping the parts of the machine in adjustment." See Kagaku gijutsucho, *Kagaku gijutsu hakusho, heisei yonen han* [Science and Technology White Paper, 1992 edition], p. 241.

35 Kagaku gijutsu kaigi, *Shimon dai 5 go: "1970 nendai ni okeru sogoteki kagakugijutsu seisaku no kihon ni tsuite" ni taisuru toshin* [The Basis for Science and Technology Policy for the 1970s: A Report Made in Response to the Prime Minister's Inquiry No. 5], 21 April 1971, pp. 3–6, 38–9. The report uses the term "life sciences" (*raifusaiensu*) rather than biotechnology, which would not gain currency for another decade.

36 Kagaku gijutsu kaigi, *Raifusaiensu bukai chukan hokoku* [Interim Report of the Committee on the Life Sciences], December 1974.

37 Kagaku gijutsucho, *Kagaku gijutsucho nenpo, showa 52 nendo* [Annual Bulletin of the Science and Technology Agency, 1977], p. 77.

38 Kagaku gijutsucho, *Raifusaiensu no genjo to tenbo: showa 49 nen han* [Current Conditions of Life Science, 1974], p. 8.

39 Kagaku gijutsu kaigi, *Shimon dai 6 go: 'Chokiteki tanbo ni tatta sogoteki kagakugijutsu seisaku no kihon ni tsuite' ni taisuru toshin* [The Fundamentals of Comprehensive Science and Technology Policy with a View to the Long Term: A Report Made in Response to the Prime Minister's Inquiry No. 6], 25 May 1977, pp. 95–7.

40 Kogyogijutsuin, *Baioindasutorii*, pp. 101–5.

41 In particular, the CST's guidelines broadened the range of bacterial hosts that could be used in recombinant DNA experiments. Brock, *Biotechnology in Japan*, p. 87.

42 Kogyogijutsuin, *Baioindasutorii*, p. 107; "Seimei o ayatsuru: kikendo ni ooji shishin" [Manipulating Life: Guidelines to Deal with the Dangers], *Asahi Shimbun*, 15 January 1981.

43 *JEI Report*, 24 February 1984, pp. 7–9.

44 Tsushosangyosho, kisosangyokyoku hen [Basic Industry Bureau of MITI], *21seiki o hiraku biaoindasutorii: sono tenbo to kadai* [Bio-Industry: Making Way for the Twenty-first Century], Tokyo: Tsushosangyochosakai, 1984, p. 248.

45 Tsushosangyosho, Baioindasutoriishitsu hen [Bio-industry Office of MITI], *Baioindasutorii bijion: sekai ni koken suru nihon no baioindasutorii* [Vision for the Bio-industry: Japanese Bio-industry's Contribution to the World], Tokyo: Tsushosangyochosakai, 1988, p. 74.

46 Nihon Kogyo Ginko [Industrial Bank of Japan], "Baiotekunorojii no shintenkai to kadai" [New Developments and Problems in Biotechnology], *Ginko chosa*, 1984, No. 4, p. 28.
47 "Baiotekunorojii," *Kogyo gijutsu* [Industrial Technology], November 1981, vol. 22, p. 28.
48 Kiban gijutsu kenkyu sokushin sentaa [Key Technology Center], *Baiotekunorojii kenkyuukaihatsu kiban ni kakaru chosa hokokusho* [Survey Report on Base Research and Development in Biotechnology], Tokyo: Baioindasutorii kyokai, 1987, p. 100.
49 Kagaku gijutsu cho, *Kagaku gijutsu hakusho*, 1992, p. 398.
50 Nikkei Sangyo Shimbun, *Seimei sangyo jidai: Baiotekunorojii no shogeki* [The Era of Bio-Industry: Biotechnology Shock], Tokyo: Nihonkeizai shimbunsha, 1981, p. 164.
51 "Jikken de usureta kikenshi: Bei de wa Teppai, Nihon de wa okureru" [Japan Lags US in Abolishing Tough Restrictions on Experimentation], *Nikkei Sangyo Shimbun*, 8 August 1981.
52 Interview with Dr. Kinji Gonda, Director in Research, National Institute of Science and Technology Policy, November 1991; July 1995. According to Dr. Gonda, scientific organizations played a crucial role in gathering information from abroad and diffusing it within the scientific and public policy community.
53 "Kigyoka sareru seimei: joho ga kigyo no shimei o sei suru" [Commercializing Life: Companies at the Mercy of Information], *Asahi Jyaanaru*, 19 December 1980, pp. 22–5.
54 "Idenshi de dai ni no Sonii ni" [Becoming the Second Sony by Way of the Gene], *Asahi Shimbun*, 6 January 1981, p. 22.
55 "Nigasu na san cho en sangyo" [Don't Miss Out on 3 Trillion Yen Industry!], *Asahi Shimbun*, 7 January 1981, p. 18.
56 "Gijutsu rikkoku e kan-zai-ro ittai de" [Technological Leadership Through Government–Finance–Labor Cooperation], *Asahi Shimbun*, 11 January 1981.
57 I. Hiroyuki, *Nihon no kagaku sangyo: naze sekai ni tachiokureta no ka* [Japan's Chemical Industry: Why It Lags the Rest of the World], Tokyo: NTT Shuppansha, 1991, pp. 83–5.
58 For a discussion of the process by which this policy was arrived at, see Brock, *Biotechnology in Japan.*
59 "'Tsusan ni Tsuzuke' issai ni," *Nikkei sangyo shimbun*, 12 August 1981.
60 Interview, Mr. Yuuichi Sakamoto, Director, Coordination Division, Japan Bioindustry Association, December 1991.
61 "10 shunen kinen tokushu: Baio/ 1981 nen/ 1991 nen/ 2001 nen" [Ten-Year Anniversary Special Edition: Bio/1981/1991/2001], *Nikkei Baio-interijiensu*, 7 October 1991, p. BI–4. Special thanks to Mr. Mitsuru Miyata, Editor-in-Chief of *Nikkei Biotech*, for kindly providing a copy of this issue.
62 *Nikkei Baio-interijensu*, 7 October 1991, p. b16.
63 Koseikagaku kaigi, "Koseikagaku kenkyu no kiban kakuritsu to bureikusuruu no tameni" [Establishing Breakthrough-Oriented Welfare Scientific Research Base], September 1987. "Hyuman Saiensu Shinko Zaidan," *Hyuman Saiensu Nyusu*, 5 August 1989. The association was later renamed as the Japan Health Sciences Foundation.
64 Interview with Dr. Yoshiaki Ui, Director of the Biotechnology Division, Ministry of Agriculture, Forestry, and Fisheries, November 1991.
65 Hiroyuki, *Nihon no kagaku sangyo*, p. 199.
66 *Nikkei Baioteku, Baio-Interijensu*, 8 October 1989, p. BI–1.
67 Interviews, Mr. Kazuaki Manabe, Project Coordinator, Life Science Business Development Department, Mitsui Toatsu Chemicals, November, 1991.

68 Baio 21 Guruppu, *Baioindasutorii: yume to genjitsu*, Tokyo: Baio 21 Guruppu, 1988, p. 38.
69 Interview, Mr. Kazuaki Manabe, Project Coordinator, Life Science Business Development Department, Mitsui Toatsu Chemicals, November 1991.
70 Itami, *Nihon no kagaku sangyo*, pp. 195–7.
71 Office of Technology Assessment, *Commercial Biotechnology: An International Analysis*, OTA-BA-218, January 1984, Washington, DC: Government Printing Office, January 1984, p. 77.
72 Drug makers in Japan often find themselves caught between two contradictory policies of the Ministry of Health and Welfare – promoting competitiveness of the industry while keeping prices low through its periodic downward revisions to drug prices.
73 Prices plunged in the early 1980s as a result of revisions in MHW's method of calculating list prices for drugs in order to narrow the discrepancy between regulated and market prices. Firms accustomed to bi- or triennial cuts in list prices of 1.6–5.8 percent every two to three years in the 1970s had to swallow cuts of 18.6 percent in 1981, 4.9 percent in 1983, 16.6 percent in 1985, and 6 percent in 1986. H. Hisashi, *Iyakuhin* [Drugs], Tokyo: Nihon Keizai Hyoronsha, 1986, pp. 148–9. It is tempting to think that such a pricing system would destroy the profitability of the industry. It does not. Regulators permit premium pricing on new, innovative drugs, while holding down prices on "me-too" products; by cutting prices across the board every two years, they ensure that competition turns on the ability to pump out a continuous stream of novel new drugs. See T. Nambu, "Characteristics of the Pharmaceutical Industry in Japan: Mechanisms of Regulation and Competition," *Review of Social Policy*, March 1994, 19–34.
74 "Prescription for Drug Makers: More R&D," *Nikkei Weekly*, 23 May 1992, p. 17.
75 The following examples are taken from Karube, *Baio no hanashi* and from company reports found in *Nikkei Baioteku, Sekai no baio kigyo 800 sha* [World's 800 Biotechnology Companies], Tokyo: Nikkei Baioteku, 1989.
76 Kao Soap also released new additions to its Sofina line of lipstick, "trumpeting the microcrystalline structure of the base ingredients and a new moisture-retaining component developed using biotechnology." See "Spring Cosmetic Lines Stress Function Over Color," *Nikkei Weekly*, 8 March 1993, p. 12.
77 "Japan Cools Biotech Spending," *Bio/Technology*, May 1992, p. 505.
78 *Nikkei Baioteku Nenkan 89/90*, p. 13; *Nikkei Baioteku Baiointerijensu*, 2 December 1991, p. BI–1.
79 *Nikkei Baiointerijensu*, 21 June 1993, BI–1.
80 Kodama introduced Western audiences to the idea of technology fusion in F. Kodama, "Technology Fusion and the New R&D," *Harvard Business Review*, July–August 1992, pp. 70–8.
81 Kodama Fumio, *Kyodo kenkyu ni okeru sanka kigyo ni kansuru chosakenkyu* [Survey Research of Companies Participating in Cooperative Research], *Kenkyu gijutsu keikaku*, 1990, vol. 5, pp. 30–50.
82 "Baio kanren shijo wa 1 cho 3000 oku en topa" [Size of Bio Market Tops 1.3 Trillion Yen], *Nikkei Baiobijinesu*, March 2002, p. 54. T. Kaminuma and G. Matsumoto, *Biocomputers: The Next Generation from Japan*, New York: Chapman & Hall, 1991, pp. 114–16; *Nikkei Baitekunorojii, Baiointerijensu*, 2 December 1991, p. BI–2.
83 For these and other examples, see Karube, *Baio no hanashi*, pp. 196–205.
84 "The Perfect Food," *Bio/Technology*, 10 September 1992, pp. 952–3.
85 "Japan Explores the Boundary between Food and Medicine," *Nature*, 15 July 1993, p. 180.

86 Office of Technology Assessment, *New Developments in Biotechnology: US Investment in Biotechnology* – Special Report, OTA-BA-360, Washington, DC: Government Printing Office, July 1988, pp. 91–2.
87 Edward Roberts and Ryosuke Mizouchi, "Inter-firm Technological Collaboration: The Case of Japanese Biotechnology," *International Journal of Technology Management*, 1989, vol. 4, 43–61.
88 "Kirin Brewery's Plunge into Biotechnology Pays Off," *Wall Street Journal*, 25 January 1993, p. B3; "Kirin ga takakuka o susumeru riyu" [Rationale Behind Kirin's Diversification Strategy], *Trigger*, May 1991, pp. 22–31.
89 National Research Council, *U.S.–Japan Technology Linkages in Biotechnology*, Washington, DC: National Academy Press, 1992.
90 Of the remainder, 38 percent were with larger American firms, 29 percent were with European firms, and 21 percent were with other DBCs. "International Strategic Alliances," *Bio/Technology*, May 1992, pp. 528–33.
91 *Nikkei Baiobijenusu*, June 2001, p. 51.
92 "Shiseido Grant: More than Skin Deep," *Science*, 25 August 1989, pp. 810–11.
93 "In Biotechnology, Japanese Yen for American Expertise," *Science*, 27 November 1992, pp. 1431–3.
94 "Academic Biotech Deals Offer More Promise than Product," *Science*, January 1994, pp. 168–9.
95 "Away from Home: U.S. Sites of European and Japanese Biotech R&D," *Bio/Technology*, December 1992, pp. 1535–8.
96 Interviews with various project participants, November 1991. On MITI's changing policies toward biotechnology, see Tsushosangyosho, Kogyogijutsuin, *Jisedai sangyo kiban gijutsu kenkyu kaihatsu seido: gijutsu rikkoku o mezashite*, 1991. Also "Ogata-Jisedai no kenkyu kaihatsu: 2 dai projekuto o togo," *Nikkei Shimbun*, 7 December 1991, p. 13.
97 Tsushosangyosho, Baioindasutorii shitsu, *Baioindasutorii bijion*, May 1988, pp. 5–44.
98 "New Development of Policy for Biochemical Industry," Tsushosangyosho, kisosangyokyoku, seibutsu kagaku sangyo ka, *Seibutsu kagaku sangyo seisaku no shin tenkai* [New Developments in Industrial Policy in the Life Sciences], September 1991 (MITI internal document).
99 For a lively account of the complex political maneuvering that resulted in KEYTECH's formation, see Chalmers Johnson, "MPT, MITI and the Telecom Wars," in C. Johnson, L. Tyson, and J. Zysman (eds) *Politics and Productivity: The Real Story of Why Japan Works*, Cambridge: Ballinger, 1989.
100 International Technology Research Institute, World Technology (WTEC) Division, "Japan's Key Technology Center Program," September 1999.
101 For details, see Kiban gijutsu kenkyu sokushin sentaa [JKTC], "Baiotekunoroji kenkyu kaihatsu kiban ni kakaru chosa hokokusho" [Report on a Survey Concerning Biotechnology Research and Development], Tokyo: Baioindasutorii kyokai, 1987, pp. 1–13.
102 "Lab Makes Name for Protein Analysis," *Nikkei Weekly*, 16 October 2000.
103 Coleman, *Japanese Science: From the Inside*, p. 79.
104 International Technology Research Institute, "Japan's Key Technology Center Program."
105 "Panel Targets 18 Public Bodies for Merger, Abolition," *Asahi News*, 4 October 2001.
106 "Govt-Funded Research Lab Closes with 276 B. Loss," *Jiji Press Ticker Service*, 12 May 2003.
107 Keidanren, Kaihatsubu, *Raifu saiensu no suishin ni kansuru kenkai*, February 1985.

108 R. Cook-Deegan, *The Gene Wars: Science, Politics, and the Human Genome*, New York: W.W. Norton, 1994, pp. 219–20.

109 Ibid., p. 229.

110 R. Landau and N. Rosenberg, "Successful Commercialization in the Chemical Process Industries," in N. Rosenberg *et al.* (eds) *Technology and the Wealth of Nations*, Stanford: Stanford University Press, 1992; Samuels, *Rich Nation, Strong Army.*

6 Conclusions

1 R. Florida and M. Kenney, *The Breakthrough Illusion*, New York: Basic Books, 1990.

2 F. Kodama, "Technology Fusion and the New R&D," *Harvard Business Review*, July–August 1992, pp. 70–8.

3 "The Health Effect," *The Economist*, 3 June 2000, p. 78.

Index

CARDIFF UNIVERSITY
PRIFYSGOL CAERDYDD